Identity, Motivation, and Multilingual Education in Asian Contexts

Also available from Bloomsbury

Language Education in the School Curriculum, Ken Cruickshank, Stephen
Black, Honglin Chen and Jan Wright
Language Learning Strategies and Individual Learner Characteristics, edited by
Rebecca L. Oxford and Carmen M. Amerstorfer

Identity, Motivation, and Multilingual Education in Asian Contexts

Mark Feng Teng and Wang Lixun

BLOOMSBURY ACADEMIC

LONDON • NEW YORK • OXFORD • NEW DELHI • SYDNEY

BLOOMSBURY ACADEMIC
Bloomsbury Publishing Plc
50 Bedford Square, London, WC1B 3DP, UK
1385 Broadway, New York, NY 10018, USA
29 Earlsfort Terrace, Dublin 2, Ireland

BLOOMSBURY, BLOOMSBURY ACADEMIC and the Diana logo
are trademarks of Bloomsbury Publishing Plc

First published in Great Britain 2020
Paperback edition first published 2021

A catalogue record for this book is available from the British Library.

A catalog record for this book is available from the Library of Congress.

ISBN: HB: 978-1-3500-9965-4
PB: 978-1-3501-9250-8
ePDF: 978-1-3500-9966-1
eBook: 978-1-3500-9967-8

Typeset by Deanta Global Publishing Services, Chennai, India

To find out more about our authors and books visit
www.bloomsbury.com and sign up for our newsletters.

Contents

Preface   vi

Introduction to Multilingual Education in Asian Contexts   1

1 Imagined Communities, Motivation and Multilingual Education in Asia   7

2 English as a Lingua Franca, Multilingual Identity, and Multilingual Education in Asia   27

3 Language Learning, Motivation and Identity in Asian Multilingual Education Contexts   47

4 Multilingual Education in Hong Kong: Motivation and Identity   63

5 Motivation and Identity of the Stakeholders: The Case of Hong Kong   83

6 The Dynamics of L2 and L3 Learning, Identity Development, and Motivation Change: A Hong Kong Learner's Perspective   109

7 Identities, Imagined Communities, and Communities of Practice: Thai Students in China   125

8 L2 and L3 Learning, Motivation and Identity: A Chinese EFL Learner's Reflection   143

Conclusion and Future Directions for Multilingual Education in Asian Contexts   159

References   163
Index   182

Preface

My fascination with identity and motivation has taken many forms during my life. I was fascinated by English words when I first heard them. From the very beginning, I realized that motivation, particularly integrative motivation, is a key factor in learning a second or other language; I kept this in mind when learning English as an L2 and Japanese as an L3. Learning these languages was not an easy task, as I was born in the countryside in south-western China, where education resources were insufficient. I did not have the chance to speak an English word to a native speaker until my second year in university. To me, the motivation to learn another language is highly complex. I set out to learn English because I enjoyed it. Then, I learnt Japanese because I thought it might afford me more opportunities to find a good job; I did not wish to return to my countryside town, which is bordered by a mountain and cut off from the outside world. My motivation to learn English and Japanese is just as much an investment in social identity. I was then motivated to become a language teacher and educator. I saw in language learning a way to turn my painful learning experience into a virtue for my students. Those factors comprise an imagined identity that has strengthened my power and motivation for multilingual learning.

This book – written in a reader-friendly format – is the culmination of my fascination towards language learning. I cannot, and will not, cover every aspect of Asian contexts; a separate treatise could be dedicated to each. This book is meant to inspire your interest in understanding identity and motivation from a fundamental knowledge perspective, to introduce some schema in Asian contexts, and to offer guidance if you are interested in identity and motivation.

It was rewarding to collaborate with Dr Wang Lixun on this book. Without Dr Wang Lixun's help in proofreading this book, contributing an important chapter (Chapter 5), and finalizing the manuscript, this book would have never been completed.

Dr Wang Lixun has teaching and research experience in Hong Kong, and I have teaching and research experience in Mainland China. However, we do not want to focus solely on these two regions. We hope that readers from other Asian regions will gain insight from reading this book, hence our decision to cover other Asian regions as well. As our workload grew, we continuously reminded ourselves that this book would be a welcome addition to the education community; it soon became a labour of love. Indeed, typing words at the holiday deserves to be a labour of love. All told, teaching and learning a second or other language is never easy. It is our hope that policymakers, planners and programme implementers from both formal and non-formal education departments, as well as from non-governmental organizations involved in multilingual education, will find this publication useful for their work. We would be delighted to hear more feedback or stories from you as you move through this book.

(Mark) Feng Teng
Hong Kong Baptist University, China

Introduction to Multilingual Education in Asian Contexts

The book responds to the sociopolitical changes in Asia and examines the manifestation of identity and motivation within Asian multilingual contexts. How do we define bilingual and multilingual education? In its simplest definition, bilingual education is the use of two languages for learning and teaching in an instructional setting and, by extension, multilingual education would be the use of three languages or more (Wright, Boun and García 2015). Generally, one of these languages is the 'home', 'native' or 'mother-tongue' language, and one is the 'dominant' societal language or a 'powerful' international language. However, as argued by Wright, Boun and García (2015), even these basic concepts – such as language, home language, dominant language, native speaker, bilingual, multilingual, and bilingual and multilingual education – are highly complex and contested constructs. Multilingual education, in this perspective, is influenced by a variety of historical, economic and sociocultural factors, and still a fad, considering the trend of globalization.

Innovative practices in multilingual education differ in diverse contexts and environments due to the plurality of language policies and education systems. The last five decades of research conducted on bi- or multilingual education suggests two major shifts in conceptualizing language(s) in education. The first shift, pertaining to the growth of anticolonial and the emergence of regionalist movements in the 1960s, is characterized by a critique of linguistic hegemony and by a claim for linguistic rights and policies aiming to strengthen non-dominant languages (Brigitta 2011). In this connection, the identity aspect and the notion of speakers belonging to homogenous imagined communities prevail. The second shift is that English language skills have become commonplace in the world's labour markets. Thus, monolingual and even bilingual English speakers may increasingly lose out to their multilingual competitors. Such a scenario would seem to provide a powerful rationale for motivating learners to develop skills in additional languages in order to maintain or gain a competitive edge (Ushioda 2017). The motivation for learning a second or third language begins to increase as it becomes more accepted that this helps learners secure an economic advantage as well as linguistic and social capital. In addition, the sheer growth in numbers of multilingual learners around the globe stimulates the growth of motivational research in multilingual learning contexts.

There are several key developments to note when discussing multilingual education in Asian contexts. First, there is a noticeable expansion regarding multilingual education in Asian contexts, both from the point of view of programme design as well as from a research-based perspective. Second, there is a growing emphasis on different types of multilingual educational initiatives. For example, language policy and planning initiatives in multilingual education at the regional and national levels are increasing. Third, there is a need to work together with multilingual education agency to identify successful strategies for language learning in multilingual settings and to facilitate the sharing of best practices in the field. Fourth, various types of perspectives, for example, motivation and identity, need to be considered when implementing multilingual education. These developments have helped make multilingual education considerably broader in scope – implemented from preschool to higher education – as well as in different contexts. Consequently, it seems more relevant than ever for both researchers and practitioners to develop an awareness of multilingual education issues, including national/regional characteristics, sociolinguistic realities, sociocultural values, educational systems, professional qualifications and requirements, sociopolitical ideologies and the like.

This book discusses multilingual education with a focus on motivation and identity, in light of the two shifts mentioned earlier. It will be a useful reference for scholars working on multilingual education, language acquisition in education contexts, motivation and identity, and language policy in related contexts. This book can be of interest to professionals in language planning, as well as to teachers and language teacher educators working in Asian contexts. This book can also be used as a textbook in courses on multilingual education for undergraduate and postgraduate students. There are eight chapters: the first four chapters offer conceptual frameworks for motivation and identity in multilingual education, and the last four chapters are empirical studies in Asian contexts.

The eight chapters in this book are organized into two sections. Section I opens with an introduction to multilingual education in Asia. It is followed by discussions on multilingual education practices in different Asian countries (Chapters 2–4). Section II contains four empirical studies.

The first chapter, 'Imagined communities, motivation and multilingual education in Asia', explores the rise of globalization and investment in multilingual education in Asian contexts (e.g., China, Singapore, the Philippines and India). Some constructs, including economic and social status, symbolic capital and investment, are discussed in order to facilitate understanding multilingual education. Implications are also drawn regarding how imagined communities might address learners' attempt to affiliate themselves with various sociolinguistic groups, how investment in language learning takes place, and how motivation can be further interpreted.

The second chapter, 'English as a lingua franca, multilingual identity and multilingual education in Asia', explores multilingual education through the lens of identity. It covers issues and concerns surrounding the spread of English as a lingua franca (ELF) and the formation of multilingual identity. In closing, this chapter, through discussing multilingual education in the Asian contexts (e.g., Hong Kong, Malaysia and Brunei) and the spread of English as a lingua franca, sheds some light on the (re)construction of identity in a multilingual learning setting and motivation in maintaining learners' interest in learning multiple languages.

The third chapter, 'Language learning, motivation and identity in Asian multilingual learning contexts', focuses on three countries: Nepal, Japan and South Korea. Readers can understand more about how the two notions of motivation and identity affect learners' multilingual practices, and how various sociopolitical factors influence multilingual practices and language learning motivation and identities. Through an understanding of multilingual learning in Nepal, Japan and South Korea from the perspective of motivation and identity, this chapter sheds light on how the status of English affects learners' identity-related motivation to learn other languages.

The fourth chapter, 'Multilingual education in Hong Kong: motivation and identity', discusses a complex array of historical, cultural-political, socio-economic and practical factors in Hong Kong, and suggests that language policy and planning for multilingual education should not be a political topic. This chapter proposes that there is a need for a suitable multilingual model from the perspectives of learner motivation and identity.

The fifth chapter, 'Motivation and identity of the stakeholders: the case of Hong Kong', investigates different stakeholders' motivation and identity in a multilingual education setting through detailed case studies from three Hong Kong primary schools. The stakeholders include school-sponsoring bodies, school principals, teachers, students and parents. Research findings show that issues related to motivation and identity of different stakeholders in the multilingual education setting in Hong Kong are complicated. It is important for policymakers and frontline practitioners to properly understand this complexity so as to implement multilingual education effectively in Hong Kong.

The sixth chapter, 'The dynamics of L2 and L3 learning, identity development and motivation change: a Hong Kong learner perspective', presents findings from interview data collected from a qualitative case study in the Hong Kong context. It explores a language learner's discursive development of identity and documents the possible change in motivation when learning English and Japanese.

The seventh chapter, 'Identities, imagined communities and communities of practice: Thai students in China', discusses the ways in which Thai learners break new ground when navigating the complex process of identity negotiation while completing their short-term studies in China. Recommendations are summarized and depicted in a model for learners in a short-term study abroad programme.

The eighth chapter, 'L2 and L3 learning, motivation and identity: a Chinese EFL learner's reflection', explores the relationships among social learning environments, individual learning motivation and the development of identity based on the first author's English and Japanese learning experiences.

Overall, the chapters in this book explore multilingual education from a number of fresh perspectives, such as motivation, identity, investment and imagined community. We hope that readers can broaden their understanding of the unique characteristics of multilingual education and gain theoretical and empirical insights. Although this is not meant to be a handbook for multilingualism, we aim to provide theoretical, empirical and practical bases for planning and implementing multilingual education. Specifically, we attempt to address issues that are relevant to the development of motivation and identity during multilingual learning. We also consider several issues, including the role of bilingualism in multilingual acquisition, the emerging issue of identity crisis, motivation attribution, and the role of culture in multilingual schools, among others. This book presents examples of multilingual contexts in different parts of Asia in order to better illustrate not only the achievements of multilingual education but also the challenges that it poses.

Understanding the special educational contexts in Asia deserves attention. More than 2,200 languages are spoken in Asia. Almost all Asian nations – in fact, any nation – are essentially multilingual. There are few monolingual nations in Asia, and English is taught in almost all Asian schools. Thus, when one considers this factor, even if a nation may seem monolingual, it is most likely at the very least bilingual. Despite the undeniable multilingualism in most Asian nations, education systems in the region generally work as if the nations were monolingual. Consequently, in most cases, only the official languages are used as the languages of instruction and literacy in education. Thus, educational systems put the learners who are not proficient in these languages at a disadvantage. In some cases, monolingual education systems in multilingual settings may even exclude some citizens altogether from education as a result of restrictive language-in-education policies. Multilingual education in Asia still has a long way to go.

This book will introduce literacy and education issues in multilingual settings in Asia. It will highlight some educational challenges that millions of learners are facing owing to restrictive language policies. Multilingual education programmes offer one solution to alleviate the prevailing situation. Yet, before multilingual education programmes can start serving speakers of ethnolinguistic minority languages, there must be some changes in these programmes. The first change is the acknowledgement of linguistic diversity. Only after the evident multilingualism in Asian societies is accepted as a fact can more supportive language-in-education policies be put in place. Therefore, the knowledge of a nation's linguistic situation is essential. A wealth of data on linguistic diversity is already available. Yet, most Asian countries have a need for more comprehensive language surveys. It is, thus, essential to gather and analyse data on multilingualism, as well as on the ways in which a society is proficient in and uses different languages. Another change is that current educational planning is based on existing facts. In multilingual nations, complex language situations should be considered in educational planning. Only after acknowledging linguistic diversity can authorities plan and implement strong and effective multilingual education programmes.

We admit that there is clearly much that remains to be done to develop a full understanding of multilingual education. In addition, there are a wide variety of conflicting ideologies, motivation theories, identity perspectives, policies and practices surrounding multilingual education throughout the world. We hope that this book will help to (1) address the theoretical foundations and present multilingual education as a current, strong and cutting-edge field from the perspective of motivation and identity; (2) provide a broad overview of the historical development and current status of the field, particularly in Asian contexts; (3) provide critical examples of policy and practice in Hong Kong; and (4) move the field forward by introducing new ideas on identity and motivation.

Multilingual education is a strong, dynamic, interdisciplinary academic field, with substantial consequences for students, teachers and communities around the world. We hope that readers can gain some insights into the pedagogical practices in multilingual education and will be able to reflect on the notions of motivation and identity while addressing the problems or challenges inherent in multilingual education.

1

Imagined Communities, Motivation and Multilingual Education in Asia

Multilingualism is viewed as a valuable resource that should be invested in language education as a means of securing learners' access to various imagined language communities (Dagenais 2003). Asia is currently one of the most exciting regions in the world and may be one of the most prominent regions in which multilingualism resides in the future. It is no wonder that Asia witnesses dynamic uses of English for various social, cultural, political and economic purposes. We traditionally limit this region to the traditional, geographical Asian countries or regions, for example, East Asia (e.g., Hong Kong, Mainland China, Korea and Japan), Southeast Asia (Indonesia, Singapore and Malaysia), and South Asia (Bangladesh, India and Pakistan). However, the concept of Asia is ever-expanding. In the modern world the word 'Asia' invokes a sense of regional integration or solidarity among Asian peoples.

In this day and age, the effects of globalization on Asian regions cannot be ignored. This chapter examines the state of multilingualism in Asian contexts. Bilingualism and multilingualism in Asia have developed and will continue its development because of human migration and coercive political campaigns. In addition, contact between languages and linguistic interference is becoming more and more common in this region. Similar to other parts of the world, linguistic diversity is a characteristic feature of Asia, where a great number of language families exist. Related to this, language contact occurs as a recurring phenomenon. Of equal significance is the fact that the Asia region is bi- or multilingual rather than monolingual.

The shifts and fluctuations in multilingual education have become visible under the recent sociopolitical and socio-economic trends. These include the development of globalization, deepening economic trade, the post-colonial search for national identities, and the increased international migration. A change has also been witnessed in the language policy in Asian contexts. Reasons included the growing dominance of English as an international language and the use of languages for national cohesion or social control. Against this backdrop, there is a need to explore the globalization, linguistic diversity, community affiliations and learners' motivation for language learning in Asia.

1.1 Language and multilingualism

Language is a system of vocal sounds and/or nonverbal systems by which group members communicate with one another. It is a critical dimension in constructing one's identity and developing awareness and psychological growth (Jay 2003). People are connected to one another because of languages. Through languages, we are able to share our internal states of being with one another. It is also a medium of exchange for reaching out to our surrounding realities and sharing the experience with others (Samovar and Porter 2004). Individuals may attempt to change the style of their language or even the language itself in order to build relationships with those they imagine or interact with (Dicker 2003). People who share the same language or dialect often share the same feelings, beliefs, and behaviours. It is no wonder that people have a bond when they share the same linguistic heritage.

When people move from school to school, region to region, languages or dialects spoken also change (Gollnick and Chinn 2006). Individuals exhibit cultural similarities and differences related to languages, gender, class, ethnicity, religion and age. Language is much more than a tool for communication. It is used to socialize individuals into their linguistic and cultural communities. This multilingual nature reflects the rich cultural heritage of people, and language diversity is an asset to a nation. This is more important when a nation needs to interact with other nations in the domains of trade, commerce, education, science and technology. However, the asset of multilingual competence is often overlooked due to the sense of ethnocentrism, or belief in each nation's self-perceived superiority of its own ethnicity or culture. From a linguistic perspective, there is no such thing as one language being better than the other. There is nothing limiting or demeaning about any language because each language can satisfy the social or psychological needs of its speakers. In fact, there are always benefits related to the existence of one language. Hence, all languages share equal importance, although society may place different levels of social statuses or functions to each language.

Language diversity is a feature of language education in Asia. Based on the concept of bilingual education (e.g., Fishman 1976), multilingual education refers to the regular use of three or more languages for teaching and learning in an instructional setting (Abello-Contesse 2013). Because of globalization and the widespread use of English, the term multilingualism has acquired a different meaning. However, there exists tensions between a monolingual ethos (the first language or the second language) and the development of bilingualism (English and national language) or multilingualism (English, national language and local languages). Grosjean (1985) suggested balanced bilingualism, which means developing similar levels of proficiency in two languages. We can also stress a need to equate multilingualism with balanced multilingualism, which refers to the development of similar proficiency in three or more languages.

However, to develop intellectually, academically and socially in multiple languages that learners have been in contact with is not an easy job to accomplish. Problems and tensions exist in the unbalanced multilingual education mode. There is also a marked tendency to place a greater emphasis on the development of foreign language rather than the first language. Likewise, there exists an emphasis on enhancing the proficiency of the national language to build a national identity. These factors, as well as learners' mental imagination of community, affect multilingual education. We may conclude that there is an increasing interest in finding effective ways to address the problems rooted in multilingual education.

1.2 Multilingual education

Multilingual education is perhaps one of the thorniest issues faced by many post-colonial states today. The historians of languages as well as the specialists in multilingualism are faced with very complex historical processes that often pull in different directions: the construction of mother tongues, medium of instruction, official languages, standard literary languages, and Creoles, apart from Anglicization (understood mainly as the spread of English either as a local or as an international language) and, last but not least, the processes of language extinction (Ribeiro 2010). Multilingual education can affect the learning of any language, from formerly highly prestigious colonial languages such as English in Singapore and Portuguese in various Asian territories as well as Creoles of colonial origin, to diverse indigenous languages (for instance, some indigenous languages in Brazil and Mexico are no longer spoken or used). In addition, each of these processes may hybridize and overlap with others in numerous and shifting ways across time. Therefore, multilingual education is becoming more important in different contexts around the world (Cenoz 2009). As proposed by Edwards (2007), multilingualism is a facet of life around the world, a circumstance arising, at the simplest level, from the need to communicate across speech communities.

In post-colonial states, schools are mostly colonial creation. This required the schools to integrate in terms of both the construct of the mother tongue and that of the standard medium. This left little room for manoeuvring towards a more non-hierarchical, empowering multilingualism. In some countries, for example India, there is a trend towards monolingualism, particularly when considering tertiary education. Although India has had a modicum of experience in using languages other than English as mediums of instruction for higher education, English is still the dominant language. The Philippines has undergone a losing battle to keep Spanish as a main language. In a similar way, the Republic of Timor Leste, a Southeast Asian nation occupying half the island of Timor, also experiences difficulties in keeping Portuguese as an official language. Although Macau manages to make Portuguese survive, it is only within restricted circles. The last extant Portuguese-medium school in Macau turned into a bilingual school (both English and Portuguese) in 2008. This situation seems to suggest that equality between different languages is still unattainable in many countries in the Asian context. Multilingual education becomes an even thornier issue when mother-tongue education is considered. This is because the mother tongue can hardly be described as a non-contentious construct. Therefore, we need to come up with new ideas or ways to rethink our current predicament involving multilingual education. There is a need to explore new paths for multilingualism to be taught and used as a boon rather than as a burden or something to be kept strictly at bay in higher education. One of the paths to be noted is the learners' imagined communities and learners' investment in learning a language.

1.3 Imagined communities and investment

The current interest in multilingual education suggests the connection among globalization, linguistic diversity, community affiliations and options in language education. Learners invest in multilingual education so that they acquire the language resources essential to access various imagined communities nationally and abroad. Imagined communities refer to 'groups of people, not immediately tangible and accessible, with whom we connect through the power of the imagination' (Kanno and Norton 2003: 241). Anderson (2006: 5) used the term imagined communities to explain the development of nationalism. It is argued that the nation 'is imagined because the members of even the smallest nation will never know most of their fellow-members, meet them, or even hear of them, yet in the minds of each lives the image of their communion'.

According to Wenger (1998: 178), imagination refers to 'a mode of belonging that always involves the social world to expand the scope of reality and identity'. Through imagination, we are 'expanding our self by transcending our time and space and creating new images of the world and ourselves' (ibid., 176). This suggests that imagination is a distinct mode of belonging to a community with which an individual creates images of the world and the self, transcending both time and space. Individuals, while joining social actions, may choose to meet ways of doing in the community – whether imagined or real – and locate, define, identify and rectify their membership through constant negotiations of their participation (Teng and Bui 2018). Imagination impacts the process of creating new identity options (Hall 1990). This process is often aided by the efforts to create new practices of self-representation and, thus, the new imagined communities (Anderson 2006).

English is increasingly becoming a language detached from any specific Anglophone community. It is becoming the representative of a worldwide global community. Hence, the process of learning English seems to be a process of learners' negotiation of their identities as members of such a global community conceived in their minds, or an imagined global community (Ryan 2006). Historically, emerging modern nation-states have promoted 'national' languages to create a sense of commonality, or a way to create 'imagined communities' with a sense of national unity and loyalty among their citizens (Bonfiglio 2010). In addition, a shift in parent's attitude has led to a change in the process of their current participation, membership alignment and their perception of the social value of each language. Finally, the changing context or the movement from one community to another tends to influence learners' development of identity and, hence, their investment in language learning.

The construct of investment was proposed by Norton (2013). Norton's proposal was based on Bourdieu's (1991) theories of capital, language and symbolic power. Based on Norton, there is a need to consider the socially and historically constructed relationship of learners with the target language and the way power relations are implicated in language learning and teaching. As noted by Norton (2013), if learners invest in learning a target language, they do so with an awareness that they would acquire various symbolic resources (language, education, friendship), as well as material resources (capital goods, real estate, money). Through this, learners can enhance the value of their cultural assets and the sense of social power. As argued by Bourdieu (1991), a legitimate language learner is an individual who is engaged in a social context, characterized by unequal struggles for meaning, access and power. This reflects the different status and power relationships between dominant and minority languages. Learners may not limit themselves to an economic rationale for investing in learning a language. They may, in practice, associate multilingualism with symbolic capital, for example, increased social status and access to communities of practice. They recognize being multilingual as a cumulative source. However, they also acknowledge that not all languages have equal importance. In multilingual education, learners' relationship to and interest in each language and the value attributed to each language in different contexts is an issue that should be considered.

Learners invest in learning a language because they believe that learning a particular language and its related education resources will enable them to gain membership in a community (Teng 2019a). They extrapolate from their own experience and create a new image of the world. Engagement, alignment and imagination in communities of practice determine their relationships with various language groups. Imagination, in this regard, is considered as a role in building learners' relationships to the practical community. Therefore, learning a language is not only learning the linguistic system of words and sentences but also a social practice that engages the identities of learners in diverse and often contradictory ways (Norton 2015). The concepts of imagined communities and investment emphasize the social dynamics and language education. Overall, they provide multiple lens for analysing learners' relationships among languages, multilingual education, power relationship and motivation. Learning a language is usually considered to occur in face-to-face communities of practice. This refers to the negotiation of becoming a certain person in the immediate situation. However, a learner's participation in an imagined world, or a learner's imagination in a community, also exert an effect on the learners' motivation. The construct of investment is similar to the construct of motivation, which is to be explored later.

1.4 Motivation

The term *motivation* is generally defined by psychologists as the process involved in arousing, directing and sustaining behaviour, or what causes a person to have a desire to repeat a behaviour and vice versa (Reeve 2009). The motivation for and causes of language change continue to be the subject of great discussion. In research on motivation, the relationship between contextual and situational influences and the self is important to the intrinsic/extrinsic approach to motivation (Bui, Teng and Man, forthcoming). According to Noels (2001), a more or less self-determined action is related to the degree to which a learner is intrinsically or extrinsically motivated. Additionally, when learners learn the language because they love it, they are intrinsically motivated, and they may internalize the learning objectives as part of their self-concept. By contrast, when a language is learnt as an attempt to achieve an external goal, individuals may be externally motivated. In this case, the learning process may be determined through analysis of context and external pressure.

As described by Noels et al. (2000), motivation is a continuum with a motivation (e.g., I am not interested in learning this language) at one pole and intrinsic motivation (c.g., I learn this language because I love it) at the other. In between these poles, different types of extrinsic motivations are distinguished: external, introjected and identified regulation. High self-perceived competence or self-determined motivation may facilitate intrinsic learning motivation (Ryan and Deci 2000). That said, the more the motivation is self-determined, the more it shifts towards the intrinsic pole. External regulation refers to the desire to learn this language for external purposes (e.g., I want to learn this language for passing the exam). Introjected regulation suggests a more internalized pressure felt by some learners while learning an L2 (e.g., I would feel guilty if I could not learn this language well because my parents expect me to learn it well). Identified regulation is the most self-determined type of extrinsic motivation (e.g., I want to learn this language because being a multilingual learner is an advantage).

Motivation has been treated as an important concept in the field of multilingual education. It includes learners' desires, positive attitudes and personal behaviours to learn a language (Gardner 2010). Gardner (2001) proposed the intergrativeness motive. This motive reflects the cultural context of L2 learning as it attempts to measure how open a learner is to the other culture that primarily uses L2. However, Crookes and Schmidt (1991) criticized such proposal. They claimed that it overlooks the educational contexts. Dörnyei (1994) also criticized it because it ignores the learners' cognitive domain. It seems that it is necessary to include the perspective of personality traits and behaviours (Markus and Nurius 1986). For example, self-representation is an issue to be considered. Three types of self-representation include what kind of person you wish to become, what kind of person you can become, and what kind of person you are afraid of becoming.

In an early study, researchers have also classified the types of possible selves into the ideal and the ought-to self (Higgins, Klein and Strauman 1985). The ideal self refers to a learner's hopes and wishes for the future self. By contrast, the ought-to self refers to a learner's sense of duty and/or obligations to satisfy the expectations of others, that is, their teachers or parents. The ought-to self is external. Dörnyei (2009) extended the concept of possible selves and included learning experiences, that is, the learning context, such as the curricula, peers and teachers. Motivation includes two components: instrumental motivation and integrative motivation. He posited that if learners wish to be successful professionals, integrativeness, that is, being a part of the L2 culture, should be regarded as the ideal self. This suggests the importance of how learners view themselves as ideal learners.

Dörnyei, Henry and Muir (2016) suggested the Directed Motivational Currents (DMCs), which is described as 'a prolonged process of engagement in a series of tasks which are rewarding primarily because they transport an individual towards a highly valued end' (Dörnyei, Ibrahim and Muir 2015: 98). According to DMCs, individual learning activities form integrated parts of a superordinate and complex motivational superstructure. It is assumed that once a learner sets in motion, they would be propelled in the direction of a goal or vision. It would be like a current that transports various life forms and objects that enter its flow. DMC includes two features: the directedness of a DMC and the enduringness of self-propelling motivational processes. This differs from the concept of intrinsic motivation, described above. Based on DMC, Bui and Teng (2019) suggested the dual-motivation system. Based on the dual-motivation system, an individual's existing language or languages (L1 and L2), especially those with closer psychotypology to the L3, may have a positive influence on L3 learning motivation. The L2 learning experience also helps to shape and sustain L3 motivation. Then, the addition of an L3 has a reciprocal and quite often negative impact on L2 learning motivation. Factors such as psychotypology, past L2 learning experience, self-confidence, perceptions of the L2 and L3 communities and even the learners' backgrounds, all contribute towards shaping and evolving the complex and dynamic relations between L2 and L3 learning.

In multilingual education, students who learn both an L2 and L3 may have a shared vision or a goal of aspiring to be multilingual. This is because learners commonly have a belief to reach across language boundaries. They would envision themselves functioning in the future as a 'task force that effectively promotes positive attitudes about multilingualism' (Dörnyei and Kubanyiova 2014: 83). However, the DMC in multilingual education may not be achieved without the visionary quality or motivational properties shared by learning an L2 and L3. Additionally, for a learner who is learning both an L2 and L3, they may have a future-oriented image of being a successful speaker in both languages. This becomes part of a person that the learner aspires to be. It also becomes a part of the learner's core identity. In such situations, it is the ideal self in learning these languages that becomes chronically accessible in working cognition. This type of target language-speaking self is related to the learner's actual lived experiences and imagined communities.

The shared visionary or motivational quality in learning both an L2 and L3 may facilitate learners out of the limited practices in a classroom and access into an imaginary world within which they would envision themselves engaged in a social interaction with other speakers of the target languages. This may be similar to Locke and Latham's (1990) goal-setting theory. They argued that certain characteristics of a goal are prerequisite in ensuring learners' efforts to concentrate on the predetermined goals. When learners have a higher level of belief in the importance and attainability of a goal, they may have a higher level of sustained behaviour. Learners may invest more in learning a language when goals are both specific and difficult. However, the goal-setting theory is not elaborate enough to explain what makes goals important and what the commitment (or investment) involves (Henry, Dörnyei, Davydenko 2015). While learners may easily form a goal, not every goal can form the stimulus for creating a powerful and enduring pathway of motivated behaviour. We need to consider several key issues: the construct of visionary qualities shared in learning both an L2 and L3, self-concordant goals and proximal sub-goals in learning the languages, and learners' motivational dynamics in simultaneously learning multiple languages.

1.5 Multilingual practices in Asian contexts

Globalization is far from a uniform process throughout the world, and multilingual practices are inseparable from the local interplay between state, market and forms of life. In order to illustrate this complex issue in Asian contexts, we have chosen to examine multilingualism in several nations in Asia: Singapore, the Philippines, India and China.

1.5.1 Singapore

Singapore, officially the republic of Singapore (also called the Lion City or the Garden city), is a sovereign city-state in Southeast Asia. The total population for Singapore was about 5.8 million in 2019, with about 4 million permanent residents. There are four ethnic groups: Chinese, Malay, Indian and others (mainly Eurasians and Europeans). Of these four groups, 74.3 per cent of the population is Chinese, 13.3 per cent Malay, 9.1 per cent Indians, and 1.4 per cent others. There are four official languages: English, Mandarin, Tamil and Malay. Malay is the national language, mainly used to serve primarily ceremonial functions, was chosen in recognition that Malay fisher-folk comprised the original population of the island, and to honour the history that Singapore was once a part of the Federation of Malaysia. Mandarin is mainly spoken by the Chinese in Singapore. Although there are about twenty-five Chinese dialects, most Chinese speakers have shifted to using Mandarin as a common language in the Chinese community. Only some main dialects were kept (e.g., Hokkien, Cantonese and Teochew). Only a small number of Indians speak Tamil. Most of them use English. Local, basilectal varieties of English, so-called Singlish or Colloquial Singaporean English, are spoken widely across different ethnic groups (Auer and Li 2007). The use of English in Singapore has roots in the nation's economic ambitions to be a global player and its communitarian political ideology. Along with the development of economic pragmatism, a situation of multilingualism and a marked emphasis on a tightly managed standard of English has been formed.

However, the multilingual situation in Singapore is complex. This, in turn, makes the language policy towards multilingual education also complex. Although the officially designated 'mother tongues' in Singapore include English, Mandarin, Malay and Tamil, there has been controversy over the real mother tongues of Singapore. We need to consider several issues in this regard. First, the new population movements in Singapore affect the outcomes of earlier language policies. There may be some differences between the immigrants' imagined communities and the actual communities. Second, there are some tensions between the government's implemented policies and people's actual practices in negotiating the languages and their meanings for a Singaporean (Lim, Pakir and Wee 2010). Therefore, unlike other Asian countries (e.g., Malay in Malaysia), a vernacular of a single group was not chosen as the national language or language for education in Singapore.

The language policy was also described as 'pragmatic multilingualism' (Kuo and Jernudd 1994:72), which means the macro- and micro-sociolinguistic perspectives should be balanced. Three vernaculars – Mandarin Chinese, Malay and Tamil – were adopted as three official languages for representing the three official races 'Chinese', 'Malay' and 'Indian'. The ex-colonial language –

English – was retained as the fourth official language. English is a neutral non-native language in Singapore and does not represent any of the Asian cultures or the mother tongue of any ethnic groups. Choosing English does not mean an advantage to any ethnic group but serves as an effective means for easing the tensions between different ethnic groups. This is the same with the implementation of Mandarin Chinese as the language among Chinese Singaporeans. Mandarin does not belong to any of the actual mother tongues of the original Chinese immigrants. The decision in adopting Mandarin as the mother tongue for the Chinese immigrants was primarily motivated by the improved status of Mandarin in the People's Republic of China (Lim 2009). Although controversies exist in terms of the implementation of mother tongues in Singapore, language policy in Singapore has been appraised as 'a unique case study of a successful programme of bilingualism and language management … an impressive case of a well-planned and effectively implemented language-policy programme', having 'negotiated carefully its language policy and the attendant-sensitive choice of a language for the medium of instruction in its state educational system' (Pakir 2004: 117).

In practice, criticisms are met in language policies adopted by the Singapore government. English has become a dominant language for science, technology, commerce and education. The proportion of the population having English as a dominant home language doubled from 12 per cent in 1980 to 23 per cent in 2000, 28.1 per cent in 2005, 32.3 per cent in 2010, and then to 36.9 per cent in 2015 (Lee 2016). By contrast, as concluded by Ng (2014), English – a non-native language with great political power, social status, educational prestige – came to replace the functions of Chinese, a language that is spoken and used by more than 70 per cent of the total population. Young Chinese Singaporeans lack motivation to learn their mother tongue due to the dominant position of English in education as well as in Singapore's society. It seems that language policy in multilingual education needs to acknowledge the complementarity between English and mother tongues. This is a challenge that needs to be acknowledged as intralinguistic considerations (reconciling a language's function as bearer of authenticity with its economic value) need to be dealt with alongside interlinguistic considerations (the desire to maintain parity or equal status among the official mother tongues) (Wee 2003). This challenge is particularly a critical issue in Singapore's language policy implementation.

Singapore is a small country, but policies towards multilingual education are dynamic due to the need to unite various ethnic groups and a continual movement of people from other countries. For example, in recent years, there has been an increase in the number of Mainland Chinese investing, studying and staying in Singapore. The increasing number of migrants from China is a significant phenomenon in Singapore, either socially or economically (Chan 2006). The impact of their presence in the current sociohistorical era raises the question of whether Mandarin is a competing language for English. Bokhorst-Heng and Caleon (2009) investigated 443 primary school students' attitudes towards English and their mother tongues. Results indicated that, apart from some Malay students, Chinese and Indian students expressed more positive attitudes towards their mother tongues. Most of them stated that they were pulled away from their cultural identity. In addition, students with a lower socio-economic status expressed more negative attitudes towards all three languages in comparison to those from middle and upper socio-economic class groups. Students who had negative attitudes might have lower motivation for learning the target languages. Indeed, English has the instrumental value in a multilingual context in Singapore, and it is one important dimension in motivating students. However, learners' cultural values (integrative function) are one of the necessary aspects to be considered, as the perception of such values may affect their motivation in learning a language. Hence, students' understanding of the meanings and values of the languages need to be considered while drawing up the language policy at the governmental level.

In addition, China's rise in the global market pushes the Singaporean government to make a balance in considering China's intentions, America's power, and the place of Singapore in the geopolitical future world. Along with the rise of China, we may witness an increasing importance of Mandarin in Singapore. The globalized power of English and the rising importance of Mandarin put the Singapore government in a dilemma, including the multilingual education policy in Singapore.

We need to consider several issues in the case of Singapore. First, language contact influences the ecology in a multilingual society, and vice versa. Second, language policy is not the only driving force which can affect the status of different languages and the respective choice, attitudes as well as motivations in language learning. Other forces in the ecology, for example, learners' attitudes, cultural awareness, and economic and social status, symbolic capital and motivation, are also important dimensions to reckon with (L. Lim 2009). Third, both the instrumental and the integrative function of motivation should be considered. Fourth, the actual communities are not the only factor to be considered in multilingual education. Language policy needs to recognize the imagined communities of immigrants from foreign countries and the language conflicts involved in this process. Finally, we need to consider the complementarity between different languages. One language should not be sacrificed to achieve the mastering of another language.

1.5.2 The Philippines

The Philippines is a sovereign island country in Southeast Asia. It consists of about 7,641 islands. It has a population of approximately 100 million. About 180 distinct languages are spoken, and multiple ethnicities and cultures are found throughout the islands. The linguistic and cultural diversity makes the issue of language policy complex in the Philippines. It is a challenging situation for implementing a language policy that can serve the whole country. Therefore, it is no wonder that language policies for the Philippines have changed a lot over the last century. In 1974 and 1987, languages used for education in schools were Filipino and English. However, more than 80 per cent of the people in the Philippines do not speak Filipino or English as their first language. Filipino was determined as the national language. The Filipino language was a linguistic symbol of national unity and identity, and it was aimed to strengthen people's national identity. English is desired because it represents the social and economic power.

As more Filipinos insist that nationalism is independent of the prescribed language of education, it is not necessary to implement Filipino as the prescribed language for education. In 2009, the Philippines Department of Education issued a policy initiating the mother-tongue-based multilingual education. Under this new policy, students in the Philippines (through pre-kindergarten to grade 3) are allowed to use their first language as the medium of instruction for all subject areas (The Philippines Department of Education 2009). In 2012, this policy was modified to include students from K to 12 (The Philippines Department of Education 2012), which means students can receive their mother tongue as medium of instruction for content subjects in basic education programme. Twelve major regional languages are also specified for medium of instruction.

Unlike Singapore, the Philippines is not a country to which immigrants flock. Although a relatively large number of Hokkien speakers from South China came and stayed in the Philippines during the 1950s and the early 1960s, the elder immigrants learnt some Filipino in a natural informal way and the younger immigrants attended school and learnt some English and Filipino. Therefore, language policies related to multilingual education are mainly made without considering the immigrants.

In practice, positive and negative results have been noticed among the language policy in the Philippines. Some of the positive results include the relatively complementary distribution of the three languages (mother tongue, Filipinos, and English) in this multilingual society. For example, the success of language policy in the Philippines may be an example case for which the vernacular is used at home or neighbourhood, English for academic, business, science, diplomacy or for wider communication, while Filipino is used for national unity and identity as the national language. This also ensures the continuing use and conservation of indigenous languages other than Filipino. These distinct languages are used and learnt in a steady state. These languages are precious linguistic resources in a multilingual society. The use of mother tongue is helpful in transforming social and educational infrastructures that breed harmful language attitudes and ideologies (Tupas 2015). However, we also need to consider that if teaching of the mother tongue goes so far, it may underestimate or disregard the realities of inequalities of multilingualism.

Negative results include the difficulties in cultivating Filipino as a language for scholarly discourse. Although sustained efforts have not been made to use Filipino for academic discourse, one does not find the motivation to do this except for a few university departments. Although some loanwords are kept in the Filipino language, there are still great differences between these two languages. The need to be literate in English alongside Filipino is challenging for most students (Gonzalez 1998). The unbalanced socio-economic development in the Philippines is also a factor to be noted. Some in the economically, culturally advantaged and affluent region may find it easier to be competent in performing higher-order cognitive tasks in English. However, those from poorer classes with insufficient teaching resources and regrettable working conditions may find it difficult to attain literacy in English.

1.5.3 India

India, located in South Asia, is the seventh-largest country by area and the second-most populous country. India has two major language families. One is Indo-Aryan, which is spoken by about 74 per cent of the population. The other is Dravidian, which is spoken by 24 per cent of the population. Other languages spoken in India come from the Austroasiatic and Sino-Tibetan language families. A national language has not been stipulated in India. Hindi, a language that has the largest number of speakers, became the official language of the government. English is used extensively in various domains, including higher education, business, and administration. English is regarded as a 'subsidiary official language' (Bhatia and Ritchie 2013: 845). Each state has at least one official language, and totally the Indian constitution recognizes twenty-two languages. Three major languages that are notable for their international presence include Punjabi, Urdu and Bengali. The former two languages are also widely used in Pakistan, India and Bangladesh. Hence, these languages are developing their own international varieties. The second major family is the Dravidian languages, including Tamil, Telugu, Malayalam and Kannada. These four languages are very important in South India. Tamil is also spoken in Sri Lanka. India also has two branches of the Austroasiatic language family: Munda subfamily and Mon-Khmer branch. Sathalia, Mundari and Ho, three languages spoken in southern Bihar, north-eastern Andhra Pradesh and broader areas of West Bengal in India belong to the Munda subfamily. Khasi, a language spoken in Meghalaya state of India, belongs to the Mon-Khmer branch.

Hence, India is a multilingual country, with Hindi and English as the two national and link languages. Hindi becomes the language of the masses while English possess the role as the pan-Indian language of the educated elite. After one and a half century, English has become an integral part of the Indian linguistic mosaic. It is no longer a language of the colonial power but a language dominant in law, science, technology, education, media and government. Although people conceived that Hindi would dethrone English after independence, the fact is that English flourished in the educational and official network of India and became a language of the Indian elite. Bhatia and Ritchie (2013) proposed a pyramid for understanding India's linguistic situation (Figure 1.1). The peak of the pyramid is Hindi and English. The second tier of the pyramid is the scheduled languages, including Bengali, Urdu, and so on, as mentioned above. Scheduled languages are those spoken predominantly in their respective states. The third tier of the pyramid is the 200+ languages with widespread currency. The base of the pyramid is the rural dialects, local vernaculars or mother tongues in the countryside.

In terms of the language policies, the government of India seems to be quite conducive to the promotion of minority languages. For example, in the third tier of the pyramid, forty-seven languages are used in primary education, and more languages are used in radio and broadcasting, fields, print media, and state-level administration. The national policy towards multilingual education in India is called 'Three Language Formula'. According to this formula, trilingualism and quadrilingualism is necessary in education. In addition to the learning of the two important languages, that is, Hindi and English, students from an early age

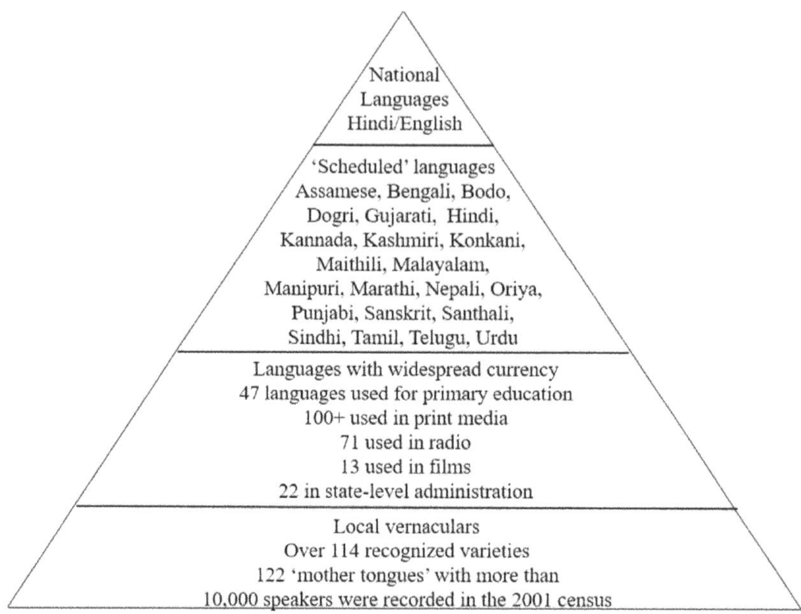

Figure 1.1 Linguistic situation in India

are encouraged to learn a third language. However, there is a public controversy on the effectiveness of the Formula in learning three languages. Despite the debate, people tend to acknowledge the underlying merit of this Formula in enhancing multilingualism and this Formula is a representative of the multilingual character of the nation. By and large, the multilingual educational policy in India is not a monolithic prescriptive model of adopting one country and one language. Although we may say the present-day result of linguistic contact and change has shaped the pattern of multilingualism in India, by and large, Indian multilingualism has been nourished naturally but not by the forces of prescriptivism.

1.5.4 China

China, officially the People's Republic of China (PRC), had a population of over 1.381 billion in 2016. It is the most populous country in the world. China is a one-party ruling country, reigned by the Communist Party of China. China is a potential superpower in the world. It has 56 recognized ethnic groups and about 290 living languages (Kane 2006). China exercises jurisdiction over twenty-two provinces, five autonomous regions (Guangxi, Inner Mongolia, Tibet, Xinjiang and Ningxia), four directly controlled municipalities (Beijing, Tianjin,

Shanghai and Chongqing) and two Special Administrative Regions (Hong Kong and Macau). China also claims sovereignty over Taiwan. The five autonomous regions have their own minority languages as additional official languages. For example, the Zhuang language has official status within Guangxi. The national language of China is Mandarin Chinese (widely called as Putonghua), which is a language that is going through the process of modernization. Putonghua is based on the Beijing dialect, and is treated as a lingua franca in China. It is fast spreading across China and is used widely in the country.

The study of English became popular after the Reform and Opening-up policy in 1988. English was taught as a compulsory subject from middle school and later from the third year of primary school. The mastery of English is widely considered as an advantage and is a required subject for entering universities. During the 2000s, there was a decreasing passion in learning English. The idea of learning English for China's modernization gradually faded due to China's dramatic achievement in economic development and the rise of identity as a Chinese (He and Teng 2019). In recent years, there has been a boom in learning Chinese. Some new terms, including 'strengthening cultural confidence', 'the Chinese dream', 'renaissance of Chinese culture', have appeared in China's new policies (Ministry of Education 2014a). One phenomenon in recent years was that the MOE has issued new policies towards English language teaching. For example, under the new policy for National Matriculation English Test (NMET), the status of NMET as a national examination was reversed (Ministry of Education 2014b).

Neither Putonghua nor English is the mother tongue of the majority of students entering school in China. Language polices in China are mainly due to the political considerations (Zhou 2003). As policies are normally top-down, students' first language (mother tongue, such as Shanghainese) is often excluded in the academic setting. Additionally, the use of their first language is prohibited in many schools. This sends a message to some students and the community that speaking the first language is inferior, both in the classroom and beyond. The result is the marginalization of a students' mother tongue and home culture.

In practice, official policies in Mainland China prioritize the development of the national language (Putonghua) and its use in commercial, political, educational and academic settings (He and Teng 2019). The result is that about 126 languages are struggling to survive and 32 are dying (Zhou, 2003). Additionally, the implementation of recent policies that honours Putonghua and devalues the English language also decrease students' motivation in learning English. Therefore, we need to rethink the hidden agenda of Chinas' two types of language policies. One is for the ethnic minority Chinese, which includes teaching Putonghua and an ethnic minority language. The other is for the Chinese majority (Han), which is the teaching of English and Putonghua through the education system. The goal of the former is for minorities to achieve competency equivalent to one of a native speaker in both their home language and Mandarin Chinese. The goal of the latter is to cultivate well-rounded talents with a mastery of Putonghua and a sufficient competency in English for a globalized economy (Feng 2007). In addition to the claimed purposes of these language policies, there is often a hidden nationalist agenda promoting national unity through spreading a national standard language (Putonghua) and suppressing the development of other languages.

1.6 Reflection

There is no doubt that linguistic rivalries and conflicts exist in the Asian region. However, an ongoing process of convergence has formed an unmarked pattern of widespread naturalistic linguistic coalescence. The linguistic situation in Asian contexts is no longer a state of separation, dominance, isolation and disintegration. In Asian contexts, enlightened by the few cases we examined in this chapter, we need to consider a large-scale diffusion of linguistic features. This kind of diffusion across genetic and areal boundaries will lead to mutually feeding relationships and reciprocity between different Asian countries. Although some may argue that antagonistic bilingualism would occur in parts of Asia, this kind of incidence will become very limited in scope and degree. The features of multilingual education in Asian contexts are likely to be long-term stable bilingualism and linguistic accommodation. We may presume that linguistic diversity is the hallmark in future multilingual education in Asian contexts.

In terms of multilingual education, there is a connection between globalization, linguistic diversity, community affiliations, and options in language education. Whether learners are motivated to learn a second or a third language is related to how they access various imagined communities while interacting with others. In some Asian countries listed in this chapter, policies towards multilingual education were mainly made based on political decisions and social considerations. Learners' imagined communities, and its impact on their motivation in learning languages, were not considered. For example, in Singapore and China, it may be a weak form of multilingual education. English monolingualism was established in Singapore while Chinese monolingualism was established in China, and this is at the expense of the learners' heritage languages. Furthermore, because of the rise of global capitalism in the twenty-first century and English is becoming the most powerful international language riding on its wings, there is a strong desire to (re-) evaluate the status of English in the education system in China.

Factors, including the linguistic sources, education, migration, media, trade and globalization, will continue to play an important role in the multilingualism in Asian contexts. Unchanged for centuries, a feature in Asian contexts is the rural populations. This can be detected in India, China and other Asian countries. Rural populations constitute the heart of many Asian countries. The most obvious linguistic vehicles for reaching the countryside may be the local vernaculars. There are still challenges in developing literacy in English. However, along with the migration from the countryside, people sense the importance of either the national language or English. In addition, the economic forces of globalization have weakened the barriers inherent to the rural and urban varieties. Even some small villages or towns, which were once inconsequential dots on the map of Asia, may receive the attention of international marketing giants and media planners. Rural areas may not be perceived as an economic basket case. The globalization and economic liberalization may bring new heights to rural marketing. The array of media forms, along with the local media form, will add a new distinct feature to multilingualism in Asian contexts.

Multilingualism will not be a marginal phenomenon in Asia, and it will not be merely restricted to educated or business communities. Along with multilingual education, multiple language identities will define features of Asian bilingualism and multilingualism, suggesting the dynamics of language usage and a constant negotiation of identities. However, the maintenance of home language will still be a challenge to many Asian countries. For example, even though the Indian constitution emphasizes the importance of safeguarding the linguistic, religious and minority rights, home language maintenance is still a salient feature concerning multilingual education in India. Similarly, the loss of many local languages in China bring doubts about the effectiveness of multilingual education. Similar phenomena can also be detected in Singapore and the Philippines. Many second-generation speakers in Asia have given up the native language to give preference to the dominant language of the region.

Hence, language shift is the norm in multilingual education in Asian contexts. Linguistic openness, linguistic resources, learners' imagined communities and practiced group membership may influence learners' motivation or investment in language learning. In addition, language conflict between two speech communities is a source of misalignment with learners' imagined communities. This kind of misalignment will be a challenge to language royalties. Although policies related to multilingual education and the social fabric aim to promote local languages, it is still an uphill battle for minor groups to maintain their local vernaculars. Due to the numeric weight, economic power, spatial distribution, personal desirability and functional power, a minor language will continue to be impoverished. Many minor languages will become endangered. The distinction between the majority and minority languages is a complex issue to be addressed in multilingual education.

Multilingual education in Asian contexts from the perspective of imagined communities and motivation provides a progressive, contemporary, comprehensive and multicultural platform for understanding the global phenomenon of multilingualism. The natural forces of linguistic accommodation, diversity and rivalry will bring complexity to multilingual education. The chapter reveals that multilingual education is not a linguistic matter but interwoven with complex factors, including language learning identities, motivations, investment and imagined communities. In multilingual education, there needs to be a balance to equip students with the necessary linguistic capital to compete in the new global world while maintaining their cultural identities. The mother tongues are also positive assets to build on for developing bilingual and multilingual competencies. Following the framework proposed by Lin and Man (2009), the continuum of L1/L2 use in school instruction, the breadth and depth of the target communicative repertoire, and the universal-elitist continuum are all important dimensions to be considered. Language, learners' imagined communities, cultural identity and motivation will continue to be components of a dynamic and viable multilingual society.

2

English as a Lingua Franca, Multilingual Identity, and Multilingual Education in Asia

There are about 7,000 languages and about 200 independent countries across the globe (Lin and Man 2009). Multilingualism is a common phenomenon. It is not only an individual but also a social phenomenon. Multilingualism refers to 'the ability of societies, institutions, groups and individuals to engage, on a regular basis, with more than one language in their day-to-day lives' (Cenoz 2009: 2). However, multilingualism is a very complex phenomenon, and different aspects of multilingualism receive varying degrees of attention. Learners exhibit different levels of proficiency in different languages. They may exhibit different motivation for learning different languages. In addition, each language has a cultural value and provides a sense of identity. Hence, the study of multilingualism in education is related to many aspects, for example, motivation and identity.

Related to motivation and identity is the issue of linguistic distance, which can influence learners' devotion of learning hours to different languages. The distance between languages is a continuum process as each language has its particular origin. Thus, language contact, in this perspective, is a major issue to be considered when exploring linguistic distance. This is because language contact can influence the most permeable levels, for example, the lexicon and the phonological levels. Linguistic differences can also affect different dimensions of multilingual education. However, linguistic differences may not be influenced by multilingual education.

In discussing multilingual education, we need to consider the macro and micro level. The macro level refers to the general vitality of the languages needed for multilingual education, with a focus on various variables, including the number of speakers for that language, the social status affiliated with that language, and the functions of that language in media or in the linguistic landscape. When different languages are used more frequently in these contexts, the macro level can be regarded as 'more multilingual' (Cogo and Dewey 2012). It is difficult to define a context as simply a 'multilingual' context or a 'monolingual' context. We may differentiate a more multilingual context (e.g., some African countries like South Africa, which has eleven official languages) from a less multilingual context (e.g., some European countries like France, which adopts French as a dominant language at the social level). The micro level refers to the individual level, for example, language learners and their social networks (Cenoz 2009). The languages used at home with parents may be different from the languages used with peers or in the academic community. For example, some Singaporean students may speak their local languages at home, but Mandarin or English with peers, and then English in the school community. In the case of international schools in Hong Kong or other similar contexts, the home language can be different from the language used at school. This is also the case with some cross-border students from Mainland China who are studying in Hong Kong local schools. They speak Putonghua at home with parents, then Cantonese with peers, and learn English at school. It seems that the macro level and micro level of multilingual education are interrelated and may influence each other. The interaction between both levels can also affect learners' motivation.

As we discussed in Chapter 1, identities of linguistic minority speakers are discursively constructed and reconstructed. The majority language is often related to a superior symbolic status over minority languages. However, we encounter questions about identity and group membership. The linguistic minority speakers may be excluded from access to, or membership in, the more powerful group. Related to this, identities are either negotiated or non-negotiable in multilingual states. In addition, when people migrate from one place to another place, there may be a change in the status of minority language or majority language. A previous minor language may become a majority language. During this process, an individual may form multilingual identities, leading to motivation change. Given the trend of English as a lingua franca in this global context, the formation of multilingual identities may become more complex. In this chapter, we provide some new ideas on multilingual education in the Asian context through the perspectives of multilingual identity. Related to this, we may need to have some basic information about the spread of English as a lingua franca and cross-linguistic differences in multilingual education.

2.1 Multilingualism and the spread of English as a lingua franca

Multilingualism is becoming more and more common. One issue to be noted is that multilingualism has many different benefits. At the individual level, learners' language skills and cognitive development can be enhanced. At the social level, citizens with multilingual skills can develop awareness of other cultures and increase mobility across countries. However, there are still many places or countries wherein the idea of 'one nation, one language' is dominant. Many languages do not own an official status or are not used in education. For example, there are fifty-six ethnic minority groups in China, and more than fifty-six minority languages are used and spoken by these groups. However, Putonghua (Mandarin Chinese) is the main language for education. Many students do not have their mother tongue as a school language. The idea of linguistic uniformity is very strong. Nonetheless, when we discuss multilingualism, we need to consider the dominant power of English.

It comes as no surprise that English has become the language associated with the process of globalization. As explained by Giddens (1990), globalization is 'the intensification of worldwide social relations which link distant realities in such a way that local happenings are shaped by events occurring many miles away and vice versa' (p. 64). The 'mutual shaping of distant realities' is due to the 'intensification of worldwide social relations' (Giddens 1990: 21) which highlights the importance of language as a primary medium of social interaction. This suggests that everyday interaction takes place within local communities. However, it is reasonable to assume that when more and more people are going beyond the local and into new communities, they are likely to construct new identities. This new order of social interaction stresses a need for a common linguistic code. In this sense, it is common to infer that English permeates the media of social interactions in many non-English-speaking countries. This includes its role in areas including the internet, satellite radio and TV, academic, business, technology and pop culture (e.g., movies, music and sitcoms).

Nowadays, English has become a lingua franca. Students from all over the world are acquiring it as a means to be a member of this modernized world. English is being portrayed as a tool for integrating into certain global spheres and is also perceived as a desirable asset or ideological endeavour with impacts on the acquisition of local languages and cultures. For example, although some Asian countries (e.g., Singapore, Malaysia) are of different cultures, history and religions, English is adapted and adopted in various domains for international and intranational communication. Asia has already become one of the dynamic areas for which English is used for various reasons. Therefore, the English language has reached undisputedly high levels of use in Asia, where some students enter school speaking English, some enter school barely speaking

English, and some are bilingual or trilingual, speaking a non-standard form of English (e.g., Singlish).

In the Chinese context or beyond, the ability in speaking and using English is considered as a benefit related to better opportunities for job-hunting. In some countries, including Cambodia, Malaysia, Mongolia or South Korea, the purpose is not to learn English as a foreign language, but become bilingual in both English and their national language. In Singapore, English is adopted as the official language rather than simply a second language. Although English is regarded as a foreign language in China, the spread of English in China is overwhelming (Hu 2007).

Along with the rising importance of English on a global scale, researchers have expressed a certain concern towards the spread of English as a lingua franca. Some consider the spread of English as a threat to other languages, particularly minority languages (Skutnabb-Kangas 2000). One opinion is that the spread of English also leads to the loss of cultural identity (Kuppens 2013). Some researchers hold different opinions and regard the spread of English as being concomitant with the use of other languages, leading to the development of multiple identities. For example, Sung (2014) argued that some Cantonese-speaking students in Hong Kong indicated a preference to foreground either a local or global identity, but some students reconciled their local and global identities, embracing multiple identities while communicating in English as an international language. Some English learners may embrace a global identity because they perceive a value in being affiliated with the global community and/or the global culture.

Despite the controversy related to the spread of English, it is still a dominant language. Nowadays, there are more non-native English speakers than native English speakers (Crystal 2003, 2008). However, we should acknowledge that the use of English as a lingua franca does not mean a delimited status or a threat to other languages (Seidlhofer 2011). Rather, English is a language for wider communication (Jenkins 2007; 2015), and entails various factors, for example, identity, code-switching and language variation (Camilleri 1996; Gauci and Camilleri 2013; Ishikawa 2016). Therefore, the use of English as a lingua franca co-constructs and reflects 'repertoires in flux' in a multilingual setting (Jenkins 2015: 76). However, the learning of English poses some challenges to the learners whose native language is significantly different from English. The cross-linguistic influence is a major issue to be considered in multilingual education.

2.2　Cross-linguistic influence in multilingual education

Cross-linguistic influence is an important issue to be noted in multilingual education. For example, learners' mother tongue is likely to have an influence on a second language, and then a third language. According to Cenoz (2003), when exploring language transfer, interactional strategies and transfer lapses need to be discussed. Interactional strategies refer to somewhat intentional switches into languages other than the target language. This is often linked to factors such as knowledge of other languages by the interlocuter or the topic of the conversation. Intentional switches are usually preceded by a pause in oral production. By contrast, transfer lapses mean the non-intentional switches. These switches are not preceded by a pause or a false start. Transfer lapses are automatic and accidental. The existence of pauses before the element from another language is a main difference between interactional strategies and transfer lapses.

One common finding related to cross-linguistic influence is that speakers tend to use or borrow more words from their first language which are typologically closer to the target language (Hammarberg 2001). For example, French-speaking English learners tend to transfer vocabulary and structures from French when they are learning English. However, Ringbom (2007) also pointed out other factors related to cross-linguistic influence. These included the level of proficiency in the source language and the target language, acquisition order of the languages, level of formality, and the specific context of interaction that can influence the amount of transfer. For example, learners with a higher level of proficiency have been reported to transfer less vocabulary while learners with a lower level of proficiency have been reported to transfer more elements from their first language (Ringbom 1987). In exploring the influence of proficiency on language transfer, we need to consider learners' proficiency in the target language as well as in the first or second language (Dewale 2001). Learners' language proficiency adds complexity to the research on cross-linguistic transfer as multilingual competency does not equal to the sum of monolingual competency (Herdina and Jessner 2000).

One issue to bear in mind is that transfer can be 'positive' and 'negative'. When specific features inherent in two languages are similar to each other, 'positive' transfer may occur. For example, there exists shared cognates between Hebrew and Arabic. In addition, grapheme-phoneme recognition in French may help French-speaking students familiarize themselves with the English alphabet. By contrast, when features in two languages are greatly different from each other, 'negative' transfer may occur because learners tend to overly rely on their first language. For example, English article system does not exist in Chinese. However, in terms of the use of English article system, Chinese learners have both a grammatical deficit (artitle underuse) and pragmatic defit (article overuse and misuse) (Robertson 2000). However, the impact of prior linguistic knowledge on the acquisition of an additional language is a much broader phenomenon. We may have to consider negative transfer, which presents an incomplete representation of the complexities in the language acquisition process. In multilingual education, having at least two previously acquired languages multiplies the potential sources of transfer, which makes the interactions between languages a complex process (e.g., Cenoz 2001; Dewaele 2001). As argued by García-Mayo (2012), the acquisition of a third language is more complex than the acquisition of a second language. These issues should be regarded as a distinct process rather than another instance inherent to second language acquisition.

Several L3 transfer models and hypotheses have been proposed in recent years. Three main models include the Cumulative Enhancement Model (Flynn, Foley and Vinnitskaya 2004), the L2 status factor (Bardel and Falk 2007) and the Typological Primacy Model (Rothman 2011). In the case of multilingual education, there exists the possibility of several sources of linguistic transfer. Understanding L3 transfer can inform us about mental architecture, linguistic representation, the interface of cognitive economy, and the ways that cannot be explored by simply investigating the transfer in various instances of bilingualism. According to Rothman and Halloran (2013), transfer in multilingual acquisition scenarios is dynamic. However, it is ultimately predictable, and, by extension, logical, based on cognitive factors. Research on L3 transfer embodies unique and independent evidence for the understanding of cognition that is related to acquisition processes.

Based on the Cumulative Enhancement Model (CEM) (Flynn, Claire and Vinnitskaya 2004), morphosyntactic transfer at the L3 state can be from either of the previously acquired grammars. However, learners can better acquire an L3 when transfer is facilitative to the learners. In other words, the learners can transfer the acquisition of L3 from L1, L2 or both. That means neither the L1 nor the L2 have their own special status for transfer. Developmental acquisition patterns are not redundant but are increasingly observable in multilingual acquisition. This makes multilingual acquisition a collective process whereby prior language learning experiences can facilitate subsequent language acquisition. A learner does not learn the same property twice in the case of L2 or L3 acquisition. Non-redundancy in acquisition is representative of cognitive economic drive. Therefore, learners may have previously acquired properties in their mind but transfer of properties from previously acquired languages may only occur when it is facilitative to L3 acquisition. Hence, transfer could be positive or neutral.

This model of CEM is supported by Leung (2007), wherein sixteen Vietnamese monolingual and forty-one Chinese-English bilinguals were involved. As the Chinese students had higher English proficiency level, they showed better performance than the Vietnamese students in terms of the acquisition of the Determiner Phrase in beginner French. However, Thomas (1990) showed that Chinese monolinguals outperformed those who are English-Chinese bilinguals in acquiring the Japanese reflexive *zibun*. A negative L2 effect seemed to have occurred. One explanation is that the CEM model has not articulated how the internal parser would be determined at the initial stages of acquisition. It seems that transfer in L3 acquisition is not done holistically. However, it is on a property-by-property basis, leading to neutralized transfer from either L1, L2, or both (Rothman and Halloran 2013). Hence, transfer in multilingualism is different from what we know in L2 acquisition.

The L2 status model proposed by Bardel and Falk (2007) suggests that the L2 has a preferred status in being a source of transfer in L3 acquisition. The role that L2 plays is stronger than the role of L1 in the initial stages of L3 acquisition. It may be because the L2 grammar is stored in declarative memory, while the L1 grammar is stored in both declarative and procedural memory (Paradis 2004). Therefore, L2 is more readily accessible and it behaves as a filter that blocks access to the L1 grammar. As argued by Falk and Bardel (2011), a possible explanation for the non-availability of L1 can be due to the cognitive differences between the acquisition of L1 and L2. For example, the learners' first language may be acquired instinctively, but foreign languages are mainly acquired through formal instruction. This is why learners would often rely on the learning of L2 for their subsequent acquisition of L3, L4 and so on. Falk and Bardel (2011) invited two groups of intermediate German learners to measure their acquisition of object pronoun placement. Among them, twenty-two were L1 English/L2 French while twenty-two were L1 French/L2 English. French exhibits pre-verbal but English displays post-verbal placement in main and subordinate clauses. German language displays pre-verbal in subordinate and post-verbal in main clauses. These results showed that both groups tend to accept more object placements, inherent in their respective L2s. The results support the L2 status model. However, one issue to be noted is that L2 transfer can be circumvented by structural or other factors. It is still not clear why factors, for example, relative structural similarity, could bypass the filter formed by the differences in declarative and procedural memory of L1 and L2.

The Typological Primacy Model (TPM) was proposed by Rothman (2011). According to this model, one of the main variables for syntactic transfer onto an L3 is the typological proximity perceived by the learners. Full transfer from either the L1 or the L2 may occur for the acquisition of an L3. Selective or partial transfer may not happen. A learner's L2 interlanguage is also important because it may be the prerequisite for locating similarities between the L2 and L3. Therefore, L3 transfer is not determined by the order of acquisition but by the linguistic structural similarities between previously known languages and subsequent language acquisition. To date, evidence for the TPM is only related to findings based on the combinations of Germanic and Romance languages (Rothman 2011). We still need to explore more unique and less closely related language pairings.

Armed with the above knowledge, multilingualism is a complex phenomenon. Language classrooms are increasingly diverse in terms of the students' linguistic profiles. Language teachers and pedagogues may face an undeniable challenge (de la Fuente and Lacroix 2015). In multilingual education, we need to consider L1–L2 transfer, we also need to consider L1–L2–L3 transfer. Stated succinctly, L1 learning can transfer to L2 achievement and even L3 learning. In addition, L2 learning may also influence L3 learning, even though the transfer is not automatic. However, this is reliant on the quality of education received in the L1 by the learners and the proficiency level achieved in their L2 learning. We may argue that there are advantages for ensuring good quality L1 and L2 instruction before proceeding to L3 learning. When students have had opportunities to develop literacy in their L1 and L2, they may make positive transfer and stronger progress in acquiring literacy in the L3. In a similar vein, stronger progress in L3 can also be made when learners have received adequate exposure to L1 and L2. Cenoz, Hufeisen and Jessner (2001) argued that L2 learning vary in terms of their cognitive demands, the extent of contextual support received by learners, and the benefits of L1 for L2 learning. However, we may also argue that academic proficiency transfers across languages because academic language proficiency is associated with common language proficiencies. For example, the skills and knowledge in previous L1 context can be used when working in an L2 and then L3, and this is the basis for us to discuss motivation in multilingual education.

2.3 Multilingual identity

Researchers have acknowledged the need to discuss identity in relation to motivation in language learning (Dörnyei and Ushioda 2009). In a globalized society, multilingual contexts are a facet of life. Multilingualism has stimulated an increasing interest in identity and its relationship to language learning. Learners build their social network in a multilingual environment. This process lays a foundation for the constant negotiation and renegotiation of learners' linguistic identity (Pavlenko and Blackledge 2004). An individual has not only multiple self-representations but also various feelings of belonging to the immediate context. However, identities are discursively constructed (Teng 2018). Most importantly, identities are embedded within social practices and broader ideological frameworks (Teng 2018).

Learners who move from one community to another, or one site to another, may encounter different partners during interaction. It is also possible for them to invoke different representations of identity. Even within the same school, there are many sites that learners may be engaged with. Each site provides learners with different opportunities, possibilities, constraints and conditions to speak and to represent themselves through language learning and use. To learners, there may be sites of first language use, as well as sites of second and third language use. What learners hear and learn within sites is critical to the development of identity. In other words, these sites provide spaces or places in which identity is enacted, where social interactions, cultures, languages, and identities are made to manifest. It is also where the 'insidering' and 'outsidering' is done, where spoken discourse is heard or not heard, is validated or remains unacknowledged, and where membership is made available or denied (Miller 2003: 46). Therefore, identity is not a fixed category, identity is 'multiple, complex, context contingent, varied, overlapping, sometimes fragmented and even contradictory along different contexts' (Baker 2006: 138). It is not surprising that learners construct and reconstruct multiple identities, particularly in a multilingual education context.

The notion of identity is central to our understanding of L2 learning. As Wenger (1998: 215) noted, 'learning transforms who we are and what we can do, it is an experience of identity'. For L2 learners, speaking an L2 is actually related to the ways in which learners negotiate with the new communities and express their identities with that language (Ushioda 2013). As discussed earlier, globalization has had significant influence on L2 identity construction. This global world can no longer be conceptualized as a community that is linguistically and culturally definable. Learning a language has a complex relationship with culture. For example, English among L2 learners indicates 'a non-parochial, cosmopolitan, globalized citizen identity' (Dörnyei 2005: 97). Some L2 learners use English but they want to preserve their L1 identity in a context of English as a lingua franca (ELF) (Jenkins 2003). Some learners display varying degrees of affiliations with their local and/or global identities in a context of ELF (Sung 2016). Language learners nowadays have more instruments and resources to convey their messages, understand others and interact with more speakers of the target language. Linguistic and semiotic repertoires accumulated from multilingual learning experiences affect learners' self-representations and mediation of identities (Teng and Yip 2019). Therefore, L2 learners in a multilingual community may possess a myriad of identity options, and this is concluded as 'multilayered modes of identity at global, regional, national and local levels' (Pennycook 2005: 41).

In terms of studying abroad, 'student sojourners abroad may encounter challenges not only to their language skills, but also to their identities' (Kinginger 2015: 6). The academic sojourns abroad are temporary. During this short-term stay, learners usually make personal choices related to their engagement with host communities and languages. Related to this, learners often encounter challenges and changes in their identity development. However, identity change is not something caused by sojourners, but it is formed when sojourners need to perform and negotiate their identities within more or less unfamiliar host environments (Barkhuizn 2017). For example, who they are, how they see and feel about themselves may be contested by others who ascribe to them identities with which they may not necessarily affiliate. We may define sojourners' identity development as multilingual identity as they possess and utilize 'a complex of specific semiotic resources' (Blommaert 2010: 102) to align with the practiced host community (Teng and Bui 2018).

Therefore, different forms of participation and interactions with different languages contribute to learners' development of multilingual identities. In a context where bilingualism is moved to multilingualism, multilingualism has taken on different meanings and goals. For example, the promotion of the local language together with the national language, on the one hand, and encouragement of using English often result in multilingual identities on the other (Larrinaga and Amurrio 2015). However, it is also argued that some learners' identity remains relatively stable and fixed because they only take English as a linguistic tool belonging to non-native English speakers while lacking motivations to incorporate their linguistic and pragmatic knowledge of English into their existent communion repertoires and failing to make that target language part of their self (Ke 2016). It is essential to allocate attention to assist learners' development of a multilingual identity. The construction of multilingual identity may help learners comfortably and confidently use various target languages in different settings.

2.4　What do we know about the Asian context?

In this section, we specifically draw upon the linguistic situation of Hong Kong, Malaysia and Brunei, three different but also interconnected contexts.

2.4.1　Hong Kong

Struggles in identity development take place while moving around a range of sites, from local (e.g., family, workplace), to national (e.g., language policy), and international (e.g., globalization). Hence, identity is neither stable nor monolithic, but constantly shifting, being fashioned and refashioned, characterized by contradiction and ambiguity. The achievement of multilingual identity is also complex, problematic and fragile. Multilingual identity, formed during learning different languages, involve negotiation of many facets, including social status, linguistic assets and group membership. These facets are tightly interconnected and simultaneously challenge the formation of multilingual identity in complex ways. This phenomenon was also reflected in Barkhuizen's (2017) study, wherein a Hong Kong student, named Max, completed a BA degree at a university in New Zealand. This is a longitudinal study, wherein Max's long-term identity development was explored before studying in New Zealand, during study, after graduation and after coming back to Hong Kong. Although Max experienced difficulties in social settings both in and out of school, he succeeded in gaining access to interaction with international and domestic students. His advanced language proficiency helped him to realize his predetermined goal, which was to cope with a new cultural context and to become a better communicator. During his study abroad, Max demonstrated three aspects of L2 identity, including (1) identity-related aspects of second language proficiency, (2) linguistic self-concept and (3) second language-mediated aspects of personal development. However, the three aspects are interwoven, showing identity as a multiple, dynamic and constantly changing notion while studying abroad (Teng and Bui 2018). Max later joined the local community and his capability in adjusting the cultural performance of his joke-telling shows his development of a multilingual identity and his openness towards identity as a global citizen. Max boosted his confidence as an English speaker but at the same time regarded his identity as a general Hong Konger in his working life years after he returned to Hong Kong.

In another study focusing on the Hong Kong context (Sung 2014), nine Cantonese speakers' experiences of using ELF inside and outside the university and their perceptions of their identities in ELF contexts were explored. Sung's study suggests the value of identity construction in ELF communication, supporting the fact that 'ELF is neither a culturally impoverished nor identity neutral form of communication' (Baker 2011: 46). In particular, variances were detected among the nine students. Two L2 learners tended to foreground their local and/ or national identities. The two learners held reservations about the formation of identity as global citizens. They attached great value to their local identity in ELF communication and they regarded affiliation with a global community as abstract and intangible. Two learners were willing to be affiliated with the wider global community. To the two learners, local and global are oppositional identity labels. They did not wish to be defined solely by the local identity because English is a language associated with the wider global community in the era of globalization. Five learners expressed their willingness to both global and local identities in ELF communication. They were happy to embrace dual or hybrid identities. They did not perceive a conflict between local and global identities because they attempted to reconcile the potential challenges in perceiving local and global values. A simplistic binary categorization between local culture and global culture should not be clearly defined for the five learners. 'Global' identity can be used to describe their attitudes towards ELF communication. We are not aiming to describe the percentage of L2 learners in different identity categorizations. We argue that learners can dynamically negotiate between the global and the local, manoeuvre within the conflicts between the global and the local and employ strategies to retain the local identity while appropriating value of the global. While having the interplay between the global and the local, it is the universalizing and particularizing forces in the processes of globalization that influence L2 learners' identity construction.

Hence, Hong Kong, a cosmopolitan city in Asia where English serves as one of the most important lingua francas for intercultural communication, is experiencing changes in ELF communication. Hong Kong has more and more non-English speakers from mainland through the channel of family ties (see more details in Chapter 4). Hong Kong also has a non-Chinese-speaking population, including first language (L1) speakers from the 'inner circle' countries (the

United Kingdom, the United States and Australia) and a substantial population of settlers and sojourners from other parts of Asia, for example, the Philippines, Indonesia and Thailand. Under the forces of globalization, it may not be appropriate to conceptualize the world as an entity comprised easily of definable linguistic and cultural communities (Pavlenko 2002).

The relationship between language and identity has become more and more complex as this inexorable link between language and identity is influenced by the nature of multicultural features and cross-linguistic differences. Chinese and English are two different languages, and L2 learners in Hong Kong may find it difficult to learn English. In addition, many Hong Kongers choose to foreground their local identities in attempting not to be another Chinese city. However, twenty years on from the handover, English is still a very important language in Hong Kong, and is still the international lingua franca. Hong Kong may no longer be a British colony, but it is still an international business hub that has earned its branding as 'Asia's world city'. It is essential to have more English in media such as radio, television and local websites in Hong Kong, and allow English teachers, both local and NET (native-speaking English teachers), to have better training in the teaching of the language in a more enjoyable way rather than requesting students to attend to tedious, outdated textbooks and exams. In today's ELF communication, L2 learners need more of an incentive to learn or improve their English skills.

2.4.2 Malaysia

Malaysia is a multi-ethnic and multilingual country. The national language is Malay, which is widely used in official domains. Malay, the language of ethnic Malays, was later named Bahasa Malaysia to unite all ethnic groups and foster a national identity. Malaysia was once a self-governing British colony, and English had been the official language until 1967. After gaining independence in 1957, the Language Act was later passed in 1967, stipulating Malay, rather than English, be used as the medium of instruction (MOI) for education from primary to tertiary level. Twenty years were given to implement this process. This period of twenty years was also called 'Malaysianization' (Kirkpatrick and Bolton 2010: 20). Mahathir, who had governed Malaysia from 1981 to 2003, exerted efforts to build an image of Malaysinization. Due to the wave of globalization, language policy in the 1990s allowed some private colleges in Malaysia to use English as a tool for science and technology. In addition, English was used as MOI for mathematics and science subjects in primary and secondary schools in 2003.

However, this policy was terminated in 2013, and English was replaced by Malay in various domains again despite a public concern for a pragmatic need of using English as a tool for having more international development.

According to the latest census data from 2017, ethnic Malays and indigenous people constitute 61.7 per cent of the total population while Chinese and Indians occupy 20.8 per cent and 6.2 per cent of the total population. Mandarin and Tamil are two major minority languages for the ethnic Chinese and Tamil communities, respectively. In addition to Mandarin, Chinese people speak many Chinese dialects, including Hokkien, Hakka and Cantonese. Although Tamil has a largest number of speakers in the Indian community, Indian groups do not share a common language but speak different languages, including Punjabis, Telugus, Sindhis, Malayalis. However, Mandarin and Tamil, as well as other local languages, were only allowed to be used in private domains. In addition, the Malaysian government carried out corpus planning for the Malay language, for example, the government aims to develop terminology and codification covering science, technology, law, medicine and other fields for the Malay language (Alis 2006). Yet, corpus planning for other languages had not been conducted in Malaysia.

The priority in language policy in Malaysia is to build national unity. Although this 'unity in diversity' agenda can help cultural, linguistic, and religious integration to a certain degree (Husin 2011), this agenda appears to be fragile as ethnic tension and conflicts in Malaysia have never stopped. The 'unity in diversity' agenda can even be regarded as a hurdle in the development of a unified Malaysian nation in this global community (Zhou and Wang 2017). Conflicts between different languages always occur in Malaysia. Blindfolded by nationalism, the Malaysian government was not able to see a significant role of English in developing Malaysia. English, a super-global language and former colonial language, was demoted from primary to tertiary education. In addition, speakers of two strong regional languages, Chinese and Tamil, are fighting against the Malay language, either explicitly or implicitly. In terms of government job employees, less than 3 per cent were Chinese or Indians (Woo 2015). These discrimination policies discouraged Chinese Malaysians from learning Malay or attending public schools and universities (Zhou and Wang 2017).

The linguistic, ethnic and cultural segregation is becoming more severe in Malaysia. The aim of language policy in Malaysia was to build national unity but in fact it caused more conflicts between ethnic groups, trapping Malaysia in a dilemma of losing many opportunities in developing business, education, and other areas for the last five decades. Along with China's economy accelerating into the world's second strongest country in the last decade, the status of Chinese as a regional language in Malaysia evolved. The promotion of English as a lingua franca in Malaysia, which was difficult in the 1950s and 1960s, can be more difficult in the future.

In today's Malaysia, learners tend to have different attitudes towards English as a lingua franca. On the one hand, as acknowledged by Lee et al. (2010: 98), 'English has played a part in making them [learners] more "open-minded", taking on more neutral views towards values that are perceived to be markers of cultural identity'. On the other hand, learners who are multilingual with English as a first language and correspondingly lesser competency in the language of their ethnic group were perceived by other learners as 'arrogant', or 'showing off' (Lee 2003). Despite being able to use English is still regarded as a social advantage in Malaysia (Zhou and Wang 2017), many learners in Malaysia seem to have lost interest in speaking and using English. As argued by Lee (2003), learners in Malaysia tend to mask their motivation in learning English because learning English does not bring them any rewards, for example, increasing their cultural capital. The cultural values that the learners can reap are not open-ended and positive. Learners may form negative dividends, including disenfranchisement and cultural displacement, in the process of learning and using English. Due to the policy in over-safeguarding Malay ethnic groups, other ethnic groups may protect their identity of belonging to their group. Hence, in multicultural post-colonial Malaysia, motivation in learning English becomes a tricky issue within certain contexts because of the complex nature in forming multilingual identity for learners in Malaysia.

2.4.3 Brunei

Brunei, a former British colony, is completely surrounded by the Malaysian state of Sarawak. The Bruneian Empire declined during the nineteenth century. In 1888, Brunei became a British protectorate. A British resident was assigned as colonial manager in 1906. The British helped terminate the monarchy in 1962. Brunei gained its independence from the United Kingdom in 1984. Economic growth during the 1990s and 2000s transformed Brunei into an industrialized, wealthy and developed country.

In terms of earlier language learning policy, Brunei aimed to modernize and become an important member of the international arena through promoting English but while at the same time, retain the local culture through using Malay as the sole medium of instruction. The 1959 constitution specified Malay as the national language but later this policy was not implemented. Reasons included a civil insurrection in 1962 and political divergence with Malaysia in the 1970s. The National Education System was introduced after Brunei gained independence in 1984. The system stipulated Malay is the MOI for primary school students grades 1 to 3. But after that English will be MOI for main subjects, including Mathematics, Science, History, and Technology. In reading the National Education System for the twenty-first century (Brunei Ministry of Education 2009), some changes were noticed. In contrast to previous promotion of Malay as the language for teaching mathematics and science from grades 1 to 3, English was adopted as MOI from primary 1 after 2011. Public concerns for undermining Malay and promoting English have dissipated, and this education system has become widely accepted in Brunei (Kirkpatrick and Bolton 2010). However, it is not an issue of whether a bilingual education system works or not. The main problem is the government schools do not provide proficient bilingual teachers and only those private schools for rich people can offer good resources for bilingual learning. In addition, it seems that Malay should not be undermined because it is an important language in constituting this country's philosophy.

Brunei is also a multilingual country. Figure 2.1 represents the linguistic repertoire of Brunei. The languages are ranked from top to bottom based on the prestige they enjoy. It seems that English occupies the most important position.

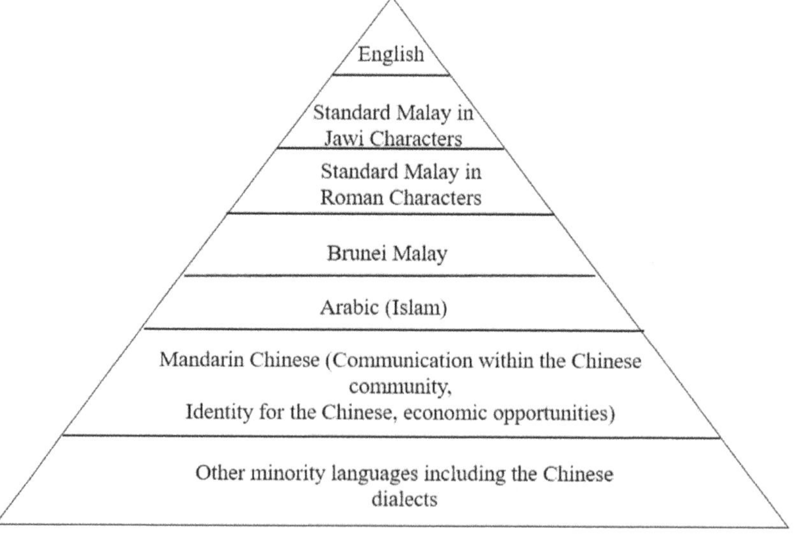

Figure 2.1 The Bruneian linguistic repertoire

The second tier of language is Malay, and the third tier of language is Arabic. The bottom language is Mandarin Chinese and local Chinese vernaculars.

An issue that needs to be borne in mind is the level of access to English in Brunei. English was only associated with the Brunei elite before (Martin and Abdullah 2002). Nowadays, English, rather than an elite language, plays a wider role in various domains in Brunei, as shown in some survey studies (e.g., Coluzzi 2012). English is used as a tool to disseminate Western cultures, which is counterbalanced by an upsurge of Islamic consciousness and desire to uphold Brunei. However, globalization pervades all aspects of life in Brunei, including religion, education, administration, language, travel and tourism, technology, cuisine, leisure pursuits, advertising and entertainment in general. The Ministry of Education has taken several initiatives to guarantee that the educational system in Brunei can deal with the challenges of globalization and technological advances. We do not agree with Kirkpatrick and Bolton (2010) that the bilingual education system is the most successful model in Asia. We do agree that despite calls in some quarters for more focus to be paid to the Malay language in the education system of Brunei, Brunei will still be likely to proceed with the current bilingual education system, which accords higher privileges to English. Indeed, Brunei has moved forward with different teaching initiatives, making English teaching a fun and enjoyable way.

However, inherent problems have been found in the language education system. For example, access to language is a big problem in Brunei. Surely, the quality, scope and variety of radio and TV programmes in English are popular in Brunei. However, in rural areas, people almost do not have access to English and pupils are struggled to learn English. During the process of being struggled to learn English, some people lose the value of local cultural products. Hence, Brunei is still trapped in a tense situation of simultaneously valuing the sovereignty of the Malay language (local identity) and the global importance of English (global citizen). In addition, while acknowledging the importance of English as a lingua franca, the language education system in Brunei ignores the language rights of minority groups. For example, Chinese and Islamic, two important languages in local communities, are not considered as a subject in public schools.

2.5 Reflection

In closing, this chapter, through discussing multilingual education in the Asian contexts (e.g., Hong Kong, Malaysia and Brunei) and the spread of English as a lingua franca, sheds lights on multilingual identity and motivation in maintaining the interest in learning multiple languages. We suggest a need to address the individual differences in multilingual education and keep reflective of the role of individuality in identity construction and motivation maintenance. Specifically, multilingual learners should be treated as active and purposeful individuals in maintaining motivations in multilingual education settings.

The dramatically increasing importance of English in today's globalizing world has yielded similar concerns to many Asian countries. English has become a major language of modernization. The globalization makes English more important. Language education policies in the Asian countries that we discussed need to ensure that citizens will have more chances to become sufficiently proficient in English. Thus, learners can use English to access knowledge and contribute to the development and dissemination of knowledge. Parental demands for improving their children's proficiency in English also make it an important perspective to be considered for the government to develop language learning policy. In addition, learners' construction of multilingual identity needs to be considered. Identity development is multiple, fluid and dynamic, but most importantly, it is individualized. The increased presence of English will threaten not only local languages but local cultures. Policymakers need to consider how to strike an equitable and practical balance between English and local/national languages. This has become a thorny issue confronting many governments in Asian contexts at the moment, and any attempts by the government would easily prompt public controversy and emotion. Each of the above-mentioned countries/regions (Hong Kong, Malaysia and Brunei) had attempted to deal with ELF, multilingual identity and multilingual education in its own way. In none of these countries, however, can it be said that the language learning policies have been uniformly successful. In extreme cases (e.g., Malaysia), the implementation of policy has yielded anger and dissent among a certain sector of population.

This chapter suggests that the link between language and identity should not be confined to native versus non-native speakers. Given the social, cultural and political concerns, there is great value in researching ELF, multilingual identity and multilingual education in the post-colonial countries/regions, for example, Hong Kong, Malaysia, and Brunei. Identity is a multilayered, non-unitary and dynamic construct. The contexts of interaction influence the formation of multilingual identity. English learners in the post-colonial context, affected by the different language learning policy in each location, negotiate a wide array of social and cultural identities. Along with the complexity of the sociocultural context for learning and using English, learners in the post-colonial contexts may perceive resistance against using the former colonial language. Learners may encounter struggles in knowing when and how to switch identities to conform to the dominant group's unspoken expectations. Using English could be perceived as distancing, offending, or annoying the local cultural identity. Identity switches equals to an actual language switch itself.

However, language affects identity in non-interactive ways. It is not the use of English that affects learners' identity development, but knowing English itself affects identity in non-interactive ways. English, a global ELF, carries within each context a particular world view and culture. Knowing English influences the way that the learners construct their vision of the world. Multilingual competency, for example, knowing English and a local language, would help learners acquire literacy through more than one window and more than one cultural lens. Multilingual learners are able to transcend their cultural boundaries and access the worldviews and ways of thinking of others. Given the benefits of multilingual education, we may need to reconsider the questions of power, inequality, resistance, and struggles inherent in multilingual contexts. Learners' complex strategic and non-strategic identity shift reflects their struggles in manoeuvring their ways in the search for acceptance and belonging, highlighting the intricate relation between language and identity. In the complex multicultural post-colonial world, multilingual learners may need to manage a complex interweaving of multiple concerns ranging from cultural dissonance to a sense of quiet empowerment.

The trend of globalization offers more opportunities for multilingual learners to constantly negotiate their affiliation with the global or local communities. Learners may be more mobile than ever before, and the mobility brings a complex situation to identity and motivation research. Therefore, multilingual education should not be exclusively associated with static categories such as nationality. In addition, the cross-linguistic influence in multilingual education has made it more complex than L2 research. It is essential to conduct more research on exploring how multilingual learners feel about their identities and the possible change in motivation. At the same time, it is essential to do more research on integrating identity and motivation in multilingual contexts, as research on this topic is still at its infant stage.

3

Language Learning, Motivation and Identity in Asian Multilingual Education Contexts

Language learning in the present chapter is defined as learning a first/second/ foreign language in a multilingual/multicultural context. Language learning shapes language learners' identities, and vice versa. Multilingualism is the opposite of monolingualism. Multilingualism is becoming more and more common in Asian contexts. Multilingual education is perceived as a useful means of enhancing learners' cognitive faculties and identity (Murray, Gao and Lamb 2011). In addition, multilingual education is regarded as a tool to facilitate intercultural comprehension. Language learning proficiency plays a role in language learners' motivation, and motivation is an important determinant in L2 learning (Dörnyei 2005). Crystal (2003) argued that speaking a global language, for example, English, can impact the learning of other languages. The impact of motivation in language learning, and its relationship to identity shift, has been an emergent topic in multilingual education.

This chapter discusses motivation and identity in multilingual education in Asian contexts. Specifically, this chapter focuses on the contexts of Nepal, Japan and South Korea. Indeed, differences, for example, historical and economic development, can be identified among the three places. In addition, a learner's development of motivation and identity is organic and non-linear, and influenced by the individual's internal feelings and the complexities of the context. Illustrating the development of multilingual education from the perspective of motivation and identity, with a focus on only three locations, was not sufficient to address multilingual education in Asian contexts.

However, the three countries have some similar elements that make researching on the understanding of multilingual education in Asian contexts valuable. First, learners in the three places possess multifaceted linguistic identities. Factors, including the mystique of the local cultures, the increasing linguistical diversity, people's perceptions of cultural associations, and political agenda, brought complexity to the development of linguistic identities. Second, English was considered to be either an extrinsic goal or an intrinsic goal to the learners. The demand for learning English as the first foreign language in the three places has increased. There has been a move towards beginning English learning at an earlier age to gain communicative proficiency, which the public believes would help the learners to succeed in future academic study. Third, multilingualism has become a common phenomenon in the three contexts and the linguistic history is complex. People use different languages in different regions. The status of minority languages has been reduced due to the need for promoting the national language and the influence of English as an international language. The learning and promotion of indigenous local languages now receives greater support. Greater public acceptance has become a hallmark for the development of alternate identities. The two constructs – motivation and identity – are dependent on the context and are socially mediated. Researching motivation and identity in the three contexts sheds light on the understanding of Asian multilingual contexts.

3.1 Motivation, identity and multilingual education

A great importance has been attached to motivation in multilingual education. Previous studies were conducted to explore motivational processes in multilingual education. For example, Sugita McEown, Noels, and Chaffee (2014) stressed self-identity internalization and how it influences language learning. Various factors that have influenced language learning included, for example, integrative orientation (Gardner 1985), L2 motivational self (Dörnyei 2005), and self-determination theory (Ryan and Deci 2000). These theories determined that identity-relevant factors were likely to be a predictor for multilingual learners' L2 motivational learning behaviours. Sugita McEown, Sawaki and Harada (2017) argued that L2 learners' motivational processes were easily affected by the role of contextual factors. However, the role of person-specific factors on L2 learners' motivational processes should not be ignored.

Gardner (1985) explained that L2 learning is related to learners' identification with the target language community. Learners who are associated with the target language community may be better able to learn an L2 because learning that language reflects a common goal. Because of their common goal, the learners develop a genuine interest in becoming closer to that language and people who speak that language. One element of motivation is that the learning context could be 'autonomy supportive' or 'controlling' (Deci and Ryan 1987). The two 'supportive' or 'controlling' situations signalled the need to explore self-determination theory (Noels 2003). Based on self-determination theory (Ryan and Deci 2000), motivation can be continually developed from a self-determined state (i.e., an autonomous state) to a non-self-determined state (i.e., a controlled state). The self-determined dimension of motivation is intrinsic motivation. Depending on whether they possess this type of motivation, L2 learners develop their pleasure and interest in learning the target language. The intrinsic motivation represents L2 learners' inherent tendency to cope with L2 learning challenges and strengthens the L2 learners' cognitive and social development for their learning capacities.

Connected to integrative orientation and self-determination theory, research into language learners' motivation has taken a new approach. For example, the development of the 'L2 Motivational Self System' (Dörnyei 2009) has spawned new discussions. A main component of the L2 motivational self-system – the ideal L2 self – that is, the L2-specific facet of learners' ideal self, was an important dimension of the language learners' motivation. The ideal L2 self was related to the integrative orientation, through which L2 learners could depend and use as a means to idealize an image of themselves as a successful language learner. L2 learners used it as a tool to reduce the discrepancy between their ought-to L2 selves (i.e., the attributes that learners possessed to meet expectations) and ideal L2 selves (i.e., the attributes for learners to gain as a speaker of the target language). Recently, in explaining motivation in multilingual education, Man, Bui and Teng (2018) proposed a dual-motivation system, defined as 'a co-existence of two distinct yet related motivation systems within a learner of two additional languages learned subsequent to their first language' (p. 84). First, 'one's L2 and L3 motivations are distinctive'. Second, 'the two motivational forces are interconnected and thus have the potential to exert mutual influence' (p. 85). Based on Bui and Teng (2019), an individual's existing language or languages (L1 and L2), especially those with closer psychotypology to the L3, may have a positive influence on L3 learning motivation. In particular, the change brought on by a new element (L3) into an existing system (L2 motivation) leads to the rise of a new system – the dual-motivation system. Factors such as psychotypology, past L2 learning experience, self-confidence, perceptions of the L2 and L3 communities and even the learners' backgrounds all contribute towards shaping and evolving the complex and dynamic relations between L2 and L3 learning drives in the dual-motivation system.

Motivation and identity are two interconnected sides of the same coin that influence multilingual learners' performance in language learning. Identity emerges from practice, discourse, and activity (Teng and Yip 2019). Identity was defined as how learners perceived who they are (Teng 2018), or in 'ways of relating the self to the world' (van Lier 2007: 58), or a person's unique qualities determined by autonomy and agency (Teng 2019b). Norton (2000) suggested the need to research identity as the centre of the learning process and L2 learning was not just the acquisition of language skills. It appears that identity is related to not only how learners become future speakers of another language but also how their identities can be nurtured (Teng 2019a). Ushioda (2011) argued that 'motivations and identities develop and emerge as dynamically co-constructed processes' (p. 21).

The two notions influence the development of multilingual education. Multiple languages are assumed to enjoy equal status in multilingual education and learners benefited from multilingual education curriculum. Motivation and identity influence students' ability to learn knowledge and foster a sense of multilingualism. However, languages are not equal and the learning of one language may influence the learning of another language. Despite the advocation of teaching multiple languages, the 'side-effects' of colonialism, the worldwide influence of English, the protection of local languages, and sometimes the choice between a colonial language and an indigenous one, have made the implementation of multilingual education challenging (Klapwijka and Van der Walt 2016). Multilingualism is not a juxtaposition or an addition of different languages. Each language has its own specific function and status and serves as a means to an end. Related to this, multilingual learning does not mean a loss of other languages. Researching learners' motivation and identities is essential to understand multilingual learning.

3.2 Multilingual practices in Asian contexts

This section aims to illustrate multilingual practices in Asian contexts. It focuses on three different but related countries: Nepal, Japan and South Korea.

3.2.1 Nepal

Nepal is an isolated and landlocked nation, located between India and the Tibetan region of the People's Republic of China (PRC). Nepal is a multilingual and multicultural country. China's and India's civilizations, which are culturally, linguistically, and racially different, influence Nepal's cultural and linguistic features. Various other factors – including economy, religions, social stratification and political history – make language issues in Nepal complex.

Before 2008, Nepal experienced instability, characterized by protests, riots, civil war, strikes and unrest. In 2008, the Unified Communist Party of Nepal won the largest number of seats in the Constituent Assembly election and formed a coalition government. Nepal abolished the monarchy and became a secular and inclusive democratic republic. After the establishment of the republic, Nepal was expected to enter a new era. However, Nepal's situation was still chaotic. Due to the political tensions, education plans were drastically limited or stopped. For example, first language education had been planned for Indo-European languages in the Terai region and for Newari in the Kathmandu Valley. However, many schools in remote areas did not have resources, including textbooks and trained teachers. The development of first-grade primary English education was hindered.

The Ministry of Education issued a planning draft in 2007 (Ministry of Education and Sports 2007), stipulating some measures for enhancing education in Nepal. The measures included (a) recognizing the cultural and linguistic diversity of Nepal; (b) a child's mother language will be used as the MOI up to third grade; (c) textbooks will be selected based on the National Curriculum Framework; (d) the governance, management and quality of English-medium schools must follow the National Curriculum Framework; (e) 20 per cent of the government's budget will be used for education; (f) recruiting new teachers; and (g) scholarships and training programmes will be provided for in-service teachers. However, the chaotic situation in Nepal made the measures difficult to implement.

In recent years, the aim of building a modern democratic nation significantly affected current language policies. Nepal is striving to build a modern political system, develop the economy, and make education accessible to more people. Related to this, Nepali, the national language, has continuously been promoted throughout the country. Nepal's language policy is featured as a 'top-down' policy. The policy did not specify the number of languages spoken in Nepal, but the 2011 census reported 123 languages spoken as a mother tongue. Other main languages include Maithili, Bhojpuri, Tamang, Abadhi, Tharu and Newari. According to the 2011 national census, the percentage of Nepali-speaking people in the country was 44.6 per cent, whereas the percentage of Maithili-speaking people was 11.57 per cent. Part I of the Constitution of Nepal 2015 contained the following provisions about the languages in Nepal: (a) all native languages spoken in Nepal are national languages of Nepal; (b) the Nepali language in

Devanagari script is used for Nepal government work; and (c) in addition to the Nepali language, provinces may choose one or more other languages spoken by the majority of the population of that province for government work (Constitution of Nepal 2015). It appeared that the government wanted to protect local vernaculars. In fact, although different languages were spoken in the same locality, Nepali became a lingua franca of Nepal as it was used in various domains, including education, administration, military and media. Minor languages lack literate tradition and are on the verge of extinction. In addition, the chaotic situation in Nepal, that is, the political instability, introduced crisis to national identity formation (Pherali and Garratt 2014). In particular, children from minority castes/ethnic communities and non-native Nepali-speaking backgrounds became school dropouts (Pherali and Garratt 2014). Educational expansion did not help with the issue of ethnic inequality.

The language situation in Nepal was strongly influenced by the British Raj in the eighteenth and nineteenth centuries. The British could not subdue the whole of Nepal but claimed the Terai and eastern part of Nepal through declaring war on Nepal in 1814. Although Nepal was never a colony of Britain and English was never imposed in Nepal, English has flourished in many of Nepal's domains as the British had contact with the Nepalese. The development of English in Nepal included three stages:

(1) The era of colonial influence from 1767 to 1850. During that stage, English represented a symbol of power as the Nepali elites conducted continuous collaboration with the British. The power of English was strengthened as the elite became more powerful.

(2) The era of English education expansion from 1851 to 1990. During this stage, the Nepalese soldiers in the British Army returned home and taught the Western ways of thought and the experiences outside the national borders to the youth in the villages. English learning became a craze and an important language in formal school education. Many private sectors also set up English-medium schools. English was not just a symbol of power of the elite; it significantly influenced the common middle class.

(3) The era of English professionalism from 1990 to the present. This is a new stage for Nepal's development. The efforts to make Nepal into a modern country, including the transmission of scientific and technological knowledge, international communication, and globalized co-operation, contributed to English professionalism in Nepal.

Two professional organizations – Nepal English Language Teachers Association (NELTA) and Linguistic Society of Nepal (LSN) – influenced English professionalism in Nepal through offering seminars, teacher training programmes, and workshops. In addition, tourism promoted multilingualism in Nepal (Sharma and Phyak 2017). Tourism has been identified as one of the major potential sectors for both individual and national economic development in Nepal. The tourism industry was particularly vulnerable during the Maoist insurgency (1995–2006). After that, Nepal started attracting a greater number of tourists. Tourism brought about a greater demand for an English-speaking workforce.

In addition, India and China, two powerful neighbours, also influenced Nepal. For example, Nepalese higher education was influenced by the Indian system. Syllabuses and assessment systems were directly borrowed from India. Many schools hired teachers educated in Indian universities. PRC, by contrast, also increased its investment, cultural exchange and heightened contact at all political levels with Nepal. The PRC government encouraged Nepalese people to learn Chinese language and culture. To do this, the PRC government sent instructors to Nepal to provide free lessons and established the Confucius Centre at Kathmandu University. For example, the global dominance of English in the tourism market was challenged by the increased use of Chinese in workplaces (Sharma and Phyak 2017). Finally, because of globalization, Nepal faced an increasing mobility of people, and generated a new context for people's preoccupation with belonging. We thus argue for the importance of language in delineating individual identities (Fuller 2007). Yet the concept of an identity, and how one creates or embodies it, has become more and more difficult to ascertain.

Overall, as delineated by Kaplan and Baldauf (2008), students in Nepal were more motivated to learn Nepali and/or English. First, because of the poverty in Nepal and the competitiveness involved in securing a job, people found it advantageous to be fluent in Nepali and/or English. In particular, English has occupied various domains in Nepal, including the tourism industry, trade, international affairs, media, education, science and technology. Local languages have begun disappearing along with the urbanization process and education reform in Nepal, influencing the formation of identities for the local people in Nepal. Some parents who speak minority languages even chose to teach their children Nepali and/or English rather than the local language because they perceived the powerlessness, prejudice, and inequality of belonging to a minority group (Fuller 2007). Because little or no support from the government has been provided to preserve the local vernacular, many minor languages in Nepal may die out in the future. Without incorporating the ethnic populations into the economic and political mainstreams of the country, revitalizing and preserving their ethnic identities and languages seems unlikely.

3.2.2 Japan

Japan has always been regarded as a monolingual nation. On 18 October 2005, Aso Taro, the Internal Affairs and Communications Minister declared that Japan was the only country that had 'one nation, one civilisation, one language, one culture, and one race' in the world. Following this, the term 'Nihonjinron' (the uniqueness of Japan) emerged. This term constituted a significant influence on the government, academic and cultural discourse of Japanese society. In essence, this term is understood to indicate that the Japanese language is different from other languages in the world and that Japan is perceived as linguistically homogenous.

Indeed, Japanese, the national language, plays an important role in nation- and empire-building. Diversity has been neither allowed nor encouraged. Even during the early modern period, some minority languages spoken in the southern and northern borders of the archipelago were suppressed because of the assimilation policy. This movement strengthened and reinforced the ideology of one whole and unified nation. By the 1920s, a standard language was designated and disseminated through education. That progress created a monolingual myth in Japan. It was certainly true that monolingualism became an enduring and strongly entrenched pillar of modern Japan. This may be traced back throughout Japan's history. Japan has never been colonized by another country. The only situation that resembled colonization was the Allied occupation from 1945 to 1951 after Japan was defeated in the Second World War. Considering no transition to the language of the occupying powers was made, monolingualism in Japan is not surprising.

English is the most widely promoted foreign language in Japan. Teaching English has attracted political attention. A common social recognition is that an English-driven change in the communication system would make Japan more competitive in the global society. However, English education in Japan has been criticized for its failure at fostering communicative language teaching. In 2002, the Ministry of Education, Culture, Sports, Science and Technology (MEXT) announced that young learners should acquire communication skills in English, and in 2003, the National Action Plan was initiated to cultivate Japanese with English abilities. English then became an elective subject in secondary school. In

2011, English-language instruction was first introduced into elementary schools as a subject for fifth and sixth graders. However, a debate over whether English should be a subject in primary school in Japan arose.

Japanese students do not appear to be motivated in learning English (Aspinall 2006). Characteristics of Japanese students are shaped by Japanese society and culture. Many Japanese students argued that due to societal and cultural influences, they were not motivated to acquire communicative English skills. For example, Aspinall (2006) described the uniqueness of Japanese students in learning English. Typical characteristics that were found to inhibit Japanese students' English teaching and learning included (a) Japanese students tended to have passive learning attitudes and were submissive to the teacher's authority; (b) Japanese students dared not display advanced proficiency in front of their peers because they were afraid of appearing over confident; (c) Japanese learners were timid in expressing their ideas because they believed that there was only one correct answer to each teacher's question; and (d) the egalitarian approach towards education was a barrier to helping advanced students or students with learning difficulties. Although Japan has entered a new era to cope with global competitiveness, many debates on English-language teaching methods in Japan still exist.

Another aspect that influences English-language education in Japan is identity. The concept of identity, particularly in Japan, is a complex matter. Traditionally, Japan is a linguistically and culturally homogenous society, wherein Japanese people seek and form positive identities through favourable comparison with outgroups or abandon identities that do not belong to their in-groups. The Japanese people regard the Japanese language as their symbol or dimension of comparison with outgroups. Even though the globalization trend has threatened the homogenous status of Japan, Turnbull (2017) argued that Japan is still a society that tends to protect and differentiate itself as a distinct in-group against the outgroup of the English language. The Japanese language represents a favourable fortress that characteristically safeguarded the Japanese identity. Fujimoto-Adamson asserted (2006) that Western culture and ideologies, and the increasing hegemony of the English language, influence Japan's national and cultural identity. Subject to this influence, Japanese people tend to stay in their in-groups while attempting to know more about the outgroups.

However, the increased pressure of globalization in recent years should never be overlooked. An increased welcoming and acceptance of the influx of English as an international language in Japanese, referred to as the *kokusaika* discourse, has become apparent. Thus, a conflict between the *nihonjinron* discourse and the *kokusaika* discourse naturally exists. Kubota (2002) identified various tensions in Japan as a result of increased globalization: (a) ethnic, linguistic, and cultural diversity was more common in the local communities; (b) English became more prevalent; and (c) a strong nationalism was endorsed by linguistic and cultural essentialism. These tensions appeared to show a conflict between a force for undermining and for supporting Japanese cultures.

Additional studies found that the safeguard of national identity influenced Japanese EFL students' English learning. For example, Sullivan and Schatz (2009) explored this issue and maintained that national identification affected Japanese university EFL students' attitudes towards English learning. In particular, the dimension of patriotism – positive identification with and affective attachment to the country – led to Japanese students' negative attitudes towards EFL learning. Indeed, it was well established that Japanese students' low level of communicative English abilities stemmed from the national culture of learning in Japan, causing students' psychological mindsets and actions to be oriented to their in-groups (Samimy and Kobayashi 2004). English learning in the Japanese context was significantly different than other contexts, such as Malaysia, where English learning is approached with more open-minded thinking. Certain forms of teaching methods, for example, communicative language teaching, have been suggested as incompatible with Japanese cultures. Hence, the protection of Japanese culture and the spread of English as a lingua franca in Japan is still causing tensions.

Finally, stating that Japan is wholly a monolingual country would not be correct as Japan has been a multilingual society for a long time. In particular, a surge of immigrants from China, Korea, Brazil, the Philippines and Taiwan since the latter half of the 1980s have introduced complexity to the language situation in Japan. The sudden increase in foreigners impacted Japan's multilingualism. In addition, the ethnic diversification has inevitably brought along many languages with their speakers. The degree and mode of foreigners' contact with the local community influence the linguistic activities of the foreigners and the locals, both positively and negatively.

Mother-tongue education, a policy of guaranteeing minority children the possibility to acquire competence in their mother tongue, was regarded as an initiative for the immigrants' individual and communal well-being. The general stance of the government in Japan is still far from promoting multilingualism in Japan. Language rights, public needs, or even the accumulation of language problems, may encourage the government to explore the issue of multilingual education, despite a common overriding ideology that Japan should be a mono-ethnic and monolingual country. The local people's increasing contacts with foreigners and their languages diminish locals' mental barriers in language consciousness gradually. Accordingly, local authorities have started to recognize the demand for multilingual education and have taken measures to accommodate the linguistic needs of immigrants. Japanese people have sensed a need to become more multilingual.

3.2.3 South Korea

Before discussing motivation and identity in learning English as a foreign language in South Korea, it is essential to consider the different phases of historical development in the country. The interactive forces of different phases – that is, Japanese colonial rule (1910–1945), division of Korea (1945–present), the Korean War (1950–1953), and the economic development stage (post-1990) – strengthened the cultural discontinuity between Korean traditional culture and contemporary culture, accelerating the modernization and influx of Western culture. In education – especially in learning English – there has always been a 'fever' among Koreans (Park 2009). Fever in learning English can be referred to as the value placed on education in South Korea, which most Koreans agree is 'a way of achieving status and power' and 'a means of self-cultivation' (Seth 2002: 9). Korean parents' urgent wishes to help children gain upward social mobility and economic prosperity have caused competitiveness in Korean society to become fiercer. A phenomenon of an English boom appeared in South Korea.

Several factors enhanced the English boom in South Korea. First, the changes in Korean government policy greatly influenced the English boom. Changes in language policy included adding English listening tests as an important part of college entrance examinations in 1991 and incorporating more communicative items in the college entrance examinations in 1994. The goal of the South Korean government in 2008 was to reform English public school education so that every graduate would be communicative in English (Ahn 2013). The English education reform in 2008 was also called the 'English Immersion Plan' (Roadmap 2008) and aimed to innovate the current teaching system in South Korea. Language policy in South Korea aimed to strive towards the enhancement of students' communicative competence rather than utilize the traditional grammar method. The importance that the government attached to English education partially initiated Koreans' English fever.

Second, the process of globalization in the late 1980s also accelerated the English boom. In addition to the deepened globalization, the economic development in South Korean society, particularly when South Korea was transformed into one of the Four Asian Tigers and ranked as one of the wealthiest nations in the world, caused people to realize the importance of learning English in the process of globalization.

Third, English became an important international language in various domains, including the economic and cultural arenas. Given the ever-increasing number of English speakers and users around the world, the status of English in South Korea has also been greatly improved.

Motivation in learning English is different for parents and students. Responding to the English-only movement in Korean society, many Korean parents sent their children to an English-speaking environment (Park 2009). They also sent their children to English villages and training camps where there would be very few to no Koreans to engage with. Many parents were still not satisfied with the outcome of their children's English learning. The extreme practice was that the Korean parents sent their children to receive 'linguistic surgery' to avoid the Koreans' common problem of 'tongue-tiedness' which caused Korean students to often pronounce the word 'right' incorrectly as 'light' (Demick 2002). However, students at different education levels demonstrated low levels of motivation in learning English in the Korean context. Reasons included the problems entrenched in the country's education system, students' learning experiences, cultural identity, the lack of role models in English learning, and the media's influence.

Although the Korean government was striving to enhance students' intercultural communicative competency, the assessment system in the Korean context was still 'examination-oriented' (Niederhauser 2012). Students were not learning based on personal interest but rather to pass the test. Although Korean schools and universities began claiming greater freedom for students to choose their majors based on interest, most of the schools or institutions have not adopted the idea. Students tended to rely on drill and practice. Although a policy was made to foster communicative teaching methods, in reality, teacher-centred classroom instruction is still the practice (Niederhauser 2012). Bored by such repeated practice that conflicted with the passion of their parents, Korean students tended not to have a high level of motivation in learning English.

Korean students' entrenched habits of passively waiting for teachers' instruction is also a concern. Most Korean students, by the time they enter college, cannot or dare not carry on simple conversations in English. Korean students are very reliant on the teacher-centred classroom: while the English teacher is speaking, the students are listening and taking notes. Their negative attitudes and lack of confidence in coping with language learning requirements make them feel less motivated. Most Korean students are not well informed about intercultural competence, although this characteristic is often advocated in the Korean government's language policy.

Korean students' cultural identity also influenced their motivation in learning English. Despite numerous invasions and occupations, Koreans have been considered *Han-minjok* ('Korean nation'), referring to how Korean people have remained remarkably homogeneous. Koreans maintain a strong national consciousness, and this consciousness became the basis of modern Korean nationalism. This cultural nationalism influenced the Koreans' cultural identity and in turn affected the multiculturalism and multilingual education in Korea (Yim 2002). For example, Korean students also perceive that saving face is more important for their self-esteem. Their strong identity as a Korean impacts their motivation towards learning English. Korean students do not like to stand out and demonstrate their English-speaking performance. The absence of English-speaking models undermines students' motivation. They fear English learning and are puzzled about ways to be successful in learning English. They may also lack confidence in reaching a sufficient level of performance in speaking and using English in the future.

The media also influences the Korean students' attitudes towards English learning. Media frequently emphasizes that foreign languages contaminate the origin and meaningfulness of the Korean language, and possibly Korean's cultural identity. This phenomenon was also called linguistic purism in Korean (Park 1989), stressing a call for protecting the standards of Korean language. Due to this phenomenon, Korean students often possess conflicting feelings about their English-learning motivation.

Similar to Japan, South Korea is a monolingual country and has always been regarded as a monocultural country. Nevertheless, multiculturalism, as well as multilingual education, has become an indispensable component of education in South Korea. The multicultural history of Korea is about thirty years long, involving immigrants mainly from China, Japan and Vietnam. Korean society is characterized by an ideology of a homogeneous society. In 2017, a plan by the Ministry of Education was initiated to support multicultural education so as to help learners, either children born in Korea or children of foreign families, to become a talented person in the society. The plan also aims to improve the multicultural understanding of all students (Support plan for multicultural education 2007). The support plan included three dimensions: promoting support for tailored instruction (e.g., recruit university student members, develop curriculum, and provide career counselling), improving the understanding of multicultural education among teachers, and establishing a solid foundation for multicultural education (e.g., cooperate with affiliated government organizations and provide support to local schools).

However, many aspects of multilingual education in South Korea are still being challenged. For example, there is still a lack of qualified teachers with relevant knowledge and teaching qualifications in multilingual education. Schools find it difficult to hire enough teachers to adapt to students' needs in multilingual education. Teachers also lack opportunities for professional development and training to improve their multicultural understanding. Accountability measures need to be developed to facilitate the active implementation of multicultural education in accordance with the background of the students and the practical conditions of the local region. Although university students were recruited as mentors to provide support services for multilingual learners, government should also provide educational support for the student mentors. In addition, there is a lack of materials for curriculum development. Organizations in the local community, including universities, support centres, and the immigration office, do not receive enough support. Multilingual education is only operating within some schools (180 schools in 2016 and 200 schools in 2017), and it still has a long way to go before its structure in South Korea is settled.

3.3 Reflection

Reflection on Nepal, Japan and South Korea has revealed that multilingualism has become an incentive as well as a necessity in these contexts. In addition, multiculturalism, with renewed and redefined ethnic identities, has become an integral part of the three contexts. Although nationalism and monolingualism have been instrumental political values, current events are changing. Similar to other multilingual contexts, how to effectively deal with globalization while at the same time maintain local culture, the relationship between languages and ethnic identities is still a dilemma. In the future, addressing ethnic groups and local languages and the widespread popularity of English language within and beyond the national context will be a challenging issue for these three countries as well as others.

Apparently, in Nepal, Japan and South Korea, conservative forces of tradition have been interrupted. Campaigns have begun for making the effort to transform English literacy from an elite, limited-access skill to one that is accessible to more people. Whereas governments in the three contexts attempt to standardize language planning activity, the impact of globalization has significantly affected the language learning policy. In some respects, globalization has had a revolutionary impact on the multilingual educational system, the different statuses of languages, and learners' motivation and identity in multilingual education. The globalization and language learning policies can also impact the status of indigenous minority languages. The complexity of various languages is regarded as a feature of multilingual education.

Some common issues have been found among the three contexts. The first issue is the increasing importance of and demand for learning English. In Nepal, many have suggested that English is a second *de facto* national language and in Japan and South Korea, learners attach great importance to the learning of English. People in each of these countries undoubtedly consider it an advantage to start learning English earlier for the purpose of gaining communicative advantages. The increasing demand has necessitated the commencement of learning English at the primary school level. However, resources, including trained teachers, materials for curriculum and academic assessment, are still insufficient to address primary school English learning (see Butler 2007 for Japan; Kaplan and Baldauf 2008 for Nepal; Seth 2002 for Korea).

Criticism of teaching and learning English at the primary school level does exist. For example, learning English at primary school is believed to hinder the learning of the Japanese language (Otsu 2004). In addition, Korean and Japanese students generally have strong identities, and most of them perceived that learning English would have a detrimental effect on their national identity and language (see Kawai 2007 for Japan; Yim 2002 for Korea). Such concerns may impact the students' motivation in learning English.

The three contexts also have some similar elements that qualify for comparison. In terms of inner environment, students were introduced to traditional educational methods, for example, the grammar-translation method, in learning foreign languages. Despite continuous encouragement for student interaction and socialization, such practices were not very common in foreign language classrooms. In a similar vein, although learner autonomy and cooperation were valued, students were always very passive in the foreign language classroom. Innovation in teaching foreign languages still requires development.

With regard to the sociolinguistic dimension, each context is multilingual to some extent. However, the dominant language is the national language. Although the general attitude towards multilingualism is positive, the practice and outcome in learning multilingual languages are not positive. The main language for instruction and communication is the national language. Concerning the sociocultural dimension, the benefits of multilingual education have been widely acknowledged. The pragmatic dimensions of learning multiple languages, for example, employment opportunities, are regarded as mainly lucrative in multilingual education. Although some students attempted to understand and speak the target languages, some students lacked motivation. In addition, students' presence and initiative were sometimes challenged because of their identity development, for example, an ideal L2 self or an ought-to L2 self. This situation becomes more dynamic and fluid when it involves the situation of learning an L3 (Man, Bui and Teng 2018). These elements form the major obstructions in multilingual education in Japan, Nepal and Korea.

When the local and national authorities do not offer adequate support to create a learning environment in which learners can have some control over their learning, they may not recognize that not all learners' identities will be conducive to motivation. Therefore, appropriate forms of learner training are needed to nurture such identities and to navigate learners' identities as learners become responsible for their learning, through dealing with external constraints (such as exam-oriented culture) and decreasing teacher control and engaging learners' voices to find collaborative, negotiated solutions in multilingual education. Multilingualism is a new linguistic capital that should be acknowledged by students and enacted in language classrooms.

Enlightened from the three contexts, exploring ways for language teacher educators to better support students for the achievement of academic success and the development of cross-cultural awareness is crucial. Through cross-cultural awareness, students can gain a better chance of achieving academic success in multilingual education and embracing the differences that make them unique. We acknowledge the linguistic and cultural diversity. Identity is the key to what makes an individual unique and the one element that should not be stripped away. Having a sense of cross-cultural differences may prevent students' loss of identity. Language teacher educators are in the position to reflect on what they are teaching and how they are teaching languages and cultures. Language teacher educators can create spaces for students to develop as bi- or multilingual citizens and agentive multilingual learners who take advantage of their varied literacies to become a member of the ever-changing global community.

4

Multilingual Education in Hong Kong:
Motivation and Identity

The use of multiple languages in education is attributed to numerous factors, such as the linguistic heterogeneity of a country (e.g., Singapore); the desire to promote national identity (e.g., India and the Philippines); or political and social change (e.g., Hong Kong). Trilingual education refers to a domain in which three languages coexist and are necessary for societal and schooling communication. Trilingual education is widespread not only in officially recognized bilingual and multilingual communities but also across the world. However, acquisition of more than two non-native languages has not received sufficient attention in scientific research in comparison to second language acquisition and bilingualism. Like bilingual education, trilingual learning can occur simultaneously or successively, formally through schooling or naturally outside school, and at different stages of life. In the process of trilingual learning, learners exhibit complex variances in motivation and identity due to the sociocultural status of each language, and their respective roles and functions in the society. This may characterize individuals or even the whole society. Against this backdrop, this chapter presents an overview of the theoretical and empirical literature of trilingual education in Hong Kong.

Hong Kong is an interesting and special case for researching trilingual education. Hong Kong was governed by Britain for approximately 154 years. Although there was no statutory provision for what constituted the official language(s) in Hong Kong between 1842 and 1974, English was by practice the dominant language in handling official matters during that period. For example, English was commonly used in the executive, judicial and legislative domains. In 1974, the government declared English and Chinese as the official languages for the convenience of communication between the government and the public. Immense public pressure was one of the main reasons for a push towards this change. The government did not specify what constituted as the official variety of Chinese in Hong Kong. Due to Hong Kong's geographic and sociolinguistic situation, Cantonese became the most often used verbal medium of communication in practice. The two official languages (English and Chinese[1]) shared equal status in use. The Hong Kong government adopted a flexible attitude towards the issue of MOI where schools had the liberty to select a language as medium for instruction (Pan 2000).

Before the 1990s, English Language and Chinese Language were the compulsory subjects in primary and secondary education (ages 6 to 18). English language was part of the core curriculum for students from primary 1 for twelve years, that is, until the end of secondary school education. Virtually all the kindergartens used Cantonese as a MOI. English was used as a MOI in some primary schools, mainly in a few international or long-established missionary schools. The official policy related to MOI in secondary schools was not rigidly determined. Schools could select which MOI they considered their teachers are qualified for and with which their students are able to cope. Therefore, secondary schools commonly used Cantonese and English for different subjects and different class levels. In many schools with English as a Medium of Instruction (EMI), Cantonese was also used in accompanying English to a varying extent in classroom instruction for easier understanding. In tertiary-level education, most of the universities adopted English as MOI. In an early study (Adamson and Lai 1997), the teaching of Putonghua, the national language of the People's Republic of China, and its use as a MOI was very restricted before the 1990s.

Hong Kong has experienced dramatic changes since its handover to China on 1 July 1997. For example, the Hong Kong SAR government issued *The Medium of Instruction Guidance for Secondary Schools* (Education Department 1997), a guidance related to MOI for secondary schools. Two new language policies were adopted. One was the compulsory mother-tongue-medium instruction policy. Another was the biliterate (written English and Chinese) and trilingual (spoken English, Putonghua, Cantonese) policy. Under these policies, Chinese (i.e., Cantonese) was encouraged to be a MOI to replace the use of mixed code (a mixture of Chinese and English) and Putonghua was encouraged to be used in teaching the Chinese Language subject. Both traditional and simplified written forms of Chinese were also encouraged. This combination of three languages became the *de facto* language policy for schools and civil services (Education Department 1997). According to the Education Bureau (formerly

---

[1] Chinese includes two different forms: the written form (modern standard Chinese written in traditional script) and the spoken form (Cantonese).

Education Department), the objective of implementing these policies was to enhance students' biliterate and trilingual abilities in primary (Hong Kong Education Bureau 2013a) and secondary sectors (Hong Kong Education Bureau 2013b).

As argued by Poon (1999), the change in the language policies after the handover is more than an educational issue involving the interests of different parties. Part of the reasons may be because the Hong Kong SAR government wants to appease the Chinese government. The Education Bureau also adopted some measures to decrease the use of English as a MOI in schools. For example, EMI schools were required to provide strategies and programmes for assisting students. In addition, at least 85 per cent of students should be able to learn effectively in English and teachers should be able to use English as a MOI. Under these requirements, only 114 secondary schools continued to be EMI schools. Over 300 other secondary schools had to choose Cantonese as a medium of instruction (CMI) (Cheng 2005a). These policies have been coercively implemented since 1997. Consistent complaints and criticisms were raised by parents, students, teachers, scholars and schools (Cheng 2005b). Additionally, individual differences among students within each secondary school increased greatly, causing difficulties in satisfying the diverse needs of students in their studies (Cheng 2009). In severe cases, CMI schools suffered from being perceived as weaker schools for less qualified students. By contrast, graduates from EMI schools had a privilege when entering universities (Clem 2008). This disparity resulted in parents' extreme dissatisfaction towards the compulsory CMI policy. After implementing the policy for about ten years, in 2008, the Education Bureau publicly recognized the problems of the existing MOI policy and considered giving more autonomy to secondary schools in making decisions related to MOI (Sing Tao Daily 2008).

In addition, along with the change of sovereignty and deepening connection with Mainland China, Putonghua has been playing an increasingly important role in the Hong Kong Education system. As an international city, a meeting point of the West and the East, Hong Kong has a strong tradition to echo the global trend in its development. Hence, Hong Kong will continue to be linguistically complex and diverse with three main languages: Cantonese, English and Putonghua. Trilingual education in Hong Kong will continue to be a special feature of the education system in Hong Kong. The Hong Kong SAR government still needs to conduct a series of language policy reforms to create a reasonable balance among the three languages in Hong Kong. As espoused by Wang and Kirkpatrick (2015), the implementation of trilingual education varies significantly from school to school, and so does the effectiveness of the trilingual education models. Thus, there is still a need to explore this issue to gain a better understanding of trilingual education in Hong Kong. In a context of growing international trends of various reforms related to trilingual education, the experiences in Hong Kong may provide a good case for understanding the dynamics of reforms, drawing theoretical and practical implications for research, as well as formulating policies and their implementation not only in Hong Kong but also in other similar places in Asia. Through overviewing the related factors and conditions in promoting or inhibiting success in trilingual education practice in Hong Kong, this chapter provides insight into how a second or foreign language can be adopted as a MOI in schools to achieve multilingualism and cognitive/academic learning, and how this possibly impacts students' motivation and identity.

4.1 Key terms and constructs related to multilingual education

Major constructs, including ideology, power and identity, are complex. Each construct has generated a voluminous literature. Policies about multilingual education are often driven by ideologies, power and politics. Language policy and planning related to multilingual education are also affected by globalization, leading to the (re)formation of identity. For the purposes of this chapter, we present some basic definitions for each construct.

4.1.1 Bilingual education

In a simple definition, the term bilingual education refers to the use of two languages for teaching and learning in an organized and planned instructional setting (Lin and Man 2009). The central defining feature is that the languages are used to teach subject matter content rather than just the languages themselves.

4.1.2 Multilingual education

The term multilingual education is the extension of bilingual education, involving the use of three languages or more (Wright, Boun and García 2015). In most cases, one of these is the 'home', 'native', or 'mother – tongue' language, and one is the 'dominant' societal language or a 'powerful' international language.

4.1.3 Ideology

The term ideology in language studies attempts to capture 'the implicit, usually unconscious assumptions about language and language behaviour that fundamentally determine how human beings interpret events' (Tollefson 2007: 26). Darvin and Norton (2015: 72) described ideologies as 'dominant ways of thinking that organise and stabilise societies while simultaneously determining modes of inclusion and exclusion'. Ideologies become problematic only when they result in policies that are implemented in isolation from the research evidence or when research evidence is twisted to be in line with ideological presuppositions.

4.1.4 Power

The term power typically includes two central meanings. The first meaning suggests that the notion of exercising power over others. Power is exercised by a dominant group (or individual or country) to the detriment of a subordinated group (or individual or country) (Teng 2018). The second meaning highlights the notion of being enabled or empowered to act in certain ways or to achieve desired goals. On the basis of these two typical meanings involved with 'power', Cummins (2001) further suggested two types of power relations: coercive relations of power and collaborative relations of power. Within collaborative relations of power, power is not a fixed quantity, but generated through interaction with others. The more empowered one individual or group becomes, the more power is generated for others to share. The process is aggregative rather than subtractive. Within this context, empowerment can be defined as the collaborative creation of power. By contrast, in societal contexts characterized by unequal power relations, it is always located on a continuum ranging between the reinforcement of coercive relations of power and the promotion of collaborative relations of power (Paia et al. 2015).

4.1.5 Identity

Prevalent conceptualization regards identity as fluid, elusive and dynamic (e.g., Norton 2013; Teng 2018). Identity is also a site of struggle, which changes across time and space (Norton and Toohey 2011). Some aspects of identities are difficult or nearly impossible to change (e.g., gender, ethnicity), but other aspects can be easily transformed through social experiences or interactions.

Social interactions constitute a major influence on the extent and the spheres in which individuals shape their identities. Each language is imbued with cultural values that shape self-awareness, identity and relationships. That said, languages play an important role in identity development (Blackledge 2004).

4.1.6 Multilingualism and the individual

The ways in which people become multilingual vary immensely (Baker 2006). Individuals may take different routes to achieve multilingualism, which is defined as the use of more than one language, either by an individual speaker or by a community of speakers (Tucker 1998). It is also associated with economic benefits for the individual. In an increasingly globalized world, multilinguals have a competitive advantage in being linguistic and cultural 'capital'.

4.1.7 Multilingualism and society

Multilingualism is the result of the population movement which, in turn, is driven by many different factors. These include changes in environment and politics, and advances in science, technology and economics. Some may argue that multilingualism is a handicap for the social development, and the use of one dominant variety is a unifying force beneficial to the harmonious development of a society. However, language is a tool rather than the cause of conflict. Elimination of diversity is more likely to give rise to the very tensions that proponents of monolingualism are seeking to avoid (Edwards 2009).

4.1.8 Language policy and planning

Language policy and planning matter in all societal contexts, especially in education. Language policy and language planning are two different but interrelated notions. The differences between these two notions are that language planning is often government-led while language policy is either a macro- or micro-sociological activity at a governmental level, national level or institutional level (Poon 2000). Language policy has long been an instrument for the promotion of a sense of imagined identity (Bonfiglio 2010). Responses to multilingualism vary a great deal in various countries. There are also many different models for managing linguistic diversity. Regardless of whether language policies are initiated by state language planners, or result from the influence of economic developments, these decisions often have social and political consequences.

4.1.9 Globalization and English

Globalization is a process of interaction and integration among the people, companies and governments of different nations. It is a process driven by international trade and investment and aided by information technology (Stiglitz 2003). Globalization has a great influence on society, environment, culture, politics and economic development, as well as policies related to multilingual education. Globalization has also created a global spread of English. Today English has become a predominant medium of global trade, finance, commerce, science, technology and the internet. English has also become a chief medium of instruction in many countries and regions.

4.1.10 Motivation and language learning

Motivation refers to the mental 'engine' that subsumes effort, want/will (cognition), and task-enjoyment (affect) (Dörnyei 1998: 122). Motivation is the incentive for learning a language and it is seemingly impossible for a learner to fulfil their language learning goals without adequate motivation. Learners' efforts, desires and attitudes towards learning a language are reflected in their motivational intensity (Gardner 1985). The description of language learning motivation can be traced back to early models on instrumental/integrative dichotomy (Gardner and Lamber 1972). In the 1990s, a lot of research studies conducted were based on Gardner's and Lambert's early sociocultural conception. For example, research by Crookes and Schmidt (1991), Oxford and Shearin (1994), among others, explored and recognized further dimensions of motivation, as well as its dynamic character (Ushioda 1996). Such argument is connected to Dörnyei's (1998) summary of the main motivational domains. Seven main underlying dimensions were concluded as follows:

1. Affective/integrative dimension
2. Instrumental/pragmatic dimension
3. Macro-context-related dimension
4. Self-concept-related dimension
5. Goal-related dimension
6. Educational context-related dimension
7. Significant others-related dimension

As argued by Humphreys and Spratt (2008), it is common for students to learn more than one foreign language. Some learn languages due to a matter of necessity while others learn as a matter of choice. Different languages learned for different reasons may trigger different motivational responses, even for learners from the same cultural background. The different responses were related to the particular sociocultural context in which the learners are engaged in. This shows a need to explore how the motivation to learn each language may vary within a certain sociopolitical context, for example, Hong Kong.

4.2 Background information about Hong Kong

Hong Kong, literally, is called 'Fragrant Harbour'. It is a Special Administrative Region governed by the People's Republic of China (PRC). Hong Kong is located on the Pearl River Delta of East Asia, covering 1,106 km². The city of Shen Zhen in Guangdong province of China borders the territory to the north. Hong Kong is composed of three areas: New Territories, Kowloon peninsula, and the Hong Kong Island. It had a population of about 7.4 million of various nationalities in 2018, which makes it the world's fourth most densely populated territory (Census and Statistics Department 2018). About 93.1 per cent of people in Hong Kong are of Chinese descent. Most of the Hong Kong people originate mainly from Guangdong province. The remaining 6.9 per cent of the population is claimed to be in the minority group. Due to the social needs for domestic helpers, the largest non-Chinese ethnic groups are from the Philippines and Indonesia, accounting for about 5 per cent of the populations in Hong Kong (around 330,000 in total). There is also South Asian population of Indians, Pakistanis, and Vietnamese, who have become permanent residents of Hong Kong. Others include Britons, Americans, Canadians, Continental Europeans, Japanese and Koreans, who are mostly working in the city's commercial and financial sectors.

The three main languages are Cantonese, English and Putonghua. Cantonese is the most common language for interpersonal communication. English and Putonghua are additional languages. The Hong Kong 2011 population census reveals that the proportion of the population aged five and over able to speak Cantonese is 95.8 per cent, Putonghua 47.8 per cent and English 46.1 per cent, respectively (Census and Statistics Department 2011). In the latest population census (Census and Statistics Department 2017), the proportion of the population aged five and over able to speak Cantonese is 94.6 per cent, Putonghua 48.6 per cent and English 53.2 per cent, respectively. There is a big difference when we compare with the population census in 1996 (Census and Statistics Department 1996), where English occupies 38.1 per cent, Cantonese is 95.2 per cent and Putonghua is only 25.3 per cent. Cantonese has maintained, and even extended, its dominant position after the handover. Cantonese gains a higher status and becomes a standard language in Hong Kong.

However, the birth rate is not high in Hong Kong. There is also a continual number of immigrants from Mainland China. For example, a daily quota of 150 Mainland Chinese with family ties in Hong Kong are granted a 'one-way permit' visa. This approximately amounts to 54,000 per year, which contributes to the growth of population in Hong Kong. In addition, Hong Kong has a deepened connection with Mainland China. Considering those factors, Putonghua may occupy a more and more indispensable position in Hong Kong. Putonghua may even overtake English as Hong Kong's second language. The increasing importance of Putonghua and the trend of globalization affect the language use and language policy in Hong Kong.

4.3 Bilingual education in Hong Kong (pre-1997 period)

Because of colonialism, the period before 1997 in Hong Kong was described as a period of 'supremacy of English'. This period was also described as 'Diglossia' (Fishman 1971), which refers to different statuses and functions allocated to the languages used in a society. English was regarded as a dominant language with a high social status in the domains of education, legislature and government administration. This situation changed slightly after Chinese was enacted as a co-official language in 1974. However, English, entrenched in Hong Kong people's heart, still secures a higher position than Chinese. English enjoys a high status in Hong Kong not only just because of colonialism, but also due to the economic situation that turned Hong Kong into one of the 'four little dragons in Asia', and a globally known centre of trade and commerce in the 1980s. The demand for English kept escalating because there was a need to provide skilled labour for the rise of economic status. Therefore, although the Hong Kong government adopted a *laissez-faire* policy towards the issue of MOI and Hong Kong schools could choose their own MOI, English remained a priority in school education. For example, secondary education was dominated by English where all subjects except Chinese subjects were supposed to be taught in English (Bray and Ko 2004). By contrast, about 90 per cent of the primary schools were CMI in the 1980s (Kan and Adamson 2010).

As Hong Kong education was called elite education in the 1970s, difficulties were not encountered in making transitions from CMI primary schools to EMI secondary schools. Mass education introduced in the 1980s, while improving the overall quality of human capital, led to a drop in English standard, as well as a struggling transition of students from primary CMI schools to secondary EMI schools (e.g., Pennington 1995). Therefore, many EMI schools adopted a mixed code (English and Cantonese) in classroom instruction. Despite these problems, there were more EMI schools than CMI schools during the pre-1997 period. One of the main reasons was that English is an international language and it accorded great value in Hong Kong society. English was attached with more importance as Hong Kong established itself as a globally known financial centre in the 1990s. There was a need to update the workforce if Hong Kong wanted to sustain its role in the global society. One issue to be considered is that the declining English standards along with the use of mixed code in EMI schools had a severe bearing on universities, which adopted English in most of their programmes (Kirkpatrick 2014). The Hong Kong government in the 1990s adopted the Streaming Policy to solve this problem (Education commission 1990). This policy assigned students to different schools (EMI, CMI, mixed code) according to their proficiency level. The Hong Kong government also undertook strenuous efforts to prevent the declining English standards. These included furthering revisions of the related syllabi in Chinese Language and English Language subjects, provision of additional resources for remedial English classes, adopting the Expatriate English Teachers Scheme in secondary schools, and additional funding for universities to run more English-language-enhancement programmes (Poon 2013).

4.4 Multilingual education in Hong Kong (post-1997 period)

Although the status of Putonghua has been improved after the transfer of sovereignty, English still enjoys a high status in the hearts of Hong Kong people. One of the main reasons is that Hong Kong continues to be an open economy after being returned to China. Despite economic crisis in the 2000s, Hong Kong is still one of the most important international financial centres on par with New York and London. Hence, English is valued by people in Hong Kong. To them, having a competitive English ability is an advantage in securing a good job. However, the political change since 1997 has brought significant impact on the language policy in Hong Kong. Officially, the Hong Kong SAR government abandoned the *laissez-faire* policy, which allowed secondary schools to choose a language as MOI for teaching. The Hong Kong SAR government imposed the 'biliteracy and trilingual' and the compulsory Cantonese as MOI policy. One of the main goals to adopt these policies was to integrate Hong Kong with Mainland China and the rest of the world. Under this policy, schools were required to be consistent in MOI and mixed code teaching was avoided. This policy led to a significant decrease in the number of EMI schools. The school curriculum was also revised to adopt Putonghua as the language for teaching the Chinese subject and Cantonese as the language for teaching other content subjects in CMI schools. Putonghua also became a subject in the Hong Kong Certificate of Education Examination (HKCEE) in 2000.

Simultaneously, Mainland China has entered a new era of modernization after the reform and opening policy since 1978. China plays an increasingly important role in the global market. In addition, after the SARS epidemic in 2003, the Beijing government issued the scheme of 'Visiting Hong Kong as an Individual Traveller', allowing more Mainland Chinese people to visit Hong Kong. Many Mainland Chinese people flooded into Hong Kong. The number of visitors from Mainland China has increased from 15 million in 2003 to 66 million in 2016 (Hong Kong Tourism Board 2016). A lot of working people, particularly in the tourism sector, need to have a good command of Putonghua to deal with the phenomenon of mainlandization, a product of the increasing contact with China. All of these factors play a pivotal role in the spread of Putonghua in Hong Kong. Overall, Hong Kong is being amalgamated into China both economically and politically, and the spread of Putonghua is one auxiliary product.

Three months prior to the handover, the government issued a stronger guidance requiring all the secondary schools to be CMI. The pro-Beijing groups reiterated that being returned to China was a great opportunity for using the mother tongue rather than the colonial language, that is, English. Nationalism became a priority in the Hong Kong education system. However, resistance from parents, teachers and schools had never been so overwhelming (Publicity of Mother Tongue 1997). Many parents and schools stressed the benefits of English in education and career development. Poon (2009) doubted the value of implementing the compulsory CMI policy. Tsang's (2008) study also revealed that due to the English requirement in universities, chances of admission into a university for students of CMI schools were only half compared to the students of EMI schools. According to Evans (2002), English-medium stream is considered to be elite education and Chinese-medium education is regarded as inferior to that.

Meanwhile, the phenomenon of internationalization has exerted great pressure on the government to raise the English standards to maintain the international position that Hong Kong had gained. Government softened the policy, allowing about 30 per cent of secondary schools to continue being EMI schools. However, as a significant number of EMI schools were cut, English standards in Hong Kong kept declining, and many students lacked the motivation to learn English. It became more competitive for students to enter EMI schools. The CMI schools became more unpopular than in the pre-1997 period.

There has been a fierce debate over CMI-EMI in Hong Kong secondary schools. The cause of the debate is the existence of the 'One Country Two Systems' model of governance. According to the Basic Law, the Hong Kong SAR government has the autonomy to decide on educational issues, including the selection of EMI or CMI. The Chinese language can be either Cantonese or Putonghua. Such autonomy is not possible in Mainland China, where the MOI for Chinese Language subject and other content subjects must be Putonghua (Kirkpatrick and Xu 2001). Facing the fierce protests from students, parents, and schools, the Education Bureau implemented the 'fine-tuning' policy in 2010. This policy was well-received by the schools because they were allowed autonomy to provide English-medium classes or partial English-medium classes. Schools seemed to be able to get rid of the labels of CMI and EMI schools and many considered this policy as an innovative idea in closing the age-long controversy related to MOI in Hong Kong (Poon 2013). However, we are not sure whether this policy is used by the Education Department to maintain the stability of MOI in schools (Fine-tuning of MOI 2015), or will be suddenly changed due to a political decision by the government.

4.5 Trilingual education in Hong Kong: Balance between political decision and globalization

The compulsory MOI policy and the 'biliterate and trilingual' policy are two features of trilingual education in Hong Kong after the transfer of sovereignty. However, policies were determined mainly by centralized political decision, which makes trilingual education post-1997 a period of dilemma (Poon 2016). Before 1997, policies about language education in Hong Kong were implemented using public consultations and rigorous decision-making procedure. An advisory system, for example, the Education Commission, compiled reports based on collected data. The agency also conducted a territory-wide consultation, revised the reports, and then finally submitted it to the Education and Manpower Branch. Although this well-established extensively used advisory system still existed after the transfer of sovereignty, such a system is no longer independent. It is controlled by the government. Professional negotiations and decisions were not made by experts from different sectors of the society. Rather, decisions were mainly made directly by the Hong Kong SAR government without policymaking negotiations or procedures (Poon 2016). The Hong Kong SAR government issued a firm guidance, requiring all the schools to adopt CMI for other content subjects and Putonghua for the Chinese Language subject. Written Chinese was also standardized based on the mainland form, including the translation of foreign names (Poon 2010). Overall, language policies prior to 1997 were conducted based on enhancing language standards of Hong Kong students. However, policies related to trilingual education after 1997 became a political move to appease the Chinese government.

These two policies, that is, 'biliterate and multilingual' policy and 'fine tuning' policy, also showed a contradiction. For example, if the aim of the 'biliterate and multilingual' policy was to enhance the language ability in Cantonese, Putonghua and English, why was there a strict demand in avoiding EMI in schools? One of the major covert goals of implementing the compulsory CMI policy was the Chinese governments' desire to integrate Hong Kong with Mainland China (Poon 2016). The compulsory Chinese policy's goal in re-integrating Hong Kong into China had adverse effects on the enhancement of English-speaking ability of the people. The Hong Kong SAR government kept the former as the priority at the expense of the latter. However, these policies, based on political decisions, were influenced by economic development. Globalization was gaining its momentum, and Hong Kong was an international financial hub. Therefore, the decline in English proficiency caused by these policies was detrimental to the government's efforts in maintaining its position in the global market. The Hong Kong SAR government then sensed a need to improve English standards. The Education Bureau adopted a compromise policy called 'fine-tuning medium of instruction policy'. Schools were given a certain level of autonomy to choose the MOI suitable for their schools. Those that already were EMI were also given six years to remain being EMI.

However, the Hong Kong SAR government may encounter a lot of possible problems relating to the policies for trilingual education in the future. One of the major problems is that Hong Kong is a legitimate region governed by the Peoples' Republic of China (PRC). Simultaneously, Hong Kong is bestowed with the Basic Law which stipulates Hong Kong as a region of 'one country, two systems'. Language policy in education is influenced by the perceptions of the role and status of languages on part of policymakers, with languages being promoted or neglected for explicit or implicit political reasons. With globalization, choices should be made regarding international, national and local languages, with concomitant tensions concerning linguistic hegemony, identity and social equity (Kan and Adamson 2016). These tensions are exacerbated in Hong Kong. Differences in ideology and governance between Hong Kong and Mainland China is the root problem for the predicament involving trilingual education policies in Hong Kong. The PRC government asserts a need for the Hong Kong SAR government to build a national identity. The Hong Kong SAR government may be forced to give up the original schedule and objectives of the 'fine-tuning MOI policy'. Protests from students, parents, and schools may continue. In the worst scenario, the aims of these policies could be twisted to be consistent with government's ideological presuppositions. More and more EMI schools may encounter problems in using English as MOI. There may be increasing numbers of CMI schools in the future. Specifically, more Hong Kong schools may use Putonghua in the future. It seems that problems have always existed with regard to the aim of 'Biliteracy and Trilingualism' in Hong Kong, and stakeholders have often had their concerns, as explained in Li (2017).

Taking all factors into consideration, policies related to trilingual education should be made based on overall planning rather than politics. There are several models available (Tucker 1998), which include

- Parental, community support and involvement are essential.
- Encouraging development of students' first language to ensure cognitive development and facilitating the acquisition of second and third languages.
- Development of the students' first language, with its related cognitive development, is more important in promoting second and third language development than mere length of exposure to these later acquired languages.
- Cognitive/academic language skills, once developed and content subject material, once acquired, transfer readily.
- Teachers must be able to understand, speak and use the language of instruction proficiently, whether it is their first or second language.
- Political considerations should not be a barrier to the implementation of innovative language education programmes.

4.6 Motivation and identity related to multilingual education in Hong Kong

Due to the complex sociopolitical and historical contexts in Hong Kong and the development of globalization, exploring the interrelations among Hong Kong people's language, ideology and identity has become very complicated. Legitimating official/national/standard languages becomes one of the most crucial agendas for the powerful (e. g., national and cultural essentialists), who want to construct and confirm national identities among Hong Kong people. Linguistic boundaries are constructed alongside citizenship and nationality. People are expected to build strong solidarity in their communities. The overt purpose of post-1997 policies was to enhance the ability of Cantonese, English and Putonghua. However, the covert aim was to promote a unified language which would unite the people and help to create a Chinese national identity. This suggests that linguistic processes such as standardization have always been intermingled with power.

However, we cannot underestimate the global force of capitalism and imperialism, which penetrates world markets in complex ways. Economic systems influenced by global forces have challenged the stability of national identities. National identities, to some extent, have been reabsorbed into larger communities – more powerful nation-states (Hall 1990). Hong Kong experienced rapid economic development during the 1980s. Even though Hong Kong was a colony of Britain, it extended beyond the economic and cultural boundaries of many countries in the world, including neighbouring countries in Asia. This expanded the symbolic power of Hong Kong culture, language and identity over other nations. English became a language for international communication rather than just being a colonized language. This also influenced the policymakers' decisions towards multilingual education after 1997.

Aronin and Ó Laoire (2004) argue that multilingualism is most adequately studied within the scope of disciplines related to language and society, with a foundation in identity theory. In the analysis of globalization, changes in MOI as well as in identities have become one of the major issues, both on societal and individual levels. Due to the social-cultural changes in Hong Kong, an indigenous identity – that of the Hong Konger – emerged. In a study conducted by Lai (2001), it was found that youngsters in Hong Kong rated English first, Cantonese second and Putonghua third in terms of importance. Those who identify themselves as Hong Kongers tend to have an affective attitude towards English and Cantonese. Being fluent in speaking English would not yield a negative image of being arrogant and snobbish. They regard it as being natural when mixing English and Cantonese in their daily communication. This linguistic practice (intertwining of English and Cantonese) seems to play a decisive role in shaping the identity as Hong Kongers. This so-called 'mixed code' is a linguistic and cultural marker in the distinctive local Hong Kong identity. After 10 years, Lai (2012) used the same research method to trace the change of language attitudes over the past years. Similar to the results concluded in 2001, Hong Kong students showed the greatest affection towards Cantonese followed by English. In relation to the instrumental values, English was rated the highest and Cantonese second. Putonghua was rated the lowest. Different from Lai (2001), Hong Kong students showed an overall improvement in being motivated to learn English, Cantonese and Putonghua. The roles and status of Cantonese and English remained stable, while Putonghua attracted more attention along with the increasing power of China in the world. The three languages have become part of the Hong Kong students' 'ideal self' and 'ought-to self' after twelve years' implementation of the policy of 'biliteracy and trilingualism'. As proposed by Dörnyei (2009), if learning a language is part of one's 'ideal self' (i.e., personal hopes and aspirations) and 'ought-to self' (i.e., sense of responsibilities), learners may show more motivation to learn that language.

Learning is a mental process that involves initial planning, goal setting, task generation, action implementation, monitoring, and evaluating (Dörnyei, Henry and Muir 2016). In Hong Kong, English was considered as a language of paramount importance and taught as early as in kindergarten. In an early study (Pennington and Yue 1994), before the transfer of sovereignty, youth of Hong Kong perceived a command over English as an essential skill and not a threat to their Chinese identity. One of the reasons for this was societal pressure and need for graduates who were proficient in both English and Chinese. This situation has not changed since the transfer of sovereignty to China in 1997 (Berry and McNeil 2005).

The Hong Kong SAR government and the community at large acknowledge the importance of learning English, and they also realize a need to ensure high-English standards in education and workforce to maintain Hong Kong's position as an international financial centre. Parents also have a high demand for English-medium education. By contrast, Chinese is accorded low status. In addition, at the level of individual Hong Konger, the English language has become both a cultural and symbolic capital and, at the communal level, knowledge of English distinguishes Hong Kongers from their counterparts in the PRC. This distinction is something that Hong Kongers cherish. They want to maintain a separate identity from Mainland China, particularly after Hong Kong was handed back to the PRC (Davison and Lai 2006). By contrast, the fear of losing one's identity may produce resistance to the norms of the new contexts or policies (Ige 2010). It appears that identity resides in the individual or groups' perception of self, reflected in their past and imagined future and how they want to be perceived or understood in the present (Pavlenko 2001; Teng 2018). It is likely that Hong Kong people have a valued sense of their historical past and an insecure fear of their own diminishing importance in the present. They prefer their identity of being a Hong Konger and fear that being reintegrated into China would make them lose this identity. It seems that an individual's or group's preferred identity strongly represents their choice and use of language, particularly within a multilingual and multicultural context.

The Hong Kong policy research institute commissioned by the Standing Committee on Language Education and Research (SCOLAR) conducted a survey on CMI school students' attitude and motivation towards learning English. Only 25 per cent of students showed strong motivation towards learning Putonghua. Unexpectedly, less than one half of the students showed strong motivation towards learning English. The Hong Kong CMI school students surveyed seemed to have low motivation in learning English (SCOLAR 2003). A myriad of factors may have contributed to Hong Kong students' low motivation in learning English. One of the main factors is the policy of compulsory mother-tongue-medium instruction. For example, when EMI schools were forced to change into CMI schools, some students only regarded English as a subject rather than a necessity for learning contents of other subjects. When English was no longer the MOI, it hinged the results of other subjects. CMI school students may only have an intention to pass the subject with minimal trouble.

The case of Hong Kong suggests that English has become a linguistic habitus for most of Hong Kong people. A command of the English language secures oneself for personal advancement. English has become a part of Hong Kong peoples' collective identity. Understanding this cautions one not to interfere with the MOI, for it suggests meddling with an individual's collective identity. The case of changing the MOI from English to Chinese in the secondary school in post-handover Hong Kong is a case in point (Chan 2002). Therefore, changing MOI should not simply be regarded as a case of educational policy decision. It is, in practice, an intent to transmute one's collective identity. Although Hong Kong has attached great importance to the teaching and learning of English, the inappropriate adoption of policy in Hong Kong fails to provide a nurturing environment for English learning. As argued by Bourdieu (1991), language can neither be analysed in isolation from its cultural context, nor can it be understood in isolation from the social condition of its production and reception. Kirkpatrick (2011) proposed that early introduction of English, along with the push for national language, is not only pedagogically ill-advised for the great majority of primary school students, but it also poses a threat to the maintenance of local languages and students' sense of identity. Without exploring the nature of language and related issues (e.g., motivation and identity), it is difficult for the Hong Kong SAR government to achieve success in handling the issue of MOI.

4.7 Reflection

After being handed back to China, Hong Kong has experienced the process of localization and mainlandization while sticking to internationalization to keep its advantage as an 'Asia's world city'. An intense interplay of these three factors contributes to Hong Kong students' motivation and identity. The intertwining of the three factors also facilitates or inhibits the growth of vitality of each language. For example, the localization movement upholds the dominant role of Cantonese in Hong Kong's social communication. The trend for internationalization urges English-language learning as a tool to maintain Hong Kong's superior status and function in the global market. The increasingly enhanced contact with China leads to mainlandization, as well as an increasing importance of Putonghua in Hong Kong. It is not surprising that the interplay of localization, mainlandization and internationalization affects Hong Kong students' motivational intensity for learning each language. The motivational intensity is reflective in the formation and reformation of identity, suggesting that a balance of these three factors is a prerequisite for facilitating multilingual education in Hong Kong.

Challenges in trilingual education in Hong Kong, one of the most cosmopolitan and internationalized metropolises, will be increasingly encountered. In Hong Kong, graduates aiming for a decent job need to master a reasonably high level of proficiency in English and Chinese. These two languages have become essential to Hong Kong's maintenance of a knowledge-based economy, socio-economic vitality, continued prosperity, cultural awareness and sustainable development. Hence, the policy concerning trilingual education in Hong Kong should figure prominently in the future and the success or failure is an example to other regions. Some researchers critically commented on the failure of trilingual education in Hong Kong. As argued by Poon (2010), the Hong Kong government has invested billions of dollars to promote biliteracy and trilingualism, but students' language standards keep declining. Related to this, we can detect some problems inherent in the development of trilingual education in Hong Kong. The first problem is that we lack a conducive language environment for using and practising English in an authentic situation. We can also say that English is hardly used for authentic meaning-making purposes among a majority of Cantonese-speaking Hong Kongers. The second problem is that the promotion of Putonghua often leads to a political conflict in Hong Kong. Speaking and using Putonghua is identified with some sort of mainland identity labels.

Finally, there is a high degree of linguistic dissimilarity between Cantonese, Putonghua, and English. For example, English and Chinese belong to different language families with diverse linguistic characteristics 'from phonology to lexico-grammar, from varying information sequencing norms to learner-unfriendly orthographies' (Li 2017: 195). Learners in Hong Kong are not likely to find the reference value of Cantonese in learning English. English has become a foreign language rather than a second language to Hong Kong learners. However, the same cannot be said of the learning of Putonghua, where some words share the same orthography with those of Cantonese. Still, it is not easy for Cantonese speakers to master the pronunciation system in Putonghua. In addition, the political conflicts between Putonghua and Cantonese may inhibit some Hong Kong learners from speaking and using Putonghua (ibid.). The term 'mother tongue education' may be a misnomer, as Hong Kong students' written Chinese and spoken Cantonese is not the same.

In the future, the road towards biliteracy and trilingualism is not a smooth one in Hong Kong. It could be a bumpy one and it could be riddled with dilemmas. Hong Kong's development into a global financial centre depended and will still depend on a bilateral and trilingual workforce. However, Cantonese speakers in Hong Kong seem to possess a collective ethnolinguistic identity. The identity can be so strong that conversing in a language other than Cantonese can be perceived as highly marked or labelled with outsiders. This may explain the odd feature in Hong Kong right now. Many students lose motivation in learning English but still need to pay an exorbitant fee to learn and practice English with other link-minded learners in a tutorial centre. This kind of hourly charge system in the tutorial centre reflects a distortion of English teaching in Hong Kong. Learning Putonghua may not be the same, but there are other problems. Many learners in Hong Kong are aware of the need to have a high level of proficiency in Putonghua, which is a key to helping them to have more opportunities in the workplace. However, many learners are not willing to speak Putonghua for meaningful practice outside the classroom. Given that the learning of English and Putonghua is confined to classroom teaching, it is not surprising for Hong Kong learners to encounter difficulties in teaching and learning these two languages.

Overall, it seems that the Hong Kong SAR government has failed to persuade the public to accept its policies about multilingual education because the government seems to has misunderstood the nature and social functions of each language. There may be potential for adopting the compulsory mother-tongue MOI policy (Education Commission 2005), but the Hong Kong SAR government has overlooked the complex array of historical, cultural-political, socio-economic and practical factors that influence language policy and planning in the Hong Kong context (Tsui 2007). Furthermore, motivation and identity were not taken into consideration during policy adoption and implementation. The choice of a suitable model of trilingual education is arguably a major educational issue confronting Hong Kong today. The Hong Kong SAR government may need a shift in mindset, not focusing solely on having separate Chinese-medium and English-medium schools, but to establish all schools as multilingual sites where Cantonese, English and Putonghua operate alongside each other in a complementary way (Kirkpatrick and Chau 2008). Finally, it may be more appropriate for the Hong Kong SAR government to use its economic and political force to pursue benefits in the global marketplace, rather than making education as a product of a political decision.

5

Motivation and Identity of the Stakeholders: The Case of Hong Kong

After the political transition in 1997, the Hong Kong government adopted the 'biliterate and trilingual' policy, aiming to help Hong Kong citizens to become biliterate in written Chinese and English, and trilingual in Cantonese, Putonghua and spoken English. Although the policy is now guiding the curriculum design in Hong Kong language education, there are no clear government guidelines on how trilingual education should be implemented in primary schools (Wang and Kirkpatrick 2013). To gain a better understanding of how trilingual education is implemented in Hong Kong primary schools, a questionnaire was designed to find out how the 'biliterate' and 'trilingual' language policy was implemented in Hong Kong primary schools (Wang and Kirkpatrick 2015). The questionnaire was sent to all the 474 primary schools in Hong Kong. These included all of the 34 government schools (7.2 per cent), all the 420 aided schools (88.6 per cent) and all the 20 Direct Subsidy Scheme (DSS) schools (4.2 per cent). The principal of each surveyed school was invited to complete the questionnaire. A total of 155 (32.7 per cent) Hong Kong primary school principals returned the questionnaire. The findings of this survey provided us with an overall picture of the current situation of trilingual education implementation in Hong Kong primary schools. The findings suggest that the implementation of trilingual education varied significantly from school to school, and the effectiveness of different trilingual education approaches varied as well (Wang and Kirkpatrick 2015).

As some questions remained unanswered after the analysis of the questionnaire survey data, follow-up case studies in three selected primary schools were undertaken. Among the questions we sought to answer, two were on motivation and identity:

1. What are the motivation and identity of different stakeholders towards the study of the three languages (Cantonese, English, and Putonghua) in the case study schools?

2. To what extent do the motivation and identity of different stakeholders towards the study of the three languages (Cantonese, English and Putonghua) vary?

In this chapter, we will focus our discussion on the motivation and identity of different stakeholders in the multilingual setting of three case study schools and how different stakeholders' motivation and identity vary, and the relevant implications to multilingual education.

Learning English in the Hong Kong context can be considered as learning a second language or a foreign language. A second language (L2) is the study or use of a language by non-native speakers in an L2 environment, which is used for 'social and learning purposes within the school or college setting' (Leung, Davison and Mohan 2014: 1). Meanwhile, a foreign language refers to a language often widely taught in schools, but it does not play a vital role in national or social life (Broughton, Brumfit, Pincas and Wilde 2002), or it refers to the use or study of a language by non-native speakers in countries/regions where that language is generally not a local medium of communication.

Hong Kong has a rather complicated language environment: although English is regarded as one of the official languages, and is adopted as the MOI by the higher education institutions, the majority of the population (around 95 per cent) speak Cantonese as their mother tongue (Census and Statistics Department 2017: 31), and English is rarely used for daily communication among local Hong Kongers. In this sense, to a small number of Hong Kongers who need to use English regularly in their profession and/or daily lives, English can be regarded as a second language, but to many others who rarely use it in their profession and/or daily lives, English can be regarded as a foreign language. As for Putonghua, because it is the national language of China, which is promoted by the government in Hong Kong, to most Hong Kongers, it should be regarded as a second language. However, as Cantonese is very dominant in the Hong Kong society, many Hong Kongers may rarely use Putonghua in their daily lives, so to an extent, Putonghua is equivalent to a foreign language to them.

Dörnyei (1998: 117) stated that 'motivation provides the primary impetus to initiate learning the L2 and later the driving force to sustain the long and often tedious learning process'. In addition, motivation determines 'the extent of active, personal involvement in foreign or second language learning' (Oxford 1996: 121). Gardner (1985) defined 'instrumental orientation' as a positive inclination for a language because of pragmatic reasons (a good job or educational opportunities), whereas 'integrative orientation' is the inclination towards a language in order to become a member of its community or cultural group. Broughton, Brumfit, Pincas and Wilde (2002: 5) pointed out when one learns a foreign language instrumentally for operational purposes, he/she wants to be able to read books in the new language, to be able to communicate with other speakers of that particular language. For example, the salesman, the science student and the tourist are clearly motivated to learn English instrumentally. This is so-called the 'ought-to self' which 'concerns the attributes that one believes one ought to possess to meet expectations and to avoid possible negative outcomes' (Dörnyei 2009: 29). This shows the learner's 'ought-to self', meaning a learner's sense of duty and/or obligations to satisfy the expectations of others, that is, their teachers or parents. In this case, the learners' language learning is deriving from external forces such as significant others, the nature of interaction with significant others, the learning environment and the broader context (Williams and Burden 1997: 138–40). To Gardner and Lambert (1972: 132), integrative motivation refers to 'the practical value and advantages of learning a new language'. If one learns a second or a foreign language for integrative purposes, s/he is attempting to identify much more closely with a speech community which uses that language variety; s/he intends to feel at home in it, and s/he tries to gain a good understanding of the attitudes and the world view of that community (Broughton, Brumfit, Pincas and Wilde 2002). This involves 'a sincere and personal interest in the people and culture represented by the other group' (Gardner and Lambert 1972). This is the 'ideal self' which represents the ideal image a learner would like to have in the future and this is derived from internal forces, for example, intrinsic interest of activity, perceived value of activity, sense of agency, mastery, self-concept, attitudes towards language learning in general, other affective states, developmental age and stage and gender (Williams and Burden 1997: 138–40).

Language learning is closely related to identity. Block (2007) viewed that Firth and Wagner's 1997 article marked the beginning of a rising interest in social theory among second language acquisition (SLA) researchers. He described the link between second language acquisition and one's sense of identity as: when individuals move across geographical and psychological borders, immersing themselves in new sociocultural environments, they find their sense of identity is destabilized and that they enter a period of struggle to reach a balance (Block 2007: 864). Norton (2013: 51) stated that commitment in language learning is an 'investment in a learner's own identity, an identity which is constantly changing across time and space'.

From Section 1.6, 'Motivation and identity related to multilingual education in Hong Kong' in Chapter 4, we understand that as Hong Kong was under British colonial rule for about 155 years, there was the emergence of an indigenous identity – that of Hong Kongers, who tend to have an affective attitude towards English and Cantonese and regard it as being natural when mixing English and Cantonese, the so-called 'mixed code', in their daily communication. This linguistic practice (intertwining of English and Cantonese) seems to play a decisive role in shaping the identity as Hong Kongers: a local Hong Kong identity. Meanwhile, Putonghua has attracted more attention along with the increasing power of China in the world and with the implementation of the policy of 'biliteracy and trilingualism' for more than twenty years, speaking Putonghua as a national identity seems to have been enhanced among Hong Kong people. Moreover, the three languages have become part of the Hong Kong students' 'ideal self' and 'ought-to self' (Lai 2012). As proposed by Dörnyei (2009), if learning a language is part of one's 'ideal self' (i.e., personal hopes and aspirations) and 'ought-to self' (i.e., sense of responsibilities), learners may show more motivation to learn that language.

Based on this framework, this chapter will discuss the motivation and identity of the stakeholders: students, teachers, parents and principals in the three languages in three Hong Kong primary schools, and the relevant implications for multilingual education in the local community and perhaps the Asian region.

5.1 Information of the three case study schools

5.1.1 School A

A co-educational school established in 1967, School A is located on Hong Kong Island. It was initially a CMI school (using Cantonese as MOI) in which all subjects, apart from English Language subject, were taught in Cantonese. In September 2008, the language policy regarding the use of MOI in the teaching of the Chinese Language subject changed: Putonghua became the MOI for the Chinese Language subject. The school is unusual in that it attracts a large number of international students. In the 2014–2015 school year, 271 students were enrolled comprising 23 nationalities, including Chinese (Hongkongers, Mainlanders and Taiwanese), Filipino, British, Canadian, Indian, Nepalese, American, Australian, French, Japanese, Thai, Egyptian, Indonesian, Pakistani, Cameroonian, Singaporean, Sri Lankan, Venezuelan, Spanish, Swiss, German,

Dutch and Nigerian. In order to help the students to strengthen their biliterate and trilingual competencies, the school implemented its own school-based Internationalized Curriculum (IC) in the academic year 2011–2012, which was based on the structure of the Hong Kong Primary Curriculum, set by the EDB Curriculum Development Institute.

5.1.2 School B

School B is another co-educational school, which is the first 'through-train' mode whole day primary school in Tung Chung, the New Territories. Aided or government primary and secondary schools implementing the 'through-train' mode have the same philosophy and aspiration for education and strive to enhance continuity in primary and secondary education. Moreover, a P6 pupil of a 'through-train' school may proceed directly to its linked secondary school without going through the central allocation process.

This school was established in September 2000. Putonghua was used as the MOI in the teaching of the Chinese Language subject until September 2008. After seeing the ineffectiveness of using Putonghua as MOI (PMI) in the teaching of the Chinese Language subject, the school decided to replace Putonghua by Cantonese as the MOI for the Chinese Language subject.

5.1.3 School C

Located in Kowloon, School C is a single-sex boy school. It has a long history as it was established in 1930. The language policy in the school has changed several times throughout the years. In 1972, Cantonese was the medium of instruction. School C started using Putonghua as the MOI for the Chinese Language subject in September 2008, starting at P2 and gradually including the later levels until all Chinese Language subject classes from P2 to P6 were PMI (Putonghua as MOI). Cantonese remained the MOI for P1. From September 2014 onwards, School C changed the policy to adopting Putonghua as the MOI for the Chinese Language subject from P1 to P4 but using Cantonese as the MOI for P5–P6.

5.1.4 Demographic information of the researched schools

Demographic information of each school is shown in Table 5.1. School C is the only school which comprises 100 per cent local Hong Kongers, while the origins

Table 5.1 Demographic information of the researched schools

Area	School Code	Origins of students			
		Local Hong Kongers (%)	Mainlanders (%)	Come from a South Asian Area (%)	Come from Other Areas (%)
Hong Kong Island	A	51	2	10	37
New Territories	B	67.4	6.8	21.8	4
Kowloon	C	100			

of students in the other two schools are a mixture of local Hong Kongers and students either from Mainland China, or from a South Asian area, or from other areas such as Canada, France and Japan.

5.2 Methodology and data collection

A multi-modal approach for the case study was adopted so as to obtain as complete a picture of each setting as possible. Our data came from student questionnaire surveys in case-study schools, interviews with teaching staff and parents, focus group interviews with students, classroom discourse data analysis, teachers' reflections, and ethnographic field research data analysis. The ethnographic field research was only conducted in School A due to limitation of manpower.

5.2.1 Student questionnaire survey

A 5-point Likert scale (Strongly Agree, Agree, Neutral, Disagree, Strongly Disagree) questionnaire survey in Chinese and English was designed to collect students' perceptions of the trilingual education approaches adopted by the three sample schools. Four hundred and five P4 to P6 students in the three schools completed the survey questionnaire (71 students from School A, 141 from School B and 193 from School C).

5.2.2 Focus group interviews

The focus group interview is a research technique that 'collects data through group interaction on a topic determined by the researcher. In essence, it is the researcher's interest that provides the focus, whereas the data themselves come from the group interaction' (Morgan 1997: 6). We employed student focus group interviews to collect the students' views on the trilingual education approach adopted by the schools. One student focus group interview was conducted in each of the three schools. In each focus group, there were eight to ten P4–P6 student interviewees. The focus group interviews were conducted in Cantonese in School B and School C, while mixed code was used in School A. In total, twenty-seven students were interviewed (eleven from School A, eight from School B and eight from School C), and each focus group interview lasted for about an hour. The focus group interviews were translated/transcribed into English.

5.2.3 Interviews with teaching staff and parents

Interviews were conducted with teaching staff including the school principals, the subject panel chairs and subject teachers. The interviews with school principals, which focused on the rationale behind the present trilingual education approaches adopted by the schools and the extent of the success of the approaches, were conducted in Cantonese and each lasted for one hour. The interviews were translated/transcribed into English. Thirty-three teachers in the three schools were also interviewed. These interviews were conducted in Cantonese and were translated/transcribed into English. Each interview lasted for about half an hour. Table 5.2 summarizes this information.

In addition, 31 parents (10 from both School A and School B and 11 from School C) were interviewed and each interview lasted for about twenty to twenty-five minutes. Cantonese was used when interviewing local parents, Putonghua was used for interviewing parents from Mainland China and English was used for interviewing parents from other areas. All of the interviews conducted in Chinese were translated/transcribed into English.

5.2.4 Classroom discourse data analysis

A total of thirty lessons in the case study schools were recorded and transcribed so as to analyse what actually happened in different lessons taught in different MOIs. Each lesson lasted for thirty-five minutes. In terms of classroom discourse data analysis, Ellis and Barkhuizen's (2005) model was followed. This involves recording authentic data which are carefully transcribed, 'unmotivated looking', rather than pre-stated research questions, selecting a sequence of utterances

Table 5.2 Information of the teacher interviewees in the researched schools

Subject	School A		School B		School C	
	Panel Chair	Subject Teacher	Panel Chair	Subject Teacher	Panel Chair	Subject Teacher
Chinese Language	✓	✓✓	✓	✓	✓	✓ (using PMI)
English Language	✓	✓	✓	✓	✓	✓
Putonghua	N.A.	N.A.	✓		✓	✓
Mathematics	✓*		✓		✓	
General Studies	✓		✓		✓	
Visual Arts	✓		✓		✓	
Music	✓*		✓		✓	
Physical Education	✓		✓		✓	
Computing	✓		✓		✓	
Total	10		11		12	

*The Panel Chair is also the Subject Teacher whose lesson was observed.

characterizing the actions/acts in the sequence, and describing and analysing turn-taking, and discussing any issues that arise. We paid particular attention to evidence of code-switching and co-/trans-languaging, and the reasons for this. We also studied the ratio of student/teacher talk in each lesson, and how questions are used by teachers and students to facilitate teaching and learning.

5.2.5 Teachers' reflections

Boud, Keogh and Walker (1985: 19) viewed reflection as employing 'intellectual and affective abilities in which individuals engage to explore their experiences in order to achieve new understandings and appreciations'. Therefore, reflective teachers think of the problems in their own teaching practices and consciously consider how those problems are related to their educational and social contexts. In this study, teachers were asked to reflect on their performance during the recorded lessons. They were asked to fill in the 'Reflection Form' focusing on the following issues:

- The MOI the teacher used in the lesson;
- The language students used when they interacted with the teacher;
- The language students used when they interacted with peers;
- Teacher's self-evaluation of the use of the MOI in conducting the lesson;

- The existence of code-mixing by the teacher and students during the lesson and the reasons for this; and
- The consideration of making use of other MOI(s) in the lesson as a supplement to facilitate students' trilingual development.

5.2.6 Ethnographic field research data analysis

Ethnographic studies support a qualitative approach, comprising extended participant observation periods and ethnographic interviews (Christensen 2011; Creswell 2013), in which researchers investigate and interpret the meaning of values, behaviours, thought processes, customs, the interactions of members and the communal language in a shared culture (Harris 1968). In ethnography, data collection is primarily through fieldwork (Whitehead 2005). Wolcott (2005) defined fieldwork as a form of inquiry that requires a researcher to be immersed personally in the ongoing social activities of some individual or group carrying out the research. Ethnographic research always involves face-to-face contact between the ethnographer and the community of study (Schensul, Schensul and LeCompte 1999). Therefore, ethnographic field research involves first-hand participation in some initially unfamiliar social worlds and the production of written accounts of that world by drawing upon such participation (Emerson, Fretz and Shaw 1995). Due to limitation of manpower, ethnographic research was only conducted in School A, in which the ethnographer observed how the three languages were used in two events on campus: the school Morning Assembly, and the Prize-Giving Ceremony and the Second Annual General Meeting of the Eighth Parent-Teacher Association. In addition, the project research assistant who acted as an ethnographer attended the school's Fourteenth Parent-Child Sports Day. The ethnographer also took photos of signs and bulletin board displays written in a variety of languages.

5.3 Discussions

In this session, the research questions will be answered through data analysis and discussions: What are the motivation and identity of different stakeholders towards the study of the three languages (Cantonese, English and Putonghua) in the case study schools? To what extent do the motivation and identity of different stakeholders towards the study of the three languages (Cantonese, English and Putonghua) vary?

5.3.1 Students' motivation and identity towards the three languages

In School A, seventy-one P4 to P6 students were surveyed (P4: 34, P5: 18, P6: 19) and eleven P4–P6 students participated in the focus group interview. In School B, 141 P4 to P6 students were surveyed (P4: 48, P5: 44, P6: 49) and 8 P4–P6 students were interviewed. In School C, 193 P4 to P6 students were surveyed (P4: 58, P5: 67, P6: 68) and 8 P4–P6 students were interviewed.

Students in the three researched schools were found generally motivated in learning the three languages as they gave an average mean score of 3.73 to item 3 (I enjoyed the trilingual education approach in the school) in the questionnaire survey. However, the more non-Chinese students the school has, the more motivated the students were in learning the three languages. Students of School A gave the highest mean score of 3.99 to this item, while students in School C, which comprises 100 per cent local Hong Kongers, gave this item the lowest mean score of 3.12. What is remarkable is that the non-Chinese students of School A showed both instrumental and integrative motivations of learning more languages, especially Cantonese. For example, a P6 student from Africa in School A said, 'I like learning the three languages because it will be more convenient for me to order food in a restaurant either in Cantonese or in Putonghua'. A P4 Filipino said, 'If I learn Cantonese, I can help my mom to translate when buying things in the market'. Another Filipino student remarked, 'In the past, I could not understand even one word in Cantonese, but now I am happy that I can understand more and more words in Cantonese'.

This data shows that the non-Chinese students were, on the one hand, eager to learn Cantonese for pragmatic purposes: they want to be able to communicate with local Hong Kongers in Cantonese (Broughton, et al. 2002) in the market and could order food in a restaurant. This refers to the 'ought-to self', meaning their sense of duty and/or obligations is to satisfy the expectations of others, that is, their parents (Dörnyei 2009). Their learning motivation was derived from external forces such as significant others, that is, their parents (Williams and Burden 1997), so that they could help, for example, their parents to translate when buying things in the market. Another external force motivating their learning Cantonese is the nature of interaction with significant others (Williams and Burden 1997). This is because if they could speak in Cantonese, they could order food in a restaurant which is a kind of reward of their learning. On the other hand, their Cantonese learning is part of the 'ideal self', which is their personal hopes and aspirations (Dörnyei 2009), and they are motivated for integrative purposes as well, as they were attempting to identify much more closely with the Hong Kong community which uses Cantonese (Broughton, Brumfit, Pincas and Wilde 2002). Deriving from the internal forces such as intrinsic interest of activity and mastery (Williams and Burden 1997), they were eager to learn Cantonese. To them, communicating with local people in Cantonese in the market is of optimal degree of challenge (intrinsic interest of activity) while having the language to order food in a restaurant provides a feeling of competence (mastery) (ibid.). We may say that these non-Chinese students are learning Cantonese as a second language (L2) which is used for social and learning purposes (Leung, Davison and Mohan 2014).

Among the three languages, the students in the researched schools were most happy with their progress in the study of Cantonese as they gave an average mean score of 4.15 to item 11 (I am happy with my progress in the study of Cantonese), ranking the second highest among all items. Moreover, they were most confident of achieving good proficiency in Cantonese when they graduated (item 16: I am confident that when I graduate I will have achieved good proficiency in Cantonese). The average mean score of this item is 4.05, which ranked the third highest among all items. However, the students from School A, which comprises 49 per cent of students coming from Mainland, a South Asian area or other areas, were less happy with their progress in the study of Cantonese and less confident of achieving good proficiency in Cantonese when compared with students from the other two schools as they gave lower mean scores to items 11 and 16. The reason accounting for the high confidence of students from School B and School C in achieving good proficiency in Cantonese is that most of them speak Cantonese at home as their mother tongue. They will not worry about their proficiency in Cantonese, regardless of the languages used in school. This shows that students from School B and School C reveal a strong sense of local Hong Kong identity and Cantonese is the language that relates to that identity (Lai 2001).

As mentioned in Section 5.1, the use of mixed code, mixing Cantonese and English, also contributes part of local Hong Kong identity: the Hong Kongers. In response to questions about the use of code-switching or code-mixing, students from School A were more accepting of switching from one language to another when studying different subjects in the school as they gave the highest mean score of 3.83 to item 4 (I find it acceptable switching from one language to another when studying different subjects in the school.) among the three schools, which is above the average mean score of 3.69. Students from this school also found code-mixing in different subjects most useful for their language development in general as they gave a mean score of 4 to item 7 (I find co-switching in different subjects useful for my language development in general.), which is above the average mean score of 3.68, while the mean scores of the other two schools are below the average mean score. The P5 interviewees who are not ethnic Chinese in School A would like their teachers to code-mix between Cantonese/Putonghua and English in Chinese Language subject lessons and between Cantonese and English in Mathematics lessons. A P5 Filipino said, 'I prefer the teachers code-switching between English and Cantonese/Putonghua in Chinese Language lessons so that I can remember the content better and learn more Chinese words'. Another P5 Filipino said, 'Most of the subjects are taught in Cantonese and we really do not understand if the teachers do not explain in English. I would like the teachers to use English to help me understand the content'. Two P4 Filipinos pointed out that they sometimes used code-mixing when communicating with local students because they thought this could be understood more easily, for example:

> '你有冇(in Cantonese) finish your homework?' meaning 'Have you finished your homework?'
>
> '我爸爸 (in Putonghua) is good' meaning 'My father is good'

Students' opinions on code-mixing varied in School B. On the one hand, the mean scores of item 4 to item 6 (I find it acceptable switching from one language to another when studying different subjects in the school; I find myself code-switching between English and Cantonese regularly during the study of the English subject; I find myself co-switching between Cantonese and Putonghua regularly during the study of the Chinese subject) from School B are above the average mean scores of the three items while the mean score of item 7 (I find co-switching in different subjects useful for my language development in general) is a bit below the average mean score of this item. In School B, about half of P4-P6 students found code-mixing in different subjects useful for their language development in general; but 15 per cent of them did not agree to this and 27 per cent of them had no opinion. On the other hand, five out of the eight interviewees said that they did not find code-mixing in different subjects useful for their language development in general. One student said, 'We can't learn a language if we are too dependent on teachers' translation'. Students from School B found themselves code-mixing between English and Cantonese while studying English, as they gave the highest mean score of 3.53 to item 5 (I find myself code-switching between English and Cantonese regularly during the study of the English subject.), which is above the average mean score of 3.41 of the three researched schools. One student said, 'We can easily understand what the teachers say if Cantonese is used to explain the English vocabularies'.

Fewer students from School C found code-mixing acceptable as the mean scores of item 4 to item 7 of this school are below the average mean scores. There are reasons to explain this phenomenon. First, all the students in School C are local Hong Kongers and are L1 speakers of Cantonese. Second, Cantonese is the major MOI in most subjects in the school. Third, teachers insist on using almost 100 per cent English in English Language lessons and almost 100 per cent Putonghua in Chinese Language subject lessons (P1–P4) and in Putonghua subject lessons (P1–P6).

Students in the researched schools showed both instrumental and integrative motivations in learning English as a second language. Students who disagreed to the use of mixed code in teaching the English Language subject showed their pragmatic purposes in learning the English language. For example, one student interviewee from School C pointed out, 'Using 100 per cent English can benefit us when we are going for an interview in the future'. This shows the pragmatic purpose of being able to communicate with the interviewer(s) in interviews in the future. Another interviewee from the same school expressed, 'It will be more difficult for us to adapt to an EMI secondary school if teachers do not use 100 per cent English. We need to get ourselves familiar with such a teaching environment', showing the learner's 'ought-to self' that he/she learnt English instrumentally so that he/she could have an educational opportunity in an EMI secondary school (Gardner 1985). A student interviewee from School B stated, 'We cannot learn a language if we depend too much on the teachers' translation'. This shows the learners' 'ideal self', which was derived from the internal forces of motivation, such as perceived value of activity and attitudes towards language learning in general (Williams and Burden 1997). One interviewee from School B showed her 'ideal self' and 'ought-to self' in learning the English language as she pointed out, 'I find learning English is easier. I enjoyed watching English TV cartoons all day long when I was small. When I found the others did something wrong in the playground, I used to scold them in English like an elder sister'. The English learning of this student was motivated by internal force (self-efficacy) and external force (the comfort learning environment, that is, watching English TV cartoons).

Regarding the issue of using Putonghua as the MOI in the teaching of the Chinese Language subject (PMIC), students from School C were more negative towards using Putonghua in studying the Chinese Language subject in the survey. They gave a mean score of 2.63 to item 1 (I find it appropriate to use

Putonghua to study the Chinese Language subject.) while students of School A gave this a mean score of 3.44. Moreover, 30 per cent of students from School C chose 'strongly disagree' regarding this item compared to only 4 per cent of the students in School A.

In the interview, the non-Chinese students in School A noted that it was easier for them to learn how to speak Chinese (Putonghua) than to learn how to write in Chinese. The reason might be that it is comparatively easy to learn pinyin (the alphabetic writing system developed for Putonghua), but it is difficult to learn to write Chinese characters. Although there are Romanisation methods for Cantonese, they are not taught in school. Some teachers allowed the students in School A to use English to raise questions in the Chinese Language lessons. The teachers would then show the students how to ask the questions in Cantonese or Putonghua and then require them to repeat the questions in Cantonese or Putonghua. A Canadian student in P4 stated, 'When we ask questions in English, the teachers will show us how to say it in Cantonese/Putonghua and we are encouraged to repeat it in Cantonese/Putonghua'.

As mentioned earlier, all students in School C are local L1 speakers of Cantonese. The P5–P6 student interviewees from School C said that they preferred Cantonese as the MOI for the Chinese Language subject and this might explain why students of this school reported enjoying trilingual education the least. A P6 student (who had been using Putonghua to study the Chinese Language subject in the past five years) said, 'I think it's better to use Cantonese to study the subject. It is because some students could not understand the teacher well when Putonghua is used'. A P5 student (who had been using Putonghua to study the subject in the past four years) said, 'I prefer using Cantonese. My Dictation performance would be affected if the words are pronounced in Putonghua as there are always misunderstandings when hearing the pronunciations'.

In addition, Putonghua grammar matches the standard written Chinese grammar and there is a slogan for using Putonghua: 我手寫我口 (My hand writes down what I say). However, students who did not favour the use of Putonghua were, not surprisingly, those who did not understand Putonghua well. As a result, they were inattentive and noisy in class as they found the Chinese Language lessons boring as expressed by a student interviewee. There were fewer interactions between teachers and students and fewer students were willing to answer the teachers' questions when using Putonghua. For example, a student from School C said, 'I also prefer using Cantonese because some of the words in Putonghua are retroflex and when we do not pronounce them properly, they will become other words with different meanings, making classmates laugh. Since we learnt Cantonese when we were very young, it is easier to understand the teachers if they speak Cantonese'.

Three out of eight student interviewees from School B used Putonghua in the study of the Chinese Language subject when they were in P1 and P2. However, they showed their preferences for using Cantonese in the study of the subject and shared similar views with the students from School C that they could easily understand the teachers in Cantonese. In addition, the mispronunciation of the words in Putonghua always made students burst into laughter, resulting in a noisy class.

Regarding the students' satisfaction of the progress of the study of Putonghua, they gave the lowest average mean score of 3.47 (the third lowest average mean score among all items) when compared with the studies of Cantonese and English. Moreover, they were least confident in achieving good proficiency in Putonghua which received an average mean score of 3.49 (the fourth lowest average mean score among all items). This is, again, the lowest among the three languages. A P5 local student from School A said in the interview, 'My Putonghua is bad. I lose my confidence in it and I don't think I can make progress in Putonghua when I graduate next year'. One P6 interviewee from School C said, 'I have more confidence in English than in Putonghua. In English, we just need to spell the words but we need to put more time on practising pinyin in Putonghua which is rather difficult. Otherwise, we cannot learn Putonghua well'. Students from School B gave a higher mean score to item 12 (I am happy with my progress in the study of Putonghua.) and item 17 (I am confident that when I graduate I will achieve good proficiency in Putonghua.) than students from the other two schools. This shows students from School B were less resistant in learning the Putonghua subject.

These findings show that students' attitudes towards PMIC varied and depended on their linguistic backgrounds and attitudes. It seems that students from the researched schools had a stronger sense of local identity than a national identity, with a preference to using their mother tongue: Cantonese, rather than Putonghua, in the study of the Chinese Language subject. This might have resulted from their belief that it is easier to learn the knowledge through mother tongue. In addition, 'few opportunities of use after school' (So 1998: 168) might be one of the factors hindering their language learning of Putonghua. Last but not least, students were less motivated in learning Putonghua and would consider learning Putonghua as a third language, mainly for instrumental value (Lai 2001: 129). The purposes of their language learning of Putonghua are to meet the expectations of their parents and teachers, and to avoid possible negative outcomes in examinations (Dörnyei 2009).

5.3.2 Teachers' motivation and identity towards the three languages

In this part, the analysis on teachers' motivation and identity towards the three languages is based on class observations, teachers' reflections and teacher interviews in the three researched schools. Teachers are categorized into language teachers and subject teachers in the study. Thirty 35-minute-long lessons were observed and video-taped and transcribed (School A: 12, School B: 11 and School C: 7).

First, regarding language teaching, the English Language subject teachers in the three schools (two from each school) were consistent regarding their beliefs and classroom practices in that they all felt it was important to provide students with a rich English-language environment. In practice, they all used 100 per cent English in their teaching and insisted that their students raise and answer questions in English so that they could practise the language as much as possible. For example: English Language subject teacher teaching P5 English Language from School A wrote in her reflection form:

> As I use English all the time in my English Language lessons, I can provide a good English environment for my students to learn and practise using English. For some less able students, it is necessary to explain some challenging English terms using a certain kind of visual aid.

> (In the interview)

> English Language subject teacher 1 from School B: I will not code-mix. I think being immersed in an English environment is the most effective way in English learning.

> English Language subject teacher 2: English Language lessons are the only chance that my students can speak in English since they all speak Cantonese as their mother tongue. Though mother-tongue teaching is more effective, it does not apply in language teaching. I believe that a language-rich environment is very important for learning English.

The Chinese Language subject teachers who used Putonghua as the MOI (School A and School C) varied in their perceptions. Those who taught the Chinese Language subject in senior grades insisted on using 100 per cent Putonghua, while those teaching the junior grades were more flexible and tolerant, explaining the content with some Cantonese and allowing their students to raise and answer questions in Cantonese. In regard to teaching the Putonghua subject (School B and School C), the teachers shared the same views with the English Language subject teachers, saying that they used 100 per cent Putonghua in class and believed this would help their students enhance their Putonghua proficiency. For example:

> Putonghua subject teacher from School C: I only used Putonghua because the students have the language proficiency to communicate in Putonghua so that the lessons can go smoothly. My students are used to and are confident in using Putonghua to communicate. There is no such necessity to code-mix. I persist in using Putonghua in the teaching of the Putonghua language to promote trilingual education.

The students also agreed that the language teachers strictly followed the MOI policies in language teaching. In general, the practice of code-mixing is relatively rare in language teaching classrooms in the case study schools.

This shows the language teachers' instrumental and integrative motivations of using 100 per cent of related language in teaching. They hoped their students' language proficiency in English and Putonghua could be enhanced in a rich language-related environment so that they would be able to use the languages to read, write and communicate with others (Broughton, et al. 2002). In addition, they would like to motivate their students to immerse in an English/Putonghua environment so that they could become members of the community and cultural groups of related language (Gardner 1985). Last but not least, they would like their students to identify much more closely with a speech community which uses that language variety (Broughton, Brumfit, Pincas and Wilde 2002) in the long run.

As for the other subjects' teachers, they were more flexible and tolerant towards code-mixing, especially when the MOI of the subjects was English for a number of reasons: first, teaching Mathematics, General Studies, Music, Visual Arts, Physical Education and Computer Science is unlike teaching languages as the focus is teaching students the subject knowledge but not the language itself; second, teachers believe students could learn and understand better in their mother tongue if the MOI of the subjects is an L2.

In non-language subjects, code-mixing is only found in Schools A and B, as Cantonese is the only MOI in non-language subjects in School C. When teachers in Schools A and B used code-mixing, they did so for a variety of reasons, including emphasis, clarification, mode shift and translation. In School A, the MOI in teaching P6 General Studies is half in English and half in Cantonese as there were nine students who are not ethnic Chinese in the class. The teacher prepared PowerPoint presentations and learning materials in both languages. Mixed code was used for instructions. For instance, she said, '仲未有書的，自己起身。Those who have no books, stand up'. In this case, the teacher just translated her instruction from Cantonese to English. This use of code-mixing for classroom management is common (Ferguson 2003). The theme of the lesson was to introduce the signing of Closer Economic Partnership Arrangement (CEPA) between Mainland China and Hong Kong. Instead of using the standard Chinese translation of 更緊密經貿關係安排, the English term 'CEPA' was used throughout the lesson even when the teacher was explaining in Cantonese. This is probably because the Chinese translation requires an additional five characters or syllables and there is no workable Chinese abbreviation (Li 2008: 83). Moreover, the 'principle of economy' is at work in bilingual conversation (Li 2000; 2008) and by so doing, the teacher can help introduce or consolidate students' bilingual lexicon (Li 2008: 84). The teacher also switched between English and Cantonese for elaboration, clarification and checking for understanding. Students answered questions in the same language as used by the teacher. This is code-mixing to help pupils understand the subject matter of their lessons and also to help establish interpersonal relations and rapport. The other teacher from School A who taught P1 General Studies used 100 per cent English in her class as the MOI is English. However, she wrote in her reflection form that she would switch to Cantonese if her students failed to follow her instructions given in English.

In School B, an English textbook is used for P3 Mathematics and the teacher used mainly Cantonese, supplemented by English as the MOI. For example, when the teacher wanted to express 'three times two equals six', she would say, '三 times 二就係六' in mixed code. In another case, the teacher said, 'There are eight hats. 個度有八隻帽!' She switched for translation and focus. In the interview with her, the teacher pointed out that using the mother tongue to explain the abstract mathematical concepts would be easier for student understanding, and the student interviewees agreed as well.

On the whole, mixed code was not frequently used in the observed lessons in the researched schools. Below are some examples of using mixed code by subject teachers (students' real names have all been replaced by pseudonyms, and underlined, English translation is in italics and in brackets):

Music teacher from School A: <u>Michael</u>, 個手冊擺係邊度？擺係邊度？放地下。(*Where do you place your handbooks? Yes, on the floor.*) OK, <u>麗明</u>, your handbook, yes, thank you <u>Michael. Gigi</u>, your handbook, don't hold it in your hands, please put it at the back, yes. Good. 祥興，個張紙唔應該抓住係手個哦，擺係地下。係啦，手擺凳下面。(*You can't grab the paper in your hand, put it on the floor and your hands on the sides of your chair.*)

G.S. teacher from School A: …… 好啦，呢段嘅key word嘞，其實我唔需要你認認真真知道太多關於佢嘅事跡，我哋間低咗呢幾個key word就夠了。係關於economic and trade exchange and cooperation with trade agreement……

   (*Ok, what are the key words of this paragraph? We need to underline the key words instead of going into details about what it says. It is about……*)

Math teacher from School B: ……distance，distance都係四十，時間唔同，距離小英、泳婷都係四十，距離除以時間，知道……(*both of them have the same distance of 40, but with different time, then distance divided by time is speed.*)

In the case studies, the language teachers preferred not to use mixed code in language teaching in general so as to provide students with a good language learning environment. Teachers teaching other subjects such as Music and General Studies, however, used mixed code for a variety of well-established reasons. Code-mixing is 'a flexible instrument of communication by the fusion of English with Cantonese' in Hong Kong (Pennington 1998: 26). Li (1998) suggests that code-mixing behaviour takes place unconsciously and Hong Kong people often cannot help mixing English words and expressions into their mother tongue, Cantonese. In addition, Tse (1992: 101) noted that in informal conversation, 'code-mixing between Cantonese and English is almost ubiquitous in Hong Kong, with Cantonese being the dominant code'. These examples demonstrate that the subject teachers revealed their identity as Hong Kongers by mixing English and Cantonese codes unconsciously, when having a conversation with their students.

In regard to using Putonghua as MOI in teaching the Chinese Language subject, the majority of the Chinese Language subject teachers of the three schools had reservations about using Putonghua as the MOI in teaching the Chinese Language subject. They did not believe that using PMI could enhance the student writing skills. In reality, they doubted the effectiveness of adopting PMI. They found that students were not motivated in class activities when PMI was adopted, resulting in less interaction between teachers and students and among students themselves. The following examples show that the Chinese Language subject teachers were not supportive to the policy of using Putonghua as the MOI for teaching Chinese ('PMIC'), while they thought students' mother tongue, Cantonese, should be used in the study of the Chinese Language subject. This displays their strong sense of local identity as Hong Kongers.

> Chinese Language subject teacher from School A: Using Cantonese is better because students are living in a Cantonese environment and they can understand better the content and can write more easily in their mother tongue.
>
> Chinese Language subject panel from School B: Students are more interested when using Cantonese as a medium of instruction. The locals like using their mother tongue to learn, while the non-locals have already been immersed in an environment of Cantonese, so it is easier for them to have their lessons in Cantonese.
>
> P2 Chinese Language teaching using PMI from School C: The advantage of using Putonghua to teach the Chinese Language subject is to let students learn the written language, and to save time on the direct translation of the content into Cantonese. The disadvantage is that there are fewer interactions among students and students are not motivated in answering questions.

The subject teachers from the researched schools also demonstrated their local identities as Hong Kongers. They all agreed students could learn better in Cantonese as this is their mother tongue. For example, the Visual Arts teacher from School A thought using Cantonese in teaching the subject could arouse the students' interests in learning Visual Arts (VA). The Physical Education (PE) teacher from School B disagreed to using English as the MOI in teaching PE when asked about his opinion if the school changed the MOI of PE from Cantonese to English. The General Studies (GS) teacher from School C pointed out that using Cantonese to teach the subject could better develop students' critical thinking and creativity. In addition, students might lose interest in science if GS were taught in English and she pointed out that telling the students the English term of the science terminologies was a waste of time. To her, using mother tongue in teaching and learning was the best way to develop students' organization and presentation skills. The Mathematics teacher from School B stated that one-third of students in her class (P3) had problems in studying mathematics as they were using English textbooks. To help them resolve the problems, a Chinese version of supplementary notes and worksheets were designed, and Cantonese was used in class for explanations so that they could understand the application questions and the abstract mathematical concepts.

5.3.3 Parents' motivation and identity towards the three languages

Ten female parents in School A were individually interviewed: five were locals, three came from the Mainland, and one from the Philippines and one from

Australia. In School B, ten female parents were interviewed: nine of them were locals while one came from Shanghai. In School C, eleven parents (three males and eight females) were interviewed. Each interview lasted for about twenty to thirty minutes. The focus of the interview was to understand the parents' perceptions of the trilingual education approach implemented in the school and their views on using Putonghua as the MOI in the teaching of the Chinese Language subject.

Parents from the Mainland were supportive of their children's learning of Cantonese as they realized Cantonese is the mother tongue of local people in Hong Kong. This echoes Bacon-Shone and Bolton's (2008: 27) view that immigrants and their children from the different dialect areas of China can (and most do) quickly learn Cantonese in Hong Kong. This shows their integrative and instrumental motivations. They had the instrumental orientation that they hoped their children were able to communicate with local people in Cantonese and eventually able to immerse in the Hong Kong community and culture.

When considering if English could be used in teaching other subjects in school, twenty-seven parents (87.1 per cent) suggested that Computing, Mathematics and the science topics in General Studies (GS) could be taught in English so that their children could adapt well to the EMI secondary schools that they all wanted to send their children to.

> A parent from School B: To small children, it will be difficult for them to learn GS in English because GS is a subject with a variety of learning content and they may not easily handle the terminologies and cannot express themselves well in English during lessons. It's ok if the science topics are taught in English as they may pave the way for their learning Liberal Studies in secondary schools.
>
> A parent from School C: The school can use mainly Cantonese, supplemented by English in Mathematics in senior grades so as to bridge the gap between the primary and secondary schools.

These parents are thus no different from the majority of parents in Hong Kong who favour EMI secondary schools (Kan, et al. 2011). In Hong Kong, parents prefer EMI secondary schools and are reluctant to send their children to CMI schools (Pan 2000: 61) because six of the eight government-funded universities are all English medium, as are all of the private universities (Kirkpatrick 2014). It is obvious that the parents' instrumental purpose is to look for better educational opportunities for their children to enter EMI secondary schools.

Thirteen of the thirty-one parent interviewees in the three schools explicitly supported the schools' policies of using Putonghua as the MOI in the teaching of the Chinese Language subject. They wanted their children to learn Putonghua for instrumental purposes. They believed that Putonghua is a global language that students need to learn as soon as possible for the future, and they thought using PMI could enhance students' writing skill in Chinese. For example:

> A parent from School A: The advantage of using PMI in the study of the Chinese Language subject is that students can write down what they say.

> A parent from School B: I prefer using PMI in the study of the Chinese Language subject. It is because both English and Putonghua are now world-wide languages. And many of my foreign friends know how to speak in Putonghua.

Those who were not in favour of this policy believed that students could learn the Chinese Language subject better in their mother tongue. Because some of the parents did not themselves speak Putonghua, they pointed out that they could not help their children and would need to pay extra tuition fees for extra Putonghua classes and tutors. This indicates the parents' local identity as Hong Kongers.

> A parent from School B: I personally oppose to the use of Putonghua as the MoI in the study of the Chinese Language subject. Our mother tongue is Cantonese and we speak in Cantonese at home and thus we cannot provide her with a rich Putonghua-language environment.

> A parent from School C: Better use Cantonese to study the Chinese language subject as Cantonese is our mother tongue. It's easier for parents to have revisions with their children when using Cantonese as the MoI of the subject. I have reservation on adopting PMI.

5.3.4 Principals' motivation and identity towards the three languages

The principals all indicated their disapproval of code-mixing, as the schools had to follow the language policies laid down by the Education Bureau. Moreover, they appeared to believe that students could best learn a language effectively without switching or mixing with other languages. In fact, they shared the same instrumental and integrative motivations of the language teachers. Moreover, they would like to motivate their students to immerse in an English/Putonghua environment so that their students could become members of the community and cultural groups of related language. In the long term, they would like their students to identify much more closely with a speech community which uses that language variety.

Principal: Teachers should avoid doing so (code-switching/code-mixing). But one or few sentences are allowed if the young students cannot understand at all. If the English Language subject teachers are trying to explain the content in Cantonese, this may bring an effect that the students would not listen to the teachers when they are using English because they know the teachers would explain in Cantonese right away. Students will become dependent on the Chinese explanation. This applies in the same way when they learn Chinese in Putonghua. Students cannot learn the target language if they are too dependent on the translation. We do not encourage code-switching but teachers may make their own judgment.

Principal from School B: The students do not have many chances being immersed in the English language environment, so I think they should be immersed in a 100 per cent English language environment during English Language lessons. This is the school policy. Meanwhile, there are many students who are not ethnic Chinese in our school, which also help to build up a rich English-language environment. We encourage teachers to use 100 per cent English in English Language lessons.

Principal from School C: 100 per cent English should be used when teaching English; or if not 100 per cent English, teachers are encouraged to use pictures or body language to express themselves but Cantonese is definitely not allowed. This is also applied to the teaching of the Putonghua subject and the Chinese Language subject using PMI.

Only the principal of School A, who shared the same views as his school's sponsoring body, was supportive of using Putonghua as the MOI in teaching the Chinese Language subject in the researched schools. He pointed out that students should start learning Putonghua, which is a global language, as early as possible. In addition, he remarked, 'Using PMI can help students in furthering studies or developing future careers in Mainland. It also can enhance students' writing skills'. This demonstrates the principal's instrumental motivation of adopting Putonghua as the MOI in the teaching of the Chinese Language subject so that his students could communicate with people in Putonghua and write in Chinese properly. More importantly, he hoped his students would have better prospects in the future in the Mainland.

The principal of School B was not in favour of using PMI in teaching the Chinese Language subject. He stated, 'I personally do not believe that PMI can enhance students' language proficiency in Chinese. I think using PMI is a gimmick and a political issue'. He firmly believed that using mother tongue was the most effective way of enhancing students' language proficiency in

Chinese. Therefore, he changed the school policy from using Putonghua to using Cantonese in teaching the Chinese Language subject. He added, 'I find my students are happier after the change. They are more involved in class and are motivated to learn the Chinese Language subject in their mother tongue'.

The principal of School C faced parents who were opposed to the use of PMI for teaching Chinese. He claimed, 'Using PMI is due to the trend after Hong Kong's return to China. It is a political issue. I personally agree to student learning in the mother tongue. If academically weak students learn the Chinese Language subject in Putonghua they may gain nothing as they cannot understand the teachers. I agree that using the mother tongue (Cantonese) can help them build up their basic knowledge in the Chinese Language subject'. Therefore, he decided on a compromise, using PMI to teach the Chinese Language subject from P1 to P4 and then using Cantonese to teach the subject in the final two years of primary school.

Both principals from School B and School C emphasized the effectiveness of using local students' mother tongue in teaching and learning at the expense of Putonghua. They demonstrated their identities as local Hong Kongers like most of their students who were not in favour of using Putonghua as the MOI in the study of the Chinese Language subject.

5.4 Reflection

The study discussed in this chapter shows that the students' attitude towards Cantonese as a mother tongue is positive. As Cantonese is their mother tongue, it is the language that they use most often in their daily life and the language that they like using most, especially in learning the subject knowledge in different school subjects. Their strong sense of local identity as a Hong Konger is demonstrated when they were most happy with their progress in the study of Cantonese and they were most confident in achieving good proficiency in Cantonese when they graduated when compared with English and Putonghua. Moreover, many were not supportive to the language policy of using Putonghua in the teaching of the Chinese Language subject. To them, Putonghua is learnt in school but not used in daily life. Their learning Putonghua is derived from external forces, showing their 'ought-to self' that learning Putonghua was to meet the expectations of parents and teachers. Instrumentally, learning Putonghua could help them communicate with people in Putonghua, and even doing furthering studies or developing future careers in Mainland as suggested by the principal from School A. Like the students, the subject teachers also demonstrated their strong sense of local identity as Hong Kongers as they were supportive to using students' mother tongue, Cantonese, in teaching. In addition, the Chinese Language subject teachers and the Putonghua subject teachers were not in favour of using Putonghua as the MOI in teaching the Chinese Language subject as well. Parents from the Mainland were supportive of their children learning Cantonese as they realized Cantonese is the mother tongue of local people in Hong Kong. This shows their instrumental orientation that they hoped their children could communicate with local people in Cantonese and eventually be able to immerse themselves in the Hong Kong community and culture with integrative orientation.

However, Cantonese is not the only language that makes up the identity of a Hong Konger, English plays a part as well. This means the Hong Kong identity depends on a bilingualism of English and Cantonese (Lai 2001). Students showed both of their 'ideal self' and 'ought-to self' in learning English with instrumental and integrative orientations. Those who were in favour of their English Language teachers using 100 per cent English in teaching would like to have better educational opportunities (i.e., entering EMI secondary schools) and better prospect in the future (i.e., performing well in job interviews). There were students who would like to gain a good understanding of the attitudes and the world view of the English-language community (Broughton, et al. 2002), for example, the student who was interested in watching English TV cartoons. The parents showed their instrumental purpose of their children's English-language learning by supporting the school policy of using English as the MOI in teaching other subjects such as Mathematics, General Studies and Computing so that their children could have better educational opportunities by entering EMI secondary schools.

Mixed code also contributes to part of an identity of a Hong Konger who is used to mixing Cantonese and English in daily communication. The non-Chinese students from School A were more acceptable to the use of mixed code in teaching and learning which shows that they wanted to speak more like a Hong Konger, and therefore their 'ought-to self' is to use mixed code when communicating with the local students. Their 'ideal self' is that they would like to immerse themselves in the Hong Kong community and culture. The subject teachers were not resistant to using mixed code in teaching, showing their identities as local Hong Kongers. They used mixed code in teaching in a natural way, just like a Hong Konger frequently mixing Cantonese and English in informal conversations.

The national identity seems to play a less important role among the students, teachers, parents and principals as the Hong Kong local identity is dominant in the study. Students and parents who were supportive to using Putonghua as the MOI in the study of the Chinese Language subject mainly had the instrumental motivation, as they believed that students who could speak better Putonghua would have better prospects in developing future careers in Mainland China.

To conclude, issues relating to motivation and identity of different stakeholders in the multilingual education setting in Hong Kong are complicated, it is important for the policymakers and frontline practitioners to understand these issues properly, so as to implement multilingual education effectively in Hong Kong.

6

The Dynamics of L2 and L3 Learning, Identity Development, and Motivation Change: A Hong Kong Learner's Perspective

Over the past few years, there has been an increase in research exploring language learning, identity and motivation. One of the main reasons for the increased complexity of identity is the phenomenon of globalization and along with it, the shifts in the range of identities available to learners (Jenkins 2007). Currently, we live in an age where English learners can have more opportunities to interact with one another than any time in history, both in person or via virtual reality. Educational institutions are also uncovering ways to promote intercultural exchange to help equip students to become global citizens. Additionally, the continuing process of internationalization brings forward the issue of identity flux in an imagined and a practiced global community.

As argued by previous researchers (e.g., Chik and Benson 2008; Pavlenko 2003), learners' experiences have an impact on their identities. For example, 'prolonged contact with an L2 and a new and different cultural setting causes irreversible destabilization of the individual's sense of self' (Block 2002: 4). It appears that identity is varied and subject to change. Furthermore, language and identity have a mutually constitutive effect (Gu 2010). Although there has been an emphasis on construction and development of learner identity, limited attention has been paid to identity development and change in motivation over a prolonged period of L2 and L3 learning experience through an in-depth case study. This study uses a narrative inquiry approach to fill this gap while exploring the identity construction and motivation change in a prolonged period of English and Japanese learning experiences.

6.1 Literature review

6.1.1 Identity

Identity is related to individuals' understanding of who they are, what kind of people they are, and how they regard others (Leary and Tangney 2003). It refers to the ways in which individuals are distinguished among other people (Jenkins 2007). In this perspective, identity is not static but relatively flexible due to the mutually constructed and evolving images of self and other (Norton 2000). Therefore, identities can be acquired and transformed while situating oneself into certain categories and interacting with others. As Joseph (2004: 224) points out, identity 'is at the very heart of what language is about, how it operates, why and how it came into existence and evolved as it did, how it is learned and how it is used, every day, by every user, every time it is used'. It is a point that is echoed in Preston's (2005: 56) concern that learners should be 'allowed to develop their personal selves as they learn a new language'.

Omoniyi and White (2006) proposed six common aspects related to identity. These included (a) identity is not fixed; (b) identity is constructed within established contexts and may vary from one context to another; (c) these contexts are moderated and defined by intervening social variables and expressed through languages; (d) identity is a salient factor in every communicative context; (e) identity informs social relationships and therefore also informs the communicative exchanges that characterize them; and (f) more than one identity may be articulated in a given context, in which there will be a dynamic of identity management. As also suggested by Omoniyi (2006), identity options range from least salient to most salient. The reviewed studies suggested that identity is dynamic, constantly changing, and subject to social processes of power. Some of the identity options are salient while others are not. As identity is constructed by language and in view of the elusive nature of language, it is complex, contradictory and multifaceted.

Therefore, language learning by its nature is a social process that involves the (re) construction of identities. As proposed in earlier studies (e.g., Lave and Wenger 1991), becoming a member of any group or community is a process linked to continued interaction and negotiation with members of that group or community. In order to be identified as a legitimate member of that group or community by its people, learners need to learn sufficient cultural and contextual knowledge. This is assumed to influence learners' formation of 'global identity', 'local identity' or 'glocal identity' (Sung 2014). This explains why identity is socially constructed. However, identity construction may be different when focusing on the learning experiences involved with L2 and L3, as it is in this chapter.

6.1.2 Motivation change

Motivation research has become a hot topic since the pioneering work by Gardner and Lambert (1972), who distinguished the concepts of 'integrative' and 'instrumental' motivation. According to Gardner and Lambert (1972), 'integrative motivation' involves a type of motive for learning a language due to a favour towards the target language and its culture. Whereas, 'instrumental motivation' refers to the practical or economic advantages of learning that language. In later work (e.g., Gardner 1985), L2 learning motivation was regarded as a conglomerate of three internal factors, including motivational intensity, a desire to learn the target language, and favourable attitudes towards the target language. According to Dörnyei (2010), motivation reflects why people have an interest to do something, how long they are likely to sustain the activity and how likely they are going to pursue it. Dörnyei and Ushioda (2011) later defined motivation as what drives an individual to make certain choices and to expend effort and engage in action. Concluded from these studies, motivation in learning a second language can be described as a process of investigating the extent to which a learner strives to learn that language because of a desire or an interest to do so, and that the two main dimensions of this process are integrative and instrumental motivation.

However, motivation is a complex and dynamic process (e.g., Dörnyei, Henry and Muir 2016), as learning a language is a process of interacting with social and contextual support or constraints. Additionally, the dynamic development of motivation may bring changes to learners' motivation (Ushioda and Dörnyei 2012). Therefore, although the mainstream research on motivation is still focused on the integrative and instrumental dimensions of L2 motivation, these two concepts are not sufficient to account for learners' motivational changes, particularly those who are learning an L2 and L3. This is because learners who learn an L2 and L3 may have multiple motivations or L2 selves, and their motivations can determine how long they will remain in the language learning process and the extent to which they might have competitions or co-existence while learning the two languages (Nakamura 2015). In general, learners' motivations are not set in stone but subject to change, which can be ascribed to their individual background and personal beliefs, their prior learning experiences, as well as the sociocultural contexts in which their learning is embedded.

6.2 The study

6.2.1 Research questions

The present study, as described by its overarching research approach, is a qualitative case study. Drawing upon the narrative inquiry approach, this study explores identity construction and motivation change of a Hong Kong learner in a prolonged period of English and Japanese learning. Two central questions that guided the study were:

(1) How does the participant discursively construct his identities over a prolonged period of English and Japanese learning?
(2) What changes in motivation does the participant display over a prolonged period of English and Japanese learning?

6.2.2 Method

6.2.2.1 Context and participant

Harry's (Pseudonym) specific case as a committed L2 (English) and L3 (Japanese) learner is explored in the present study. This study details part of a research project with a focus on learners who study at a university in Hong Kong, where English is the medium of instruction and Japanese is an additional language for learning. Invitations were sent to ten potential learners who simultaneously learn English as L2 and Japanese as L3. Two participants, who shared their stories, were selected. This study reports on one learner, a Cantonese-speaking Hong Kong citizen born locally. Harry was chosen to be the focus of the study because he is a committed learner, who has joined different intercultural contexts interacting with different L1, L2 and L3 speakers in both academic and social settings. In addition, he is an English and Japanese language learner. Aged 25, Harry had learned English since kindergarten. He was considered as an advanced English L2 learner. Upon commencing university studies in Hong Kong, he began to learn Japanese. After graduation, he worked as a research assistant at the time of data collection for this study. Since this is a qualitative case study, the findings of the study are not meant to be generalizable to all L2 (English) and L3 (Japanese) learners in Hong Kong or any other context. A focus on Harry does, however, provide knowledge about the multiple layers of identity development and motivation change in a particular case.

The present study is an in-depth case study, tracing identity development and motivation change in a Hong Kong language learner. Hong Kong encountered rapid sociocultural, political, economic and educational changes after the transfer of sovereignty. The currents and counter-currents make Hong Kong an important context to study on its own as well as a case to compare with patterns elsewhere. While in some respects the nature of Hong Kong's colonial transition seems unique, Hong Kong has similarities with other post-colonial regions. Therefore, Hong Kong appears to be an appropriate and unique location for investigating the impact of language learning experiences on learners' identities.

6.2.2.2 *Data collection and analysis*

Data was collected through six rounds of semi-structured interviews. Interview is an effective way to provide a window into the interviewee's mind which could not be directly observed. It is also useful to explore the ambivalences and complexity in the learners' life and experiences (Jenkins 2007). The first round of interviews focused on the learner's primary learning and life experiences. The second round focused on his experiences in secondary school. The third round focused on his learning experience during university, including English and Japanese learning while being an exchange student in Britain. The fourth round of interview explored his experience using English and Japanese inside and outside the university. The fifth round considered the participant's work life and Japanese and English learning. The sixth round of interview focused on his personal deep reflection on his identities and motivations in learning Japanese and English. The emphasis of each interview was on how Harry perceived his identities and his possible change in motivation during the given respective phase of his life.

All of the interviews were audio-recorded and conducted one-to-one with the first author in Cantonese, with occasional code-mixing between Cantonese and English. All the interview data was translated into English. Each interview lasted approximately from sixty to ninety minutes. Email correspondences, although not subject to data analysis, were also used to follow up on the interviews. Interviews were conducted every two months to capture the complexity of the participant's identities and motivation. Thus, this qualitative case study lasted for a year.

The collected data was analysed through a constant comparative approach (Corbin and Strauss 2014). Following the thematic analysis, the themes of identity and motivation emerged from the data were recursively evaluated through rereading and examining the original data. By cycling back and forth between the different rounds of interview data on his language learning experiences, we aimed to showcase how his identities were inextricably linked with his change in motivation while learning an L2 and L3. Finally, through rigorous data and theme checking, Harry himself shared his thoughts on the themes and the earlier version of the data analysis. His feedback and comments were considered for further revision of the study.

6.3 The findings

6.3.1 'Who I am': Experiences from learning two foreign languages

According to Harry, Britain and the English language were very naturally integrated into his early life. Such learning experience, to some extent, has shaped how Harry regards himself at the beginning of his English-learning phase. Harry reported,

> When I think back to my childhood, there are two things that come into my mind immediately, which are Britain and English. Even though I was born and raised in Hong Kong, my connection to English and Britain has been a major factor in shaping my life. (Interview 1)

Although Harry studied English in Hong Kong primary schools, English became more than just a second language to him. It was a language for Harry to socialize with others, to become a legitimate member of the imagined community, and learn more about himself through interactions with others. Harry stated,

> My parents always took me for vacations in Britain. From the time I was quite young, I visited Britain often and it was not just one place. It seems like my imagined second home, and I needed to learn English to be part of it. (Interview 1)

After starting high school, Harry experienced academic pressure from tests or assessments. Although Harry attempted to uphold his original identity, he feared being ostracized by his in-group(s). Harry began to accept some aspects, for example, the assessment system, which is deemed necessary by the dominant society. Harry stated,

> I really disliked the tests administered by the school. This assessment system graded us into different levels of communicative skills, but it may not reflect one's real competence in speaking English. I need to be admitted into a university. I had no choice but to adapt to the assessment system. (Interview 3)

During high school, Harry also had thoughts of changing his identity from an 'English test-taker' to 'English user'. However, identity modifications were only made if they did not threaten his prescribed identity. He expressed his ideal identity of being an English user. Harry explained,

> During the test, we first stated 'I agree with you'. Then we repeated our partner's points and expressed our opinions. It is very formal. But in practice it is not the case. We were just test-takers, but the society needs us to be English users. (Interview 5)

Harry reported some changes in his self-image after studying at university. He transformed his identity by working through certain conflicts within his environment and achieved a stable sense of self as an English speaker. He stated,

> I had more opportunities to speak English in university. I was happy because I did not need to care about the evaluation system. Learning English in university was overall a positive experience to me. (Interview 4)

After being an exchange student in Britain, Harry expressed some changes that occurred to his identity. Harry preferred to fashion a global identity. His aim and passion for a British accent showed his desire of belonging to a wider global community. An aim to pronounce like a British individual, that is, with a British accent, seemed to play an important role in the construction of his global citizen identity. He stated,

> It is English who brought us together. It makes me become a global citizen when sounding like a British. (Interview 3)

Culture is affiliated with the formation of identity (Holliday 2010). During Harry's learning experience, he formed a cultural identity: a feeling of belonging to a group. It is a decisive force for Harry to learn English, and that cosmopolitanism gave him a greater sense of shared citizenship. According to Harry, English provides a common framework for cultural identities. This influences his internal cultural realities. He formed an identity that is practically associated with international society, as he revealed himself,

> We come from different cultural background. We have different first languages, but then because of English, we have things in common. We are all different but then we are all the same at the same time. (Interview 3).

However, after being an exchange student for some time in Britain, Harry believed that native English speakers are not necessarily superior English communicators than non-native speakers. Harry persisted that the non-native speaker status would not cause negative perceptions of his identity as an authentic

English learner. He did not believe in having any strong feelings of inferiority or insecurity because of his non-native accent. He became less interested in seeking a British accent, even though he once wished for a British accent. He insisted that effective communication depends more on the content of the conversation. Therefore, the native/non-native dichotomy should be de-emphasized. He stated,

> There is no one standard British pronunciation. Sometimes, it is even difficult for some British people to understand another British accent within a local community. It is also difficult for us to pronounce like a native speaker. In addition, the content is the most important dimension in communication. (Interview 3)

In addition, Harry realized that after studying in Britain, he exhibited more traditional Hong Konger-like thoughts and behaviour in his culture, customs and beliefs. He suggested that a Hong Kong English accent affiliates him with his local Hong Kong identity. As he navigated the intricacies of the new reality, 'Hong Konger' became a frame of reference for his construction of identity. Therefore, his Hong Konger identity had been strengthened with the context of studying in Britain. Spontaneous comparisons with his home culture stood out for Harry as he tried to negotiate the meaning of his identity. He stated,

> I am not a native speaker and I was not brought up in their culture. I am from Hong Kong. When I talk about Hong Kong, my home place, how vibrant and beautiful Hong Kong is, then I would feel more like a Hong Konger. I should not feel a sense of displeasure in speaking a local accent. (Interview 3)

During his time as an exchange student, Harry experienced anxiety while talking to native English speakers. This experience seemed to be connected to his lack of self-confidence in using English. Hence, the act of speaking before natives was at times a rather stressful, even intimidating, experience for him. This included a fear of making mistakes and of being ridiculed or judged for the imperfections. This exemplifies Harry's feelings of insecurity and vulnerability in figuring out how to adapt to the novelty of talking to English native speakers. He stated,

> It could be of a bit intimidating when I talk to native speakers at first. I obviously think more about my sentence structure or the words or the vocabularies or some stuff like that. I don't know how they perceive me. (Interview 3)

The difficulties that non-native English speakers encounter in communicating with native speakers can be attributed to not only their relative unfamiliarity with the language but also cultural differences. Harry experienced emotional discomfort while communicating with some locals in Britain. He felt especially insecure when engaging with unsupportive people within the unfamiliar environment. When feeling threatened, insecure or vulnerable from engaging with dissimilar others, Harry attempted to either assert or redefine his previous self-images as a Hong Konger. Harry stated,

> I had a terrible experience in talking to a local in Britain. He judged the umbrella movement in Hong Kong as a post-colonial issue. He may think he knows a lot, but he knows nothing about Hong Kong, which is so complex that even the media news had only covered a fraction of it. We are in different positions. (Interview 3)

Harry later labelled himself as bilingual because of his equal competence in both Cantonese and English. A social need to have competence in both languages plays a key role in strengthening his willingness to identify himself as a bilingual learner. According to him, speaking English and Cantonese well helps build a professional image in Hong Kong, and it is important for his job-hunting. Identity is socially constructed and influenced by the negotiations that Harry experienced in his language community. For example, he would post English messages via Facebook, or some other platforms and would think how local friends and international friends respond to the posts. Through this, Harry felt more 'glocal'. He stressed a need to move towards the construction of a 'glocal' identity rather than a simplistic binary categorization of 'local culture' versus 'global culture'. He said,

> English major students often focus on how to improve English, but they seem to have ignored the fact that we should learn both languages well. Particularly now there is a continual movement to protect Cantonese against Mandarin Chinese in Hong Kong. Cantonese is one feature of Hong Kong that we cannot lose. We are global, but we are also local citizens. (Interview 4)

Later, Harry began to learn Japanese. His reasoning for doing so was because he had thought about immigrating to a new country, for example, Japan, due to the social dilemma and conflict between Hong Kong and Mainland China. He experienced struggles in locating his 'self'. He thought of moving to another place. He said,

> In recent years, immigration to other countries is a hot topic in Hong Kong. The strict control imposed by the Beijing government is a threat to the system in Hong Kong. Hong Kong is no longer what it was. We are losing our home. I want to learn Japanese because I may find my new home in Japan. (Interview 5)

However, Harry still insisted he is a Hong Konger. For him, even though Hong Kong is losing its core values, he still regarded Hong Kong as his home. He was struggling between leaving and staying. He reported,

> Hong Kong is losing its core value. I want to leave, but I have lived here for many years. It is my home. I want to leave but I also want to stay in Hong Kong. (Interview 6)

6.3.2 Motivation change during learning the two languages

Harry expressed an integrative motivation towards learning during his initial years of learning English. He was attracted by the beautiful and dynamic nature of the language. He stated,

> I like learning English, which is not just a second language to me. Although I cannot say it is my mother language, it has special meaning for me. I learn English because it is a beautiful and dynamic language. (Interview 1)

Harry also had a positive attitude towards Britain. He had visited the country many times. He emphasized how much he had enjoyed his visit. He said,

> I enjoyed my visit to Britain. The people, the scenery, and the life attract me. (Interview 1)

In addition to his fondness of Britain, he also mentioned his interest in British history. His fascination with history seems to strengthen his love and interest in learning English. He said,

> I have always been fascinated by the history of Britain. Hong Kong was once a colony of Britain. I feel like I can't truly understand the history of it unless I have some knowledge of the language itself. (Interview 2)

In line with the overall positive attitudes towards Britain, Harry also reported on his positive encounters with British people, describing them as friendly and open. He stated,

> During my time in Britain, I found that everyone was so helpful. I liked the culture. Everyone was very open and friendly. (Interview 2)

However, Harry also described learning English for exams as difficult. He stated he was demotivated by the continuous drilling and practices. He stated,

> Learning English in my secondary school was a difficult time for me. I had to practice again and again for the test. It was like drills. I didn't like this kind of

exam-oriented practices. I once thought of giving up English learning in class. (Interview 3)

Harry was motivated for different reasons after being admitted to university. For example, the desire to communicate with a partner is a factor that accelerates his language learning. Harry stated a need to learn English and know the culture well to enhance communication with native speakers. He said,

> There is a strong connection between language and culture. I learn English, and then to know the culture, I need to communicate with English native speakers. (Interview 5)

After working as a research assistant, the English self-image seemed to be strengthened because it has become one part of his job requirement. Harry reported,

> Even though I got a job now, I have to keep learning English anyway. In Hong Kong, you need English if you want to excel. (Interview 5)

The process of being motivated to learn Japanese was quite different. If learning English can be categorized as an 'ought-to self' (education domain) and 'ideal self' (being integrated to target language and culture), learning Japanese was a process of forming 'ideal self'. As a learner who began to learn Japanese at university, Harry experienced two stages for the Japanese learning process. Harry said,

> The initial motive for me to learn Japanese was because of a favour towards Japanese culture (manga, anime). I am now thinking of immigrating to Japan, which is one of the biggest motives for me to learn Japanese. (Interview 6)

From the interview data, it is evident that Harry has positive and clear English and Japanese self-images. In addition, the L2 self and the L3 self do not seem to compete. This could be because the English and Japanese self-images are connected to different domains of his future life. He stated,

> I use English for my career. I imagine myself actively using Japanese in the future. I don't think there is competition in learning these two languages. (Interview 6)

Harry's ideal English and Japanese self-images seem to share three similar domains (extracurricular, career, interpersonal) of his life (Nakamura 2015). The education domain is the difference in learning English and Japanese. In addition, the learner possessed a social need for learning Japanese for immigration (social domain). However, the multiple L2 selves do not seem to interfere with each other because the role of each language's self-image is distinctive. He said,

I like watching anime and reading manga. In addition, I like watching English movies. Learning English and Japanese can be good for my future jobs. For example, I want to teach Japanese children English in the future. These are three similar motives for me to learn English and Japanese. However, I don't need to learn Japanese to pass various exams, and English is not a language for me to immigrate. I had a clear vision on learning the two languages. (Interview 6)

6.4 Discussion

This is an in-depth case study tracing identity development and motivational change over a prolonged period while considering the individual learner as a reflective agent. We can perhaps conclude from the data that experiences in learning an L2 and L3 is a process of overcoming struggles. These struggles include staying motivated, modifying or maintaining an identity in social interactions, and understanding who a learner should be and how that relates to the language learning community, the local sociocultural context and the imagined global community.

Overall, the findings of the study point to a recurring theme of identity flux. Harry seemed to embrace hybrid identities during the process of learning English. Studying in Britain was Harry's first lengthy stay abroad. He reconciled his local and global identities. He became less, not more, desirable of his imagined identity as a global citizen. His perceptions of social and cultural disparity led to recoiling, that is, a discourse of superiority of local identity rather than an active engagement with the global identity. The increased complexity in identity development became salient while studying abroad (Meinhof and Galasinski 2005). During this period, Harry's conscious belief that a native-like English accent is somewhat better was not so important. He also expressed a desire to retain some aspects of the L1 accent in the L2. Such tensions are further complicated due to the norms provided by the native-speaking community. Harry negotiated and reconstructed his local identity through social interaction. During the identity transformation, he experienced self-discovery, validated the sense of self, questioned, challenged and casted off certain practices and beliefs that he had taken for granted his entire life.

As suggested by Pavlenko and Blackledge (2004: 12), 'any analysis of language practices needs to examine how conventions of language choice and use are created, maintained, and changed, to see how language ideologies legitimize and validate particular practices, and to understand real-world consequences these practices have in people's lives'. In Harry's case, a practiced identity – a Hong Konger identity – comes into play. New values – strong attachment to local culture and beliefs – are assigned to his practiced identity option. These were not previously valued by Harry. Initially, Harry aimed for a strong affiliation with the global community. As revealed in the data, this shift may be because Harry's strong awareness of his local identity and the values attached to it. Another possible explanation alludes to the fact that the global community and/ or the global culture is intangible. Specifically, Harry expressed the difficulties in grasping a native-like accent and being engaged in the abstract global community.

Therefore, however essential a sense of global community has become, in and of itself, it may not be adequate for personal identity formation and meaning. It may be too abstract, too divorced from actual societies with their highly idiosyncratic histories and mythologies (Sung 2014). Learners may acquire a far more particular identity, located concretely in space and time. This has become increasingly necessary in facing the growing resurgence in local affiliations. Vast collectivities, based upon very thin, abstract commonalities, seem unable to replace local associations with their richly textured, highly particular cultures. As argued by Baker (2011), identity and culture need to be approached in a flexible and non-essentialist manner. A global community should be dynamic and diversified to accommodate the varieties of identities, cultures and languages, while allowing them to develop simultaneously.

However, as argued by Joseph (2004), some of 'Hong Kong English' speakers, a variety many speakers themselves deny, regard differences between their English and standard British English as errors. It seems that the learners in Joseph's (2004) study reject the notion of a local identity in their English. Documented by Jenkins (2007), some L2 learners had a desire to promote an L1 identity in their L2 English. It is a kind of 'love–hate' tension with native English. Suggested by Sung (2014), some learners may possibly project varying degrees of affinities with the global and local communities. For example, some learners may possess hybrid identities without being hostaged to the meanings of either their local or global communities while other learners may prefer to foreground either their local or global identity. In the present study, a learner may have hybrid identities towards the global or local community. Hence, it is not reasonable to state that either local or global identity should be the only facet of English learners' identities. They should be considered as complementary facets. In this chapter, Harry is possibly an agent in constructing his identities, exhibiting changing identities, from global to local and then to glocal, during the process of learning English.

Due to the trend of globalization and learners' accumulated experiences in studying abroad, L2 learners may embrace more complex identities than before. We may argue that L2 learners' conflicting identities are increasingly fluid and dynamic when they encounter changes in their learning contexts. For example, Harry in the present study expressed a favour towards native English pronunciation, but having a local accent is also an aspect of his local identity as an exchange student. Identity is not fixed or static to nationality, ethnicity, creed, but constantly changing due to the social context (Park 2012). Harry experienced an identity flux from a 'global identity' to a 'local identity'. During the identity transformation, he experienced struggles and confusion. This can be explained by Omoniyi's (2006: 30) proposed model of 'hierarchies of identities'. According to this model, 'a cluster of identity options … are … distributed on a hierarchy based on ratings from least salient to most salient'. Therefore, identity options are always co-present, and multiple identities exist.

Existing literature on identity negotiation proposes that certain identities are made available to learners to assume or resist in social interactions (Blackledge and Pavlenko 2001). When learners enter a new context, they may grapple with feelings of insecurity and vulnerability. They need to figure out how to adapt to the novelty of it all. In the case of Harry, identity negotiation occurs when his secured self-image is threatened while encountering difference or unfamiliar contexts in being an exchange student in Britain. Identity negotiation is a transaction where learners 'attempt to evoke, assert, define, modify, or challenge, and/or support their own and others' desired self-images' (Ting-Toomey 1999: 40).

In addition, during the process of identity negotiation, learners may feel secure while engaging with supportive people in a familiar environment. However, when they feel threatened, insecure, or vulnerable upon engaging with dissimilar others, learners may put more importance on their self-image or perception of themselves. They may also either assert or redefine existing self-images (Swann, Milton and Polzer 2000). For example, Harry secured his identity as a Hong Konger because of his unhappy interactions with native English speakers in Britain, particularly about the political movement in Hong Kong.

The data also showed that Harry experienced anger, annoyance, vulnerability and processed emotions from middle school to university. He embodied a flux in identity. Due to a fear of not belonging to or separating from social groups in high school, Harry deterred himself from adjusting values and experimenting with self-identity. Harry described experiencing a sense of vulnerability after an encounter with the requirements of assessment. This may explain why Harry did not modify his self-image when his social identity was threatened. He felt a level of vulnerability when confronting differences. For example, after starting university, and due to the supportive environment, Harry rationalized, observed, avoided and, finally, chose to support existing self-images. This reveals that modifications to self-image were made by using rationalization and observing in a supportive environment. Therefore, satisfactory identity negotiation outcomes result from feelings of being understood, respected and affirmatively valued, or a supportive environment (Ting-Toomey 2005). It also suggests that learners attempt to negotiate their identities within multiple positions imposed by school and the broader social discourse (Gu, Mak and Qu 2017).

In terms of motivation for learning an L2 and L3, Harry displayed a wide range of motivational change. Harry began to learn Japanese in university, although the initial motives were because of a love of anime (extracurricular domain). He later learned Japanese due to the social need for immigration (social domain). Then, he imagines himself working as an English teacher at a Japanese school (career and interpersonal domain). This illustrates how Harry's ideal Japanese self-image has developed to encompass multiple domains throughout his learning history. Overall, Harry expressed a high level of integrative motivation towards learning English (L2) and Japanese (L3), which included positive attitudes towards target cultures and the languages. Regarding instrumental reasons, Harry considered the value of English for passing exams or for job-hunting.

Unlike Henry's (2011) study, which explored the competition or interference between different L2 selves, the present study supports that an existing L2 would not affect the construction of L3 self. As Harry's case indicates, when a learner can clearly identify an L2 with domains in the present and future life, he may not have competitions or conflict in constructing a viable L3 self-image. Thus, the language might not lose out in the competition for motivation. The development of a strong L2 self does not necessarily have a dampening impact on the development of L3 self. Thus, an existing L2 self might not conflict with L3 self. The learner may be able to change the power relationship among multiple L2 selves depending on his/her identification with possible L2 selves in domains of use (Nakamura 2015). It may only happen in a situation where the learner has limited learning capacity for learning a third language, and a cause of competition among different L2 selves may occur, as suggested by Csizér and Dörnyei (2005). However, this might not always be the same. In this study, although Harry has learned a global language, that is, English as an L2 and that L2 is linked to all the domains of his future selves, he can still establish ideal selves in learning a third language. As multiple L2 selves can coexist within the same domain, the dominance of a powerful L2 does not in itself hinder the construction of additional L3 self-images. Thus, Harry formed motivations in learning an L2 and L3.

6.5 Reflection

Some implications can be drawn from these findings. First, the learner's identity flux indicates that English teachers should not just train students' language skills but build an awareness that learning English is intricately related to learners' identity construction (Gu 2010). Multilingual education teachers may also need to re-evaluate their pedagogical practices.

Second, learners who have had a chance to study in an English-speaking country tend to find themselves simultaneously immersed in multiple cultures and juggling a flux in terms of their identity. Identity is a continual process of integrating new experiences and moulding values, roles and self-images based on the changing context. However, this does not mean that the identity in flux equals to identity crisis. We may need to view each learner as a unique blend of diverse contexts and global encounters.

Third, language teachers need to consider whether students can manage multiple L2 selves in learning an L2 and L3. When multiple ideal L2 selves can coexist without any competition, the learners are more likely to stay motivated to learn a language. If not, the learners may struggle to stay motivated. Therefore, there is a need for language teachers to know what their students' L2-specific self-images are and to rethink how they can encourage their students to imagine domains of their future L2 self in the classroom.

Finally, the relationship between language and identity is complex. The findings raise the question of how Hong Kong English learners negotiate the complicated as well as changing social context and position themselves somewhere between English-speaking cultures, the local culture and Mainland China's influences. This issue has become complex in the era of globalization and Hong Kong's transition period after the transfer of sovereignty.

7

Identities, Imagined Communities, and Communities of Practice: Thai Students in China

Along with the popularity of Chinese culture, an interest in learning the Chinese language has boomed. Chinese is increasingly becoming prevalent around the world due to China's steadily rising economic status. The number of foreigners who come to China to learn Chinese is also increasing. Thus, learning Chinese is emerging as a promising education trend. In terms of learning Chinese as an L3, establishing an identity is assumed to be perplexing in nature.

Recent decades have witnessed an abundance of research on students' language learning and identity development while studying abroad. Despite the significance in researching the complex relationship between language and identity, the voices of Thai students studying Chinese in China have not been heard much (Teng and Bui 2018). The present study focused on sixteen Thai students' experiences while studying abroad in China for one year and explored their imagined communities, the development of identity, the way they presented themselves to others in communities of practice, and how the transformation of learners' imagined identities influenced their motivation in L3 learning practices. We aimed for a detailed account about the process of identity construction and motivation in language practices related to imagined communities and communities of practice, and how their memberships in the imagined future may be shaped.

7.1 Theoretical notions

7.1.1 Language learning and identity

Language learning is closely related to identity. Drawing upon post-structuralist theory, Norton (2000) claimed that 'identity' was not a fixed construct but should be explored from an individual's experiences in the broader social, cultural, economic, and political world. In this sense, identities, which are usually formed through struggle, are transformed across time and space, negotiated during movement across contexts, and reproduced in situated practices or social interactions. Researchers have also explained identity negotiation from the perspective of 'positioning theory', which refers to identity as a discourse taking place between individuals (Blackledge and Pavlenko 2001). In other words, identity is constructed during social interaction and each member has a position while simultaneously reacting to the other person's position. In addition, individuals entering new communities may grapple with feelings of insecurity and vulnerability while attempting to figure out their appropriate positions in the new environment (Young, Natrajan-Tyagi and Platt 2015).

7.1.2 Imagined communities

Norton (2001) connected the concept of imagined communities to language learning. Since then, there has been a growing interest in exploring learners' imagined communities (Kanno and Norton 2003), which refer to the communities that an individual intends to belong to someday while using target languages (Norton 2001). Imagined communities have been established based on an individual's past experiences and future aspirations (Yim 2016), and hence, their actual and desired memberships in the 'imagined community' affect their learning trajectories (Pavlenko and Norton 2007). Therefore, each learner's own imagined communities are related to his or her identity.

7.1.3 Imagined identity

'Imagined identity' refers to an identity that is constructed while imagining relationships between oneself and other people and about things in the same time and space with which the individual has no straightforward or direct interaction in practice (Norton 2001). According to Gao (2012), an imagined identity is the way by which a learner positions his/her memberships or is positioned by others in an imagined world which, to some extent, affects learners' cultural identifications and language practices. Imagined identity was defined as a fluid construct, and not immediately tangible or readily accessible (Kanno and Norton 2003). In an attempt to better understand language learners and their imagined identities, previous studies suggested that a language learner was a participating social agent, and the sense of agency was related to the larger sociocultural and historical social practices (Norton and Toohey 2011).

7.1.4 Communities of practice

Communities of practice have been described as groups of people who share a concern or a passion negotiate to be a self-actualized agent in the immediate situation or for something they do, and learn how to improve it while they interact regularly (Wenger 1998). Language learning is also situated in learners' experiences of participation in the community. Learning is the process of developing identities of mastery, and participation is essential in the foreign language learning context. Through legitimate peripheral participation, a newcomer becomes a full member of the community through sustained efforts and the guidance of old-timers (Lave and Wenger 1991). Therefore, learning – including learning a language – has been described as the process of becoming a full participant in a sociocultural practice, constructing an identity, and becoming a different person through communities of practice.

7.1.5 Investment

Norton (2000) proposed a post-structuralist construct: 'Investment'. This construct focuses on the complex relationship between language learner identity and language learning commitment. As Norton (2000) suggested, investment – the efforts or movements that learners would like to make in order to acquire a second/additional language or cultural capital – complements 'fixed' and psychological constructs of motivation and seeks to connect a learner's commitment to learning. Darvin and Norton (2015) argued that the construct of motivation considered the individual to have a unitary and coherent identity with specific character traits. Investment, by contrast, views the learner as a social being with a complex identity that may change across time and space while having social interaction. Because identity is fluid, multiple, and formed in a site of struggle, how learners invest in a target language is contingent on the dynamic negotiation of power within different communities (Darvin and Norton 2015). Hence, investment may be complex, contradictory and in a state of flux (Norton 2013).

7.1.6 Motivation

Similar with investment, motivation refers to a driving force which helps learners sustain the long and often tedious learning process. Indeed, all the other factors involved in L2 learning, including the social, historical, linguistic and individualistic factors, combine dynamically over time to co-construct learners' motivation (Dörnyei 2014). Without sufficient motivation, even individuals with the most remarkable abilities may not accomplish long-term goals. However, high motivation can make up for considerable deficiencies both in one's language aptitude and learning conditions (Dörnyei, MacIntyre and Henry 2015). Hence, given the central importance attached to motivation by teachers and researchers alike, the relationship between motivation and language learning has been the target of a great deal of research during the past decades.

7.2 Gaps in previous literature and the present study

A recent trend has explored learners' identities while studying abroad. For example, in Trentman's (2013) study, American students who studied abroad in Egypt wanted to belong to an imagined community of Egypt. In order to realize this aim, they demonstrated the identities of cross-cultural mediators and dedicated language learners. However, the communities of practice in which they participated while abroad were different from the communities in their imagination. The communities of practice also afforded differential opportunities to demonstrate their identities, which led to both alignments and misalignments between reality and imagination. The degree of alignment between learners' expectations and the realities that they encountered affected their interaction in the Arabic language. Likewise, in Umino and Benson's (2016) study, an Indonesian student's experiences while studying abroad in Japan suggested that opportunities for interaction in Japanese were limited due to the learner's peripheral participation in institutionally organized communities of practice. Towards the end of his fourth year in Japan, this learner succeeded in becoming a central member of an informal, self-organized community of practice that consisted mainly of local Japanese friends who were more supportive of his interactions and language development. Du (2015) also investigated twenty-nine American college students' identities and their investment in studying Mandarin Chinese in China for one semester. Monthly informal individual interviews revealed that while some learners' self-representation of Americans was strengthened, some learners struggled for legitimacy within the new community believing that learning Chinese was an advantage to them. To access more powerful Chinese networks, strengthen their perceived 'foreigner identity', and to be accepted by the target community, they sought to increase their symbolic and material resources. Therefore, satisfactory identity negotiation outcomes and willingness to invest in learning a language appeared to be related to feeling understood and respected.

In an era of rapidly changing economic, sociocultural and political contexts around the world, learning a language entails complex and often contradictory relationships that challenge conventional practices and beliefs. Within the purview of previous literature about identity, motivation, and studying abroad, research that has investigated the perspective of Thai students studying Chinese in China was not found. It is not clear to what extent Thai learners' experience identity challenges or how they are motivated in learning Chinese as a third language during their study in China. Research concerning this topic is invaluable as more and more Thai students choose China as their destination for study. The present study utilized the ethnographic approach commonly adopted in the line of research on imagined communities and education (e.g., Dagenais 2003) and explored the complexity of learning the Chinese language as a third language by Thai students. The present study also concentrated on the negotiation of identity, the interaction taking place between Thai students and local Chinese people, and how their imagined identities and communities of practice influence their learning pedagogies and motivation. Two questions that directed this research study include

1. How do the Thai students develop a sense of self before and after their stay in China?
2. How do their communities of practice affect their experiences in China and motivation towards learning Mandarin Chinese as a third language?

7.3 Method

7.3.1 Context

A group of Thai students entered a programme at a university in south-western China specifically designed for Thai college students who had learned some Chinese in their country and aspired for better proficiency in the language. This programme was the product of a cooperation between a liberal arts college in Thailand and a university in southwest China. The programme runs for one year, and the learners attended twelve periods per week. Main courses included Speaking Chinese, Chinese Grammar, Chinese Culture, and China History. All learners were required to complete additional daily homework, a mid-term exam, and a final exam. Programme participants also attended some extracurricular activities with local students, including hiking, a cultural communication festival, and travel, providing them more opportunities to communicate with local students.

7.3.2 Participants

Among the thirty Thai students who were enrolled in the programme, sixteen volunteered to take part in this study. Participants ranged in age from twenty-two to twenty-four. The participants were at the end of the third year studying for their undergraduate degree and planned to spend the final year in China. Nine of them began their Chinese studies in college and had learned Chinese for two to three years as a third language in Thailand before they came to China. Their first language was Thai, and their second language was English. None of the participants were heritage speakers of any Chinese dialect. None of the participants began studying Chinese prior to beginning tertiary-level education. Several of the participants had a high proficiency in the language, and three of them passed level six of the HSK exam. All were permanent residents of Thailand and while some of them had travelled to China before, none of them had stayed in China for more than a month. Participating learners signed consent forms on a voluntary basis and were told that they could withdraw from this study at any time. All names used in the present study were pseudonyms.

7.3.3 Data collection

Data was collected through regular semi-structured interviews about their feelings on being a foreign student in China. Each interview lasted fifty to seventy minutes and was conducted every three months. The interviews focused on several aspects, including participants' personal history, feelings, attitudes, and internal conflicts concerning learning Chinese before and after coming to China; personal experiences, such as interactions with different people in their lives, and the various emotions that arose from these experiences; and overall reflections on the learning associated with different emotions, and how the participants perceived themselves as Chinese learners at the end of the programme. Participants were invited to share their thoughts and feelings regarding specific issues, for example, how they regard their relationships with local students during their stay in China.

The first author also attempted to elicit critical stories which produced strong emotional resonance and made an impact on their self-understanding.

To prompt learners' greater emotional intensity and detail, the interviews were conducted in the language preferred by each participant. Two chose to speak Chinese, and fourteen chose to speak Thai. None of them chose English. The first author transcribed and translated the Chinese verbal responses into English. For those who chose to speak Thai, a helper with a mastery of Chinese and Thai was invited to interpret during interviews, and then transcribe and translate Thai into English. A total of sixty-four interviews (sixteen students, four interviews each) were recorded, yielding a total of more than 115,000 words of transcription.

7.3.4 Data analysis

Data analysis was conducted through thematic analysis, with the participants' identities, imagined communities, communities of practice, and investment designated as the units of analysis. Open coding, axial coding, and selective coding were used to generate categories. Informed by previous studies (Du 2015; Strauss and Corbin 1990), overall, three rounds of data analysis were conducted. First, the data was carefully and chronologically read and reread by the author. A code was entered when a piece of data illustrated or implied a unit of meaning related to the learners' imagined identities or possible explanations for motivation towards language learning. The second round involved re-examination of the existing codes, with an emphasis on the relationships between codes through repeated comparisons that formed the basis of tentative categorization of these codes (Strauss and Corbin 1990). In the third round, the tentative categorization was reorganized, exploring the ways in which learners' identities interact with imagined communities and motivation in learning Chinese. As a result, three major themes were identified, including (a) capacity or struggles in locating a self: the imagined community of study in China; (b) awareness and determination in discovering a self: communities of practice and variation; and (c) partial success in validating a self: motivated or demotivated for further study.

Following the identification of the themes, the author thoroughly re-examined the themes by reviewing the original data and then composed narratives. This process of deconstructing, constructing, and reconstructing the social meanings of the identified themes by writing narratives provided insights into the process of identity negotiation (Barkhuizen, Benson and Chik 2014). The constructed narratives were also shared with the participants to validate the data analysis results and to obtain additional insights.

7.4 Findings

7.4.1 Locating a self for the imagined community: Expectations and struggles in China

The predominant theme that emerged from the collected data was an imagined community of studying abroad in China. Students envisioned belonging to this imagined community. Their imagined communities expanded the range of possible selves, for which some of them were willing to seek certain kinds of educational opportunities they might otherwise not seek. For example, ten Thai students described their feelings before travelling to China as 'excited and anxious'. They were excited because it was the first time that they had the opportunity to practise Chinese in a real-life situation. All the Thai students reported an interest in studying abroad in China and nine of them reported they were primarily motivated by a desire to travel and to experience Chinese language. For example, Josh reported, 'I like travelling, and I see studying in China is a great experience for me' (Interview 1). Five students saw overseas placement in China as an opportunity to secure an advantage when hunting a future job. For example, Snow stated, 'I look forward to studying in China as this will enhance my proficiency in Chinese and help me get a better job in Thailand' (Interview 1). Four expressed that studying abroad in China would be a chance for them to enhance cultural awareness and would provide a means for exchanging ideas and values with local students, to help the participants learn more about and appreciate cultural differences, compare different educational systems, and facilitate both personal and professional development. For example, Steve stated, 'I am excited to experience different cultural differences, which is good for my future development' (Interview 1).

However, despite the participants' desire to belong to this imagined community of studying abroad in China, most students expressed worries about their stay in China. Common reasons for the anxiousness included separation from family and friends and worries about family responsibilities. Apple stated, 'The reality of leaving home is pretty scary. I made my whole family drive me to the airport. But ultimately, I didn't want to say goodbye to them' (Interview 1). Other reasons included health and safety risks, and culture shock. News media seemed to be the primary source that influenced learners. The development of a sense of an imagined community appeared to have been promoted independent of a particular locale. For example, Jennifer stated, 'I am not sure about the life in China. I only know from the news that everything in China is highly controlled. I am not sure whether I can handle the culture shock in China' (Interview 1).

The struggles in locating a possible self can reframe the learners' perception of possibilities in a future community. In addition, whether learners view themselves as peripheral or legitimate members of their imagined community is likely to affect their perception of learning opportunities while studying abroad (Teng and Bui 2018). For example, Jesse stated, 'I am worried it might be difficult for me to adapt to the life in China as my Chinese is not good enough. It may be difficult for me to perform well while studying in China' (Interview 1).

The learners' willingness to be engaged in the imagined communities strongly influenced identity construction and engagement in learning. It appeared that when learners imagined themselves bonded with their future community members across time and space, they felt a sense of being affiliated with the future community. For example, although five Thai learners studied Chinese in Thailand, they envisioned themselves as authentic Chinese speakers in China. In their imagination, they would be recognized members of a Chinese-speaking community, and Chinese would be one of the most important means of gaining this future affiliation. Those learners were able to relate their visions of the future to their prevailing actions and identities. It seemed that what had not yet happened could have been a reason or motivation for certain future actions. In addition, the influence of globalization and transnationalism on language learning was observed. For example, Sam stated, 'China is one of the biggest trading partners of most of the ASEAN countries, and may continue to feature prominently in considering the globalisation and "one belt, one road" initiative. I can see the value of studying Chinese in China' (Interview 1).

By contrast, the imagined communities imposed constraints on some learners. For example, language ideologies in the imagined communities influenced the social value of learning Chinese for five learners. Entrenched beliefs or ideas about the status of specific languages were a source of attitude judgements towards the target language. In addition, beliefs or ideas about language ideologies were established from learners' sociocultural experiences, indicating that language ideologies are multiple and diverse across cultures and individuals. For example, Becky reported, 'It is difficult to remember the Chinese characters. Chinese seems to have similar cultural elements with Thailand. But the languages are totally different. From Thai language, to English, and then to Chinese, it is a big language conflict' (Interview 2).

7.4.2 Discovering a self: Communities of practice and variation

After settling down in China, the Thai students expressed overall positive experiences during their study and living in China. Specifically, ten learners expressed that the environment was hospitable and members of the local community were willing to communicate with them. However, it was the first time visiting China for four students and their identity as a Thai person did not become immediately apparent because they had similar physical appearances to Chinese individuals. They wished to establish a contrast between themselves and others and wanted some special attention as a foreigner, but sometimes they were treated as Chinese persons. Reactions to the locals' attitudes ranged from 'feeling happy, to feeling uncomfortable, to breaking down in tears' (Steve, interview 2). Two wanted to be treated as a Chinese person with standard Mandarin Chinese, saying that 'we want the locals to speak Chinese normally to us rather than speaking slowly' (Eric, Apple, interview 2). Six wanted special attention or treatment as a foreigner, saying that 'we did not want to be treated as a local as we were different from locals' (Maurice, Jesse, Steve, Sabrina, Becky, Ben, interview 2). Three students enjoyed the attention that locals paid to them when knowing they were from Thailand and said 'we appreciated that the local friends arranged everything well for us' (Jesse, Apple, Snow, interview 2).

A recurring phenomenon was that the students were 'ripped off' by vendors or taxi drivers once those people knew that they were not locals. The Thai students expressed that they were especially vulnerable because they were new to the customs and the embedded rules in bargaining. Difficulties with responding to this phenomenon included their language proficiency. For example, when Jennifer attempted to buy something from a vendor, the vendor charged her 10 Yuan rather than 2 Yuan because she could not express her thoughts well. When she tried to argue with the vendor, she felt it difficult to express what she intended to say (Jennifer, interview 1). Liz stated similar experiences, although she could speak Mandarin Chinese quite well. She said that when she wanted to buy something from a vendor, she was charged 15 Yuan even though the price was only 5 Yuan. Later, she found that some locals would charge higher prices when a customer could not speak the dialect (Liz, interview 2). However, Liz later placed herself in a stronger position for resolving similar situations using language skills. She said that when she calmly told the vendor that other people had bought the item at a lower price, the vendor became embarrassed (Liz, interview 3). Even when Liz had negative experiences, she defended herself and demonstrated at least a modest connection to the communities of practice through the advantage of language skills.

Among the Thai students, ten of them reported that studying and living in China presented them with a new perspective. For example, Ben and his friends planned to travel to other cities in China. They were very astonished at the speed of the express train in China. In contrast, they regarded 'the train in Thailand is very slow and never on time' (Ben, interview 2).

By contrast, nine Thai students reconstructed their identities as Thai. When encountering differences, the individuals may not have been actively engaged with the local community but may have recoiled into a discourse of national identity. The negative experiences they encountered while staying in China reinforced their national identity. To them, the love for their native country grew stronger as time went by. Five of them expressed discomfort about the life in China and they were very nostalgic about their country. For example, Anna said, 'I miss Facebook, Twitter, and Line. Although I want to share my life with my friends, most of the apps I used in Thailand are blocked in China. I miss my friends. I miss Thailand' (Interview 3). Another student, Laura, also possessed the same feeling. Although her father moved to Thailand from China thirty years ago, she insisted on asserting her identity as Thai after living in China. Although many people assumed that she was Chinese and she spoke Chinese well, she chose to speak Thai or English and attempted to enforce her identity as Thai. She expressed her motive to come to China was to find out why her father left China and moved to Thailand. After staying in China, she found she was fundamentally Thai.

The learners who had split identities might have found it difficult to negotiate their group affiliation. Four Thai students said they looked forward to the life in China and the learning of Chinese (Interview 1). But later they said they were not independent, mature, confident, or ready to try new and different things, as they had expected to be (Interview 2). This reversal was quite interesting since before coming to China, they imagined they would be legitimate members of a Chinese community. After arriving in China, they regarded themselves as peripheral members of the communities of practice.

7.4.3 Partial success in validating a self: Motivated or demotivated for further study

One prominent issue that emerged during the Thai students' stay in China was whether to just 'pass' and to be recognized as a foreigner, or to be considered 'one of them' (i.e., a Chinese person) through making the investment to learn the target language and to match the cultural and linguistic norms of the local community. Instead of clinging to their native language, all sixteen students mentioned a need to study Chinese. Almost every student talked about how amazing it had been because of their Chinese-learning experiences, and ten of them took great pride in their proficiency and improvement in Chinese. The improvement in language learning encouraged them to invest more in their Chinese learning. Becky reported 'an excellent experience when she used her language skills to bargain for the best price' (Interview 4). In addition, eight Thai learners expressed pride in their language proficiency and felt superior to other foreigners who could not speak Chinese. Sabrina mentioned, 'I was happy when Chinese people were astonished at my Chinese after knowing that I am from Thailand. They said my pronunciation of Mandarin was better than some Chinese people' (Interview 4).

Six of them mentioned motivation to further their study. Their responses implied a value for learning Chinese, which mainly included the material and symbolic resources (Norton and McKinney 2011). For example, they perceived Chinese as a skill that would help them achieve success in their future career and that learning Chinese was crucial as more and more Chinese people are travelling to Thailand. David expressed in interview 1 and interview 2 that 'Chinese is a critical language in Asia. It would be a marketable skill'. Five of them expressed they could also gain symbolic resources through studying Chinese. David stated, 'I am learning the most difficult language in the world. The structure of the language is hard but interesting and beautiful' (Interview 3). Another symbolic resource that the Thai students noted was the ability to mediate between cultures that they regarded as conflicting or frequently misunderstood. Apple explained that learning Chinese would allow her to help promote the Thai culture. She said, 'Chinese people do not often understand our Buddhism religion. It seems that most Chinese people do not have any religion. Knowing Chinese is a tool for me to explain our faith and culture to them, and let them know more and respect our culture' (Interview 4).Some Thai students, while studying in China, earned partial success and the material and symbolic resources. The success helped the learners centre around the potential to enhance their studies, form positive attitudes, gain success in future careers and promote cultural understanding.

However, eleven learners expressed they did not belong to the community and it was impossible for them to gain authentic access to the community. As stated by Sabrina, 'It is impossible to build social and institutional relations within the communities. Chinese people always think we are foreigners, and being a foreigner means an outsider to them' (Interview 4). In this regard, the learners' future trajectories in their future communities were concrete and tangible. They regarded life in China as a short stay. While the transnational imagined communities existed in relation to the Thai students' pasts, they were unable to build future images that matched the image of the community that they had left behind. The failure in building future images formed a new type of incongruence between these images, which influenced their negotiation of membership or identity. In these circumstances, they had to reimagine their community according to certain ideologies and reject their efforts at renewing their existing membership.

Learners' struggles in current situations partly influenced what they have formed in their imagined communities, and motivation differed in the 'real' world but also in imagined worlds. Transforming from 'peripheral members' to 'legitimate participants' (Lave and Wenger 1991) seemed to be impossible for the Thai students. The process of striving to achieve one convergent end point did not appear to be a homogeneous and unitary process. For example, David stated, 'I found I was only a traveler in China. I may not stop my further learning of Chinese, but I could not join here' (interview 4). While facing the diversity and variations in actual practices and membership, some were in conjunction with their imagined communities, but some were not, and this discrepancy should be viewed from the perspective of a learner's negotiation of identity rather than a unitary procession from 'peripheral' to 'legitimate'. These factors demotivated the learners' Chinese learning as a third language.

7.5 Discussion and conclusion

In summary, the examination of the three themes revealed that the Thai students' identity formation while studying abroad in China was a non-linear process. An imagined community was first created when they separated from their home culture and home identity. Following this, they moved to a new community where realities may or may not align with their imagination, for which they fashioned a new identity. During this process, they experienced self-discovery. For example, they perceived or developed new things from both a global perspective and a national identity and finally, they validated new aspects of their identities. Learners who were agentive perceived the possibilities as opportunities then re-incorporated themselves into their home culture, bringing with them the values and insights of their experience abroad and expending more investment in language socialization practices. In contrast, those who failed to perceive the affordances embedded in communities of practice found their identity negotiation and self-presentation challenging, and finally retreated from motivation in language learning.

In relation to imagined community and identity negotiation, imagination was determined to affect a language learner's identity negotiation and language practice (Teng and Bui 2018). For example, the Thai learners' visualizations of imagined communities as a legitimate member of a Chinese community stimulated them to make extra efforts towards learning pedagogies and practice. To belong to this community, some demonstrated identities of dedicated language learners and cross-cultural mediators. The students needed a desire to belong to the imagined community to gain a return on their investment in Chinese, both for success in future careers (material resources) and acting as cross-cultural mediators (symbolic resources). However, despite the desire to belong to the imagined community that the learners possessed, the extent to which they were involved with the communities of practice varied a lot. While the communities of practice allowed some learners to invest in becoming a dedicated learner, some felt trapped within the communities of practice and lacked motivation for their predetermined learning goals. For example, David and Steve – although dedicated to their Chinese learning, and capable of employing their language skills to gain greater and more authentic access to the local community – found it difficult to be a legitimate member of this community due to the relatively closed policy towards foreigners in China. In addition, when learners felt that communities of practice did not align with their pre-imagined communities, some of them chose to discontinue, as was the case with Laura, who wanted to find out why her father left China and moved to Thailand. After staying in China, she found she was fundamentally Thai.

In addition, imagined communities affect learners' transnational language practices in a continuum of past and future communities while they try to negotiate their membership among those of the past, local communities and the ones that they wish to be part of in the future (Teng 2017). For example, the Thai learners were often informed by their past and present experiences, and their imagination had allowed them to form images of themselves and the community that they were in. This delineated the reciprocal relationship between the imagery of future communities and their present and past experiences. While their future trajectories reflected their imagined communities, and guided their practices, their imagination was also conditioned in part by their past experiences (Kanno and Norton 2003). Along with this process, identity was enacted, and this could reach out to learners' imagined states, which are within the actual states constructed upon the concrete practices they are engaged in. Therefore, the identity of the Thai students was secured, strengthened, and altered by means of the complex identifications which they incorporated within themselves, principally through the process of habituation, the rules, norms and ideals constitutive of assorted historical practice.

The fact that the Thai students in China experienced a noticeable identity development was not surprising as identity is established or strengthened through other people (Meinhof and Galasinski 2005). While studying in China, the Thai learners encountered new customs, practices and beliefs, which may question or challenge their own, and ultimately produce changes to their identity. However, no matter what realities they encountered, for those who sensed that their presence in a new context was accepted by others, they may have perceived that their self had been validated, as experienced by Ben and Ann in the present study. Jackson (2008) suggested that if the learning environment is supportive and friendly, students may be more willing to accept a new culture and reinforce their identity and be more motivated to learn and use the new language. By contrast, if learners perceive the sojourn abroad too daunting or unfriendly, they may retreat from the realities and thus reduce efforts for their language learning. Identity appeared to be negotiated and reconstructed when learners were understood, respected and affirmatively valued during their experiences abroad. For example, six Thai learners in the present study expressed studying in China was an opportunity for them to acquire material and symbolic resources. They perceived that they were affirmatively valued, and they felt they were legitimate speakers of Mandarin Chinese. With this positive self-image formulated in their minds, they were more likely to become more motivated and exert more effort into learning the target language and communicating with Chinese local speakers.

Furthermore, identities for those who planned to study abroad were complex because the learners did not know the people, events, circumstances and stories in their future immigrant lives, yet in the mind of each lived the image of their ongoing construction, performance and negotiation. The process of identity construction was not only complex, but also non-linear, and dynamic (Norton 2000). For example, David and Steve imagined they would be legitimate learners but they later became peripheral learners in the communities of practice due to the policy towards foreigners in China. Identity was observed as a complex system consisting of many active elements. During this process, the learners adapted themselves and changed their behaviours along with their interactions with other members. Identity construction was a non-linear process because the changing behaviours of the learners were not proportional to their causes or what they had imagined. This process was also changeable as more cultural information flowed in and out of the system during the interaction process.

Larson-Freeman and Cameron (2008: 158) proposed that 'language learning is not about learning and manipulating the abstract symbols, but it is enacted in real-life experiences, such as when two or more interlocutors co-adapt during an interaction.'

Finally, the Thai learners encountered challenges during their study abroad in China. The challenges to the learners' identity negotiation included their foreigner identity, otherness, and lack of language proficiency. However, the moment-by-moment agentive positioning involved in dealing with variances in communities of practice helped them actively take advantage of and even create opportunities to use the language. As a result, the learners made critical discoveries about their identity, developed a more sophisticated national and global perspective, and further validated their sense of self as a cross-cultural mediator. Consequently, successful language learning depended heavily on the initiative of the learner, and the precondition for a learner to take actions in his/her learning was to have a personal sense of motivation. As Allen (2010) suggested, study abroad was a learning context that emerged from the dynamic interplay between the learner's intentions versus those in his or her community of practice. Positive attitudes displayed by members of the Chinese community helped boost the Thai learners' confidence in speaking and using Chinese, and form a positive sense of being a legitimate, respected, and valued member of the local community. Such positive self-images or self-representations may have been a source that stimulated them to talk with Chinese speakers, thus leading to higher motivation in language practices.

7.6 Reflection

Drawing upon Thai students' experiences of studying Chinese in China, this chapter offers us a window into some issues and challenges that study abroad students and educators may face today. While this chapter has centred on a Chinese-learning community in China, many of the elements that are discussed are apt to resonate with other parts of Asia who are investigating study abroad learning with other populations. For example, the formation of cultural and linguistic identity in imagined and practiced communities and its relationship to motivation in language learning is an issue confronting study abroad researchers. In addition, national identity shifts from a passive to an active identity in the global context. The study abroad experience foregrounds the importance of the 'cross-cultural' experience. However, for most of the Thai students participating in this study, the critical encounter of study abroad was with the reformation of their national identity or self. The experience of study abroad is not simply a private individual experience. Instead, how students perceive their imagined communities and practiced communities has implications for motivation and language learning. Learners with an exclusionary, closed understanding of the self may seek to create one type of inner community and may not find it easy to be engaged with the local community. In contrast, learners who have a more open, inclusive, sense of global outlook may be more willing to be engaged with the local community. They may also form integrative motivation towards learning the target language.

This chapter focused on a short-term study abroad experience. Based upon the findings of this study, we make the following recommendations for study abroad learners and study abroad programme administrators. Recommendations are summarized and depicted in a model (Figure 7.1). We assume that the recommendations proposed, while essential to Thai students who study abroad in China, will stand up to the test of good pedagogy for all study abroad learners. First, the elements of study abroad programmes should include novelty and intensity. Learners should be allowed to become immersed in cultural and academic challenges both in and out of the classroom. The cultural environment should afford diverse opportunities for foreign students to interact with local students. The cross-cultural communication can be used as a primary learning

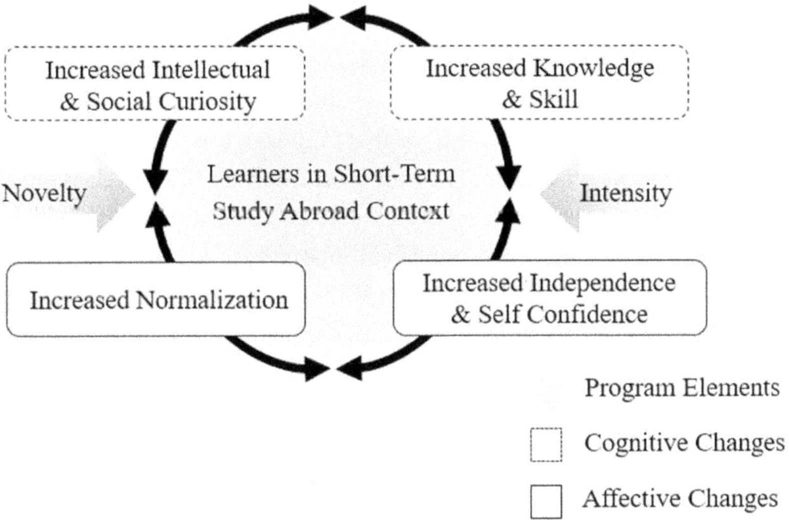

Figure 7.1 Recommendation for learners in short-term study abroad programmes

tool to heighten foreign students' experiences and involvement. The types of cross-cultural activities include structured field work, home stays, and co-curricular activities that require them to interact with local students. In addition, foreign students should be given the support that help them constructively confront and engage with the differences that come with the novice abroad experience. The Thai students experienced a number of developmental levels due to short-term study abroad. The way we assess short-term study abroad outcomes should reflect variety. Traditional measures of educational success on short-term study abroad focuses too much on academic aptitude and intercultural skill. However, we may need to consider other dimensions, including increased knowledge/skill, intellectual and social curiosity, social and emotional growth (e.g., confidence).

Finally, students' motivation in language learning is a fluid and dynamic process. Learners may encounter a lot of problems while studying abroad. We may consider different ways to enhance learners' language proficiency regardless of their level of desire for language competence. Language educators have a number of roles to play. For example, prior to a sojourn abroad, the instructors should provide guidance in selecting a programme prioritizing language and cultural learning. The instructors should also foster learners' social interactive abilities (sociolinguistic, discourse, or pragmatic) and provide guidance on how these skills can be best learned while having interactions with the lost community members. In the study abroad programme, language educators should promote students' engagement in the practices of host communities, providing support in interpreting these practices, and preparing students to take specific advantage of language learning opportunities. After joining the study abroad programme, the instructors can reflect on how to integrate foreign language study abroad into the curriculum with a mandate to educate students as global citizens. Overall, endeavours should be made to ensure that language learners studying abroad enjoy access to – and engagement in – the local communities as well as guidance in their interpretations of learning experiences and motivation dynamics.

(A revised version has been published in *Applied Linguistics Review*: Teng and Bui (2018). Thai university students studying in China: Identity, imagined communities, and communities of practice. *Applied Linguistics Review*.)

8

L2 and L3 Learning, Motivation and Identity: A Chinese EFL Learner's Reflection

English is a core part of public school education around the world, much as is math and science. In the past decade, policies on the appropriate introduction of English in schools have been reformed. While policy shifts to the early introduction of English helps the younger generation, it does not produce measurable improvements across the adult population for quite some time (He and Teng 2019). For example, the recent English Proficiency Index (EPI) ranked China as one of the low proficiency countries according to the average level of English-language skills among those adults who took the EF test. China has a strong Confucian culture that values education. Emphasis has been placed on English study in China, both in the public school system and through the enthusiastic use of thousands of private English training centres. Yet, the level of English among adults is below the average of 58.58 out of 100. This is particularly striking when compared to the astoundingly high achievements in other Asian countries. An over-emphasis on rote learning, relatively low levels of exposure to English speakers in everyday life, and teacher-student ratio which impede conversation practice all contribute to the problem. There are many Chinese students who have spent a great amount of time, money and effort in memorizing a lot of English words and sentences but have achieved limited results. It is puzzling why so many years of effort yielded so little success.

Research has consistently supported the role of motivation in learning a foreign language (e.g., Gardner 1985; Gu 2009; Ushioda 2016). Motivation is an important variable in attaining successful language acquisition. However, according to Ushioda's (2009: 218) person-in-context relational view of motivation, language learning involves a 'self-reflective intentional agent, inherently part of and shaping his/her own context'. This recommends the necessity of paying attention to learner voices and facilitation of learners' motivation and identity.

This chapter attempts to explore the first author's personal experiences in learning foreign languages (Japanese and English) using an autobiographical approach. The data is presented as a case study with longitudinal inquiry. The primary discussion is on the role of motivation and its interaction with identity in a foreign language learning environment. The discussion of motivation also relates to attribution theory. It is expected to provide an entire album rather than a single photograph, with a goal to further our understanding of the role of motivation in foreign language learning.

In this chapter, a relevant theoretical background is provided first, followed by a detailed account of the context in which the first author of the book learn two foreign languages, that is, English and Japanese. The option for an interpretative autobiography approach is then justified. Following this, the overall foreign language learning experiences of the first author will be discussed, focusing mainly on motivation and identity.

8.1 Theoretical background

Motivation is a significant variable in successful foreign language learning. Learners who are motivated are more likely to exert effort, embrace a desire to achieve the goal and hold a positive affect from learning that language (Gardner 2001). In addition, motivation is related to the cognitive processes of noticing and attention, which are important to the learning of a second or foreign language (Schmidt and Watanabe 2001). An interesting issue to be noted is that motivation plays a role in guiding learners to notice and pay attention to certain language features, particularly in the context of learning a foreign language where input enhancement of target language is not sufficient (Crookes and Schmidt 1991). However, other factors such as learners' attribution, self-efficacy and social contextual factors also need to be considered.

Attribution refers to the explanations that learners give for their success or failure in learning a language, for example, locus, stability and control (Hsieh and Schallert 2008). No matter how much learners are willing to learn a foreign language, they may not put much effort into studying it if they perceive it beyond their control. By contrast, if learners believe that they have the capabilities to perform well, they may deploy control over the study, as described as self-efficacy by Bandura (1997). The two notions come from learners' self-perceptions and can influence their expectancy, values, emotions and beliefs about their competence, which, in turn, influence their motivation in learning the target language.

Previous studies have also drawn attention to some aspects of motivation, for example, the dynamic character and temporal variation (Dörnyei 2001). The complexity of motivation suggests a need to account for the ebbs and flows of a learner's motivation. In addition, motivation is not static but evolves and fluctuates along with the changing context. Even during a single L2 course, a learner may show a certain amount of changeability; in the context of learning a language for several years, motivation is likely to go through diverse phrases. As argued by Williams and Burden (1997), motivation changes along a continuum: first initiating the reasons for doing something, then deciding to do something and finally sustaining the effort or persisting in doing something. This process can also be explained as three distinct phases of the motivational processes proposed by Shaoib and Dörnyei (2005):

1. Preactional stage: Motivation needs to be generated. The generated motivation leads to the selection of the goal and tasks for a learner to pursue.
2. Actional stage: The generated motivation needs to be actively maintained and protected. It is also called *executive motivation*, and it is particularly relevant to the sustained activities such as studying an L2, where learners are exposed to many distracting influences, including irrelevant distractions, anxiety and off-task thoughts.
3. Postactional stage: This stage is also called motivational retrospection, which is related to the learners' retrospective evaluation of how things went.

When learners successfully manage their emotions, or affective factors (e.g., motivation, anxiety, empathy and self-esteem), it can lead to successful learning of a foreign language. This may influence the construction of identity as successful L2 users.

8.2 The study

The present study attempts to look at the language learning experience of the first author of this book in a retrospective way. The data is presented as a case study with longitudinal inquiry. As each learner's language learning histories is regarded as uniquely constructed by events, desires, decisions, strategies, beliefs, actions and particular perceptions (Murphey, Chen and Chen 2005), adopting an autobiographic approach is an effective means to explore personal life and practice. The term 'autobiography' is used to refer to an approach to research that focuses on the analysis and description of social phenomena as they are experienced within the context of individual lives (Benson 2005). In the field of foreign language education, Benson and Nunan (2005) have proposed the possibility and usefulness of investigating learners' stories through researching autobiographical accounts. According to their study, the research based on first-person accounts of long-term process of learning a second/foreign language can be best described as 'autobiographical' research (p. 2), involving first-person analysis of experiences of foreign language learning. Following this, the current study is an autobiographical research providing insights into the long-term experience of learning foreign language from personal perspective.

Autobiographical studies may be insightful here. Firstly, an autobiographical research can be used to examine what an individual is really feeling – to bypass the problems public face in China – and to understand the individual's definition of major concepts such as motivation, identity and success. Secondly, autobiographical research can provide insights into what a subject really feels over time and not what the learner is supposed to feel. Thirdly, private definitions of the situation and beliefs can be more readily studied free from the public pressure of appropriate responses. Finally, the subject's cumulative effects over a longer duration can be observed.

8.2.1 The formal learning environment

This section provides information about the university (JU, a pseudonym) and the Foreign Language School (FLS) where the first author conducted his learning. The description of the context might help explain the possible constraints and support that the first author experienced. This also explains why an interpretative qualitative research approach was appropriate.

JU, the university in which the first author studied was a non-prestigious, teacher-education university. It is located around 100 kilometres away from the provincial capital of an economically underdeveloped province in central China. JU began to recruit BA students in 2003, also the year that the first author entered the university.

The FLS = is composed of three departments: English, Japanese and college English department. The English department was mainly for training business English professionals and prospective English teachers. Compared to other prestigious universities, the general entry requirement and English proficiency level for the BA English programme was relatively low. In addition, 2003 was the year that accompanied rapid expansion of the Chinese tertiary education, therefore, getting a place in any programme in JU was not highly competitive among secondary school graduates.

The English department offered proficiency courses for learning fundamental English skills in the first two years. These courses included listening, speaking, reading and writing, and so on. Students enrolled in some professional courses from the third year, for example, business courses and advanced English courses (linguistics, literature, lexicology, phonetics, etc.). In addition to these courses, students needed to study various courses not related to English, for example, politics, philosophy, mathematics, introduction to Mao Zedong thoughts, Chinese and so on. Generally, proficiency courses for learning English accounted for about 60 per cent of the whole curriculum in terms of teaching hours. In the second semester of the final year, students were required to participate in a working practicum (WP) or a teaching practicum (TP). To increase students' job opportunities, the FLS tried to find a number of companies as WP or TP sites. However, most of the WP or TP sites could only accommodate a relatively limited number of students (e.g., up to ten). In addition, finding companies or schools to accept students to conduct a semester-long WP or TP was difficult, which was why students were given the freedom to find their own sites for WP or TP. Overall, more than 90 per cent of the students were encouraged to find their own sites for WP or TP. The city where JU is located is not an economically advanced city in the province, therefore, many students had to seek employment opportunities outside the city, in economically prosperous towns of the province, or other provinces, where they could get a better pay.

Before entering the university, the first author studied in a middle school, which was located in a small town in the western part of China. Generally, students could not have access to adequate facilities when studying in a small town or rural community in China. In addition, one of the most important issues in secondary school education is the passing rate in important external examinations (e.g., national examination for entering universities and colleges). This is an agenda of high priority for secondary schools. Every year, there was a ranking list of success rate for this examination. In other words, the students being admitted to university in proportion to the total number of students in a secondary school provide an important measuring standard. This way, schools with a lower rate often feel the pressure and are forced to do the utmost to get more students admitted to universities in the upcoming years. In order to achieve this goal, many courses, including English, were designed for examination-oriented purposes. Most of the teaching sessions were focused on various test skills.

Similarly, the university education system puts too much emphasis on individual's test-taking skills. Although reforms towards quality-oriented education have been called for, most of the teachers were trying to help students obtain a good performance in academic study and prepare students for all kinds of examinations. This is reflected by one phenomenon that teachers teach in order to let the students pass the exam for getting admission into a graduate school. Other high-stakes external examinations include two tests for measuring English major students' English proficiency: Test for English Majors (TEM)-4 and TEM-8. Both tests are national proficiency tests administered by the Ministry of Education in China. TEM-4 is scheduled in the second academic year, and TEM-8 is scheduled in the fourth academic year. Many universities regard the passing rate of the two tests as a major measurement of English graduates. Apart from the external examinations mentioned above, the university administers various kinds of end-of-semester tests for each subject. At the end of each semester, students need to pass all the tests, which are the prerequisites to register for a new semester.

In summary, students had to prepare for all kinds of tests, learnt many compulsory courses not related to English, and overcame the job-hunting stress. The English-speaking practice in classroom, in this regard, was rather limited.

8.2.2 The first author's narratives on his English-learning experiences

As a Mandarin Chinese native speaker, I started to learn English as a second language (L2) from middle school. I was fascinated by the alien sounds when I was first exposed to English. I wanted to learn more and understand more about English. I thought it was impressive when an individual was able to speak a few words in English. The spark of curiosity was ignited at that time. My first English-language learning started with memorizing the alphabet. As I was in the remote countryside at the time, I did not have opportunities to learn English before middle school. However, I believed that I was ready to learn English, and I had confidence that I would succeed.

I studied English in the secondary school system from 1997 to 2003. At that time, the dominant means of instruction was the traditional grammar-translation method. My first English teacher was a fresh college graduate. He always encouraged us to learn English words by rote. He spent one month in teaching us the alphabetical letters and some simple English words. What we did at that time was to follow him and read aloud the words repeatedly.

In order to be admitted into a university, I also worked hard to get a high score in the exam. After six years of secondary school English study, I chose English as a major at university due to my personal interest. Studying English in a university provided me with my first opportunity to be taught by native English speakers. My motivation to learn English was then closely related to the desire to communicate with native English speakers and know about their culture. To further improve my English, I also tried self-instructional methods such as listening to tapes, watching movies, reading books and magazines and watching English-learning programs on TV.

I started teaching English after graduating with a degree in English education. This job lasted for two years and required me to speak both English and Chinese in class. I then entered graduate school to study English education in Australia, where I was completely immersed in a natural English-learning environment. My biggest frustration resulted from the lack of cultural awareness embedded in the English language. Colloquial idioms usually have cultural events linked to them. Understand speakers' gestures or facial expressions was sometimes more important than understanding the spoken words. I realized that there was a great deal more to function in English. One year after completing my MA, I started teaching English, and taught for six years before coming to Hong Kong to do my PhD. My motivation to learn English now was to survive in academia.

Overall, my English-learning environments can be separated into four major phases: formal school instruction, informal self-instructional, natural learning environments and then self-instructional learning. The formal learning environment corresponds to the six-year education period in secondary school. The informal self-instructional learning environment includes the times that I taught myself English through self-study. It also includes the time that I spent in teaching English. Finally, the natural learning environment was the time when I had been immersed in the target language country. These learning environments have gradually moved from a relatively structured environment to a more naturalistic environment in which I have more control. These environments will be discussed in the framework of motivations to show how these variables have influenced my English-learning experience and language achievement.

8.2.3 The first author's narratives on his Japanese learning experiences

I began to learn Japanese as a third language (L3) in 2003, which was the first year of my university education. The interest in that language and the culture intrigued me to study Japanese through self-instruction. Overall, my Japanese learning experience was based on informal self-learning, which made it a very exciting experience for me. It was when I realized that a foreign language should be learnt with a focus on the target culture. I joined a group of Japanese speakers who came to China for learning Chinese. I seized every opportunity to speak and use Japanese with them. In the beginning, I was frightened that my Japanese would not be understood by my Japanese friends and that they would think I was less intelligent because of the inevitable speaking errors. To my astonishment, no one ever complained about having a hard time understanding me. In fact, they appraised my spoken Japanese and encouraged me to further my study. We all got along quite well. At that moment, my Japanese speaking abilities and confidence soared.

I discovered that there are two Japanese languages and different dialects among Japanese speakers. The first language is for daily use among friends and acquaintances, as well as for TV programmes. The other language is used as academic language in books, materials, and journals. I realized that there were many skills I needed to obtain to become an efficient communicator in Japanese. I discovered that I needed to understand the culture and the context in a more extensive way. I knew this was a matter of exposure and time. I believed that, over time, I would acquire greater language skills. In the meantime, I realized that I was doing the right thing that I had always wanted to do: communicating with Japanese native speakers and learning about their culture.

As I needed to learn Japanese and English at the same time, I naturally compared and embraced the differences between the two languages. I was often surprised to learn how the two languages manage to convey the intended meaning. I did not learn Japanese due to the pressure of passing an exam. Along with the enhancement of Japanese language proficiency, I took Japanese language proficiency test 1 simply to demonstrate my ability in this language. Overall, the main motivation for me to learn Japanese included an expectation of using Japanese to travel around Japan, translating Japanese materials into English or Chinese at a company, and reading Japanese books and manga during my leisure time.

8.3 Discussion based on the first author's experiences

My motivation to learn English was unfixed, dynamic and subjected to the changing context. My initial motivation to learn English was to be admitted into a university because studying in a university was the only way to help me get success at that time. In this connection, the main motivation for learning English in secondary school was exam-oriented. My motivation for learning English at university was due to a desire to communicate with native English speakers and know more about their culture. As my formal learning environment did not help me achieve the goal, I kept looking for other ways to achieve it, for example, through informal self-study. When I was able to set a goal for learning, my motivation to learn English grew. If achieving that goal is salient, then more proximal goals may develop, for example, the motivation to learn English was later to survive in the academic research circle. It seems that motivation is not a stable state but a dynamic process that fluctuates over time. A variety of factors had either a negative or a positive impact on my motivational disposition. During the L2 learning process, several salient 'motivational transformation episodes' (Dörnyei 2001) had significant motivating potential to structure my motivational disposition, putting me on a new track. For example, having native English teachers teach the course helped me to set a goal to communicate with native speakers and know more about their culture. Studying in Australia helped me understand what was needed for cultural communication and regain control over my own learning. This shows the importance of adopting a process-oriented perspective in motivation research.

According to attribution and motivation theory, I should have decreased my effort because the L2 instruction in the formal instruction had not prepared me sufficiently to communicate with native speakers or sufficed me with a practical skill for using English. This disinterest and frustration should have lowered my efforts and changed my perceptions about learning. On the contrary, I tried even harder. In light of failure, I increased my effort to improve my approach for self-studying, for example, extensive reading of English materials. Many of the students did, in fact, give up at this point because they were trapped in the recycling predicament of test practices. I could see that they really were not studying much, and they blamed their failure on the fact that it just was not possible to learn English or learning English was just for passing the tests.

Indeed, we were instructed to memorize some phrases and vocabularies in order to pass various tests from the time we begin learning English. In retrospect, this may have had a negative influence. I knew that memorizing grammatical structures was necessary to obtain good grades, but I also believed that I should learn English for pragmatic purposes. Although I may have been pushed to memorize a lot of words and language structures, rote learning for passing tests was not central to meeting my main goal, which was talking with and understanding people. It seemed likely that, although frustrating, I partitioned language learning goals at this point – one for my internal interest and the other for the formal demands of school. At this juncture, I formed both integrative and instrumental motivation (Gardner 1985). According to Gardner and MacIntyre (1995), instrumental motivation may be particularly effective at increasing effort. In an autobiography study (Lim 2002), instrumental motivation was shown to have a limited capacity to sustain effort. It seems a weakness in Gardner's (1985) proposal. It may have something to do with the fact that there was a subtle shift in goals for me. I became motivated to perform well in school, to get good grades, and to be perceived as a good student by teachers. I, then, sensed a need to speak and use that language and study ever harder in order to achieve my personal goals. Somehow, I had managed to learn English, satisfying the demands of the schools as well as meeting my personal interest. Deep in my heart, I believed that good grades were within my control and I knew getting good grades was not really related to achieving my ultimate goal, so I continued my self-study.

Many researchers would say that I exhibited an integrative motivation for learning Japanese from the beginning. I had a keen desire to learn and a great curiosity, fondness, and predisposed positive orientation towards people who spoke the language. According to Gardner's (1985) integrative motivation, I should have been very enthusiastic about my Japanese studies. My interest in learning Japanese language and its target culture indeed motivated me to persevere. However, learning a third language (Japanese) seems to be slightly different from what was proposed in the L2 motivational self-system. According to Dörnyei (2005: 105), 'The ideal L2 self is a powerful motivator to learn the L2 because of the desire to reduce the discrepancy between our actual and ideal selves'. The ought-to L2 self represents the L2-related attributes that one believes one ought to possess, and it is imposed by external authorities rather than the learners' own desire and wish (Dörnyei 2009). Learning an L3 seems to be more related to the ideal L2 self but less related to the ought-to L2 self. For example, if a learner feels pressured to learn a language in order to avoid the unfavourable end-state of not learning it, the ought-to self might be a strong driving force for learning.

However, I did not have such experience in learning Japanese. Hence, an individual is less likely to claim an ought-to L3 self as acquiring a third language is primarily because of personal interest rather than external requirements. Nevertheless, learning a third language is also related to one's learning experiences. We can claim it as L3 learning experience, which refers to the motivational impact of immediate third language learning environment and experience (e.g., the positive impact of success or the enjoyment of communicating with native speakers). Without joining a group of Japanese speakers in a Chinese-learning programme and getting support from the Japanese speakers during the interactive process, it would have been difficult for me to continue my study of Japanese. The engagement with the actual language learning process and experiences gave me great inspiration and motivation to further my L3 learning.

Despite the challenges and setbacks during the learning of two languages, I never lost my interest in them. I tried and tested various strategies to see which one was more suitable for my learning. The confidence in conquering the trial-and-error process helped me believe that I could control my learning pace. I understood and accepted that I might not be able to perfect the two languages, but I identified a road map for actualizing the self-guides. I kept my vision alive, which was to achieve the self that I aimed to realize. I could do what I wanted – express my ideas to others using those languages – which gave me great inspiration and motivation to continue to improve. It seems that during the lengthy and tedious process of mastering a second and third language, enthusiasm, commitment, persistence and confidence were key determinants of my success. The motivational sequence moves from initial vision creation, through a number of reality checks, to test whether the vision of an ideal L2 self is achievable in practice (Hadfield and Dörnyei 2013). Other self-guides – the feared self and the ought-to-self – are then evoked as further motivational forces and finally work is done on strengthening and enhancing the vision, making it more precisely targeted to appropriate real life. Once these steps are completed, two processes succeed them: Mapping the journey, which relates to operationalizing the vision by providing a road map for actualizing the self-guides, and keeping the vision alive, which aims at locating strategies that will activate the ideal self (Figure 8.1).

I started learning English to get good grades, then for loving the language, and later for academic work. By contrast, I first learnt Japanese for personal interest, then for career advancement, followed by my interest in the language as my current career does not require knowledge of Japanese. It appears that the overall self is not single, fixed or permanent. Rather, it is a collection of a number of different shifts, and sometimes even contradictory selves. Additionally, despite my belief that learning two languages is controllable and, over time, I would acquire greater language skills, I realized that there were many skills I needed in order to be an effective communicator of English or Japanese. I discovered that I needed to understand culture and context in a more extensive way. It appears that there is an obvious discrepancy between the current/actual self and the ideal future self. Self-discrepancy theory states that learners should be motivated to

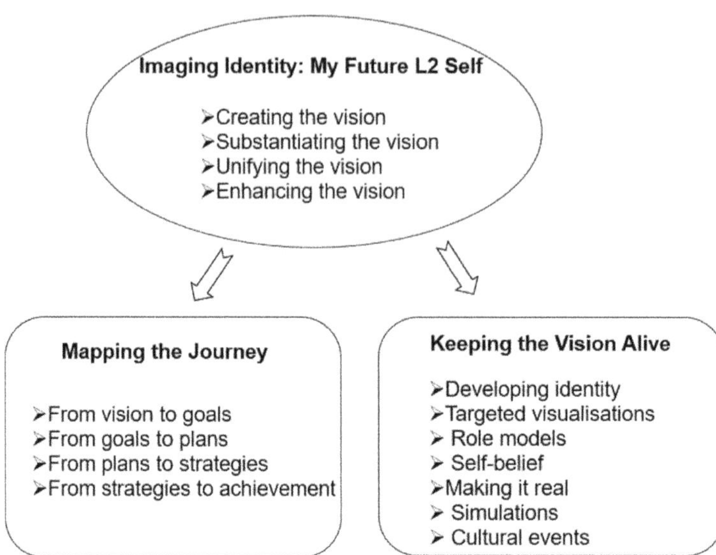

Figure 8.1 Schematic representations of the sequencing of the motivational process

reduce this discrepancy so that their current self can approach the vision of their ideal self (Higgins 1987). Hence, motivation means a desire to reduce the gap between present and ideal selves. In order for the discrepancy to be perceived and, thus, for this desire to exist, a vision of an ideal future self is a must. Most learners have some idea of an ideal future self, but this may not be substantial, elaborate or vivid enough to motivate them.

Nevertheless, I managed to see my future self as being fully prepared, confident and able to learn these two languages. Thus, it is important to raise awareness about an individual's future desired self. This can be done through building up a detailed image, which is both vivid and imagined as a possible reality. The more detailed and vivid the vision, the more ideal self will come to form. Furthermore, the more the visions seem to be an achievable reality, the greater is the motivation to achieve it. This might also enable a learner to create a vivid and detailed vision of his/her future possible L2 identity.

To me, becoming a proficient learner of English and Japanese is a way of reorienting myself in the society – a process wherein I attempted to summon my own strategic use of personal experience, talent and resources to upgrade my access to cultural capital and share my knowledge with others. Put succinctly, my efforts in learning English and Japanese can be regarded as an 'investment' in my social identity (Norton 2000). I wanted to break free of the confining circumstances of a countryside person and aimed to become a person in my imagined community.

I was frustrated at the availability of limited resources due to my background and I aimed to overcome the shortcomings. I was also motivated by the perceived benefits of learning languages in order to profit my career. Therefore, my personal motives, my motivation in learning English and Japanese, and the meanings I ascribed to the pain-staking learning process can be interpreted from the sociocultural worlds and my personal imagination about my future identity.

During the process of learning two languages, I sensed a 'competition' among the languages (Csizér and Dörnyei 2005: 657). When I spent time learning English, I often wondered if I had sufficient time to learn Japanese. I embraced ideal images for two languages. But they sometimes cause interferences with each other. It is not as proposed by Dörnyei and Chan (2013) that, positive attitudes towards a particular L2 may negatively influence an individual's attitude towards additional languages. I always kept a positive attitude towards both English and Japanese language. I did not have a formal learning environment for Japanese. But my ideal Japanese self was strong due to my interest in Japanese and Japanese pop culture (e.g., anime, manga). However, competition indeed occurred. For instance, I stopped spending time on Japanese after I started my academic job, leading to the weakening of my ideal Japanese self.

Multiple ideal L2 selves, as indicated in Nakamura (2015), are firmly linked to an individual's future self-image and they can exist together. In addition, coexisting ideal L2 selves do not inherently interfere with each other. Thinking of future languages, I could state that L1 (Mandarin) reflects my Chinese identity, and the self-images associated with my first language would not diminish even if I am not able to imagine a future self to whom that language is relevant. English will be useful for my future as a researcher, defined as a career domain. By contrast, Japanese played a role in my personal hobbies, defined as an extracurricular domain. Therefore, I have positive and clear English and Japanese self-images, which are related to different domains of my life. These L2 selves do not seem to compete with each other. This could be because the English and Japanese self-images are connected to different domains of the future life. However, competition between the L2 and L3 may occur due to the limited language learning capacity.

8.4 Reflection based on the first author's experiences

Some implications were concluded in the present study. Firstly, in terms of multiple language learning, each language has distinct L2 selves, and each L2 self has connections with different domains of a learner's future life. For example, Japanese-specific L3 self appears to be linked to an extracurricular domain. English-specific L2 self appears to be linked to the career domain.

Secondly, the development of a strong L2 self in English does not necessarily have a negative impact on the establishment of L3 self in learning a third language. The competing relationship among multiple L2 selves is dependent on the learner's identification with possible L2 selves with regard to the domains of use. One can establish ideal L2 selves in additional languages using a clear identification of different domains of uses for an L2 and L3, meaning different ideal multiple L2 selves can coexist. Hence, the dominant L2 self does not hinder the establishment of additional L2 self-images in learning a third language. However, competition between L2 and L3 may occur due to a learner's limited language learning capacity.

Thirdly, motivation, particularly integrative motivation, is a key drive for learning a second and a third language. Integrative motivation, not instrumental motivation, shapes learning through various learning stages. Although instrumental motivation plays an important role for many learners, a shift from being more instrumental to becoming integrative is essential to sustaining effort and improving learners' self-efficacy. In addition, building a learning environment that is solely dependent on instrumental factors may fail to produce the expected effects.

Fourthly, the nature of being motivated to learn a language is complex. Becoming a speaker of English is a way of reorienting learners themselves. It is a mission to summarize the strategic use of personal experiences, talent and resources to upgrade access to multicultural capital and share knowledge with others. Related to this, motivation towards English and Japanese language learning is just as much an investment in social identity. It is a bid to break free of the confining circumstances of being from the countryside and to become a different person. Hence, the mission to me is explicitly linked to professional aspirations. Although I cannot say that I am ashamed of my background, I was frustrated at the limited perspectives it offered, and I had a desire to move beyond it. Hence, my motivation in language learning and the meaning that I ascribe to multilingual competence can be related to the dynamism of sociocultural context over time. Learning English and Japanese to me has instrumental value, but precisely I longed for the prestige of those languages. I was also motivated to become a language educator. I saw in language learning a way to turn my painful learning experience into a virtue for my students. Those factors formed an imagined identity that strengthened my power and motivation to upgrade my multilingual learning.

Finally, motivation is shifting, dynamic, constantly changeable, flexible and dependent on learners' internal goals or environmental factors. This may explain why the L2 identity transforms constantly. According to the EF index, China is listed as one of the low English proficiency countries in learning English. This may be explained through a reflection on my personal experience. Although most Chinese students learn English due to an instrumental motivation – either passing a test or gaining an advantage during a job-hunt – my overarching aim was to be able to use English, especially with people from the target language cultures. I also had the same purpose for learning my third language. It appears that obtaining a certain test score is not the major purpose for my language learning, and my relative success was mainly due to my capacity to form a goal outside the education system.

As my motivation was from my internal pursuits, rather than the rewards mediated by others, I persevered through the struggles and challenges inherent to the learning of a foreign language. This gave me better control over my learning process, leading to sustained effort and better performance.

The main feature of today's English education in China is the over-emphasis on test skills. The government in China tends to use examinations as gatekeepers of access to schooling, indicators of learning outcomes, and as a means of quality control. I do not argue that tests should be abandoned. I argue that as the major guides and organizers of classrooms, and by unfolding information and evidence in terms of validity and consistency of tests, teachers could reach a relatively sufficient level to assist students in varied aspects of foreign language learning: learning styles correction, motivation enhancement, learning guiding, learning attitude fostering and self-assessment.

Conclusion and Future Directions for Multilingual Education in Asian Contexts

The remarkable fact behind the increasing use of English is that there are more and more non-native English speakers who learn English and use it for international communication. Research in motivation has generally looked at different languages separately by examining the process of acquiring one language or multiple aspects of competence acquisition in different languages. However, boundaries between languages and identities exist and multilingual education cannot be separated from the exploration of motivation change and identity development involved in learning L2 and L3. This book tries to break new ground by exploring L2 and L3 learning, with a focus on motivation and identity, as well as implications for multilingual education.

This book has reported research on multilingual education, particularly in the context of Asia. As noted, there have been a considerable number of studies which focus more on the outcomes of multilingual education or attitudes towards different languages. However, the scope of research is somewhat limited. One possibility is to adopt a more multilingual approach with a focus on identities in multilingual learning rather than multilingual competence. Another possibility is to include a critical interpretative perspective which emphasizes the way identities are formed in relation to institutional and historical practices and power relations. Finally, it is also possible to explore new areas in multilingual education through the perspectives of motivational dynamics. This book may not cover all aspects on multilingual education, but it is a starting point from the perspective of motivation and identity.

Additionally, this book illustrates that multilingual education is dynamic as it involves multiple practices and challenges. Some of these challenges are related to learners' identity flux and motivation change, and whether multilingual learners are able to identify the link of each language to a different domain in learners' self-image. Multilingual education can also take different forms because multilingual learning is related to the sociolinguistic context. To conclude, we list several key underpinning themes of this book. They are:

1. Motivations in learning an L2 and L3 are two quite distinct yet related systems, where L2, L3 or any subsequent languages deserve discrete statuses.
2. Constructs of language need to be reconsidered in fostering multilingual education, that is, symbolic capital, investment, economic and social status.
3. Political considerations should not be a barrier to the implementation of innovative multilingual education programmes.
4. There is a need to revisit boundary and intercultural sensitiveness involved in moving from a community to a new one.
5. Multiple L2 selves can coexist without competition if the learner can identify the link of each language to a different domain in the learner's self-image. However, competition between an L2 and L3 may occur due to the limited language learning capacity.
6. In line with the nature of identity, motivation can also be a multiple, dynamic, fluid, multiple-framed process.

Bilingual and multicultural programmes in the future will have major consequences for policymakers in Asian contexts. In particular, the development of multilingual education influences the hiring of new teachers and the development of responsive teacher-education programmes. This book presents richly contextualized accounts of multilingual education in Asian contexts. An understanding of multilingual education practices in some Asian countries help researchers have an understanding of how language teaching and learning is shaped by the social, cultural and linguistic systems. We also understand that we need more future studies to document and theorize full range of ways in which learners are apprenticed to non-native languages. For example, there is a need for longitudinal studies on motivation in multilingual learning context. There is no doubt on the importance of motivating learners for language learning. The problem is how we can foster students to have strong motivations for learning languages. Some key conclusions from the book might be that we can expect a more pragmatic acceptance of a lingua franca and common-sense use of English and a continued enthusiasm for multilingual learning. However, how multilingual education system can better serve the motivational dynamics of multilingual learners is currently a critical problem in educational institutions.

The second prominent issue in Asian multilingual education is how we can better lead multilingual learners' identity development to fit with the needs of developing multilingual learning. For example, in what way can we reinforce the cultural richness of the varied minority groups while upholding the policy of bilingualism or multilingualism? Hence, one emerging issue in future multilingual education is language and identity. Multilingualism was more nuanced when it came to reflections on the impact of language on identity. One concern is about maintaining a sense of national identity in the face of globalization and the increasing use of English as a lingua franca. Multilingual learners' identities are constantly being negotiated and shaped within all forms of multilingual learning practice. Within multilingual education, this negotiation takes place in several languages and reflects the material and symbolic resources of the different social groups. Given the complexity in identity construction and the influence of identity construction on multilingual learning, we surely will encounter challenges in multilingual education.

We have also concluded that we now face new challenges rooted in new types of work and ways of multilingualism in the twenty-first century and in the extraordinary scope of contemporary population movement. Such challenges – combined with unbalanced economic and social development, in particular the crisis and threats to social cohesion – make policy and practice on multilingual education more challenging. If we are to continue to make progress, there are many questions still to be answered. Of particular importance, we suggest the following directions: (1) provide support for national, regional and local policies, international and national/regional communication, community cohesion, and linguistic development; (2) acknowledge the status of English to improve communication and mutual understanding; (3) facilitate resources for teacher training, pedagogies for multilingual classroom and the development of plurilingual repertoires; (4) harness existing linguistic capital, for example, the immigrant communities, to link formal and informal multilingual learning within and beyond classroom as a major part of educational provision; and (5) enhance the multilingual use of the worldwide web and support better global understanding.

But there is still much left to do. We have just started to extend existing discussions of multilingualism. This work is important, but it tends to cover only a small part of Asian multilingual contexts. It has had less to say about how we could actually help learners harness linguistic repertoires more effectively in multilingual pedagogy and assessment practices. In addition, addressing identity and motivation requires us to ally our growing understanding of the complexity, reciprocity and porosity of multilingual repertoires with the ongoing need for the achievement of bi/multiliteracy. Related to this, we have to acknowledge the ongoing structural inequalities that many multilingual learners encounter and the extent to which the education policies can impinge upon, and often delimit, learners' educational and wider opportunities. Multilingualism, in itself, is no panacea. Multilingualism is not always situated for the individual contextually in terms of their existing and current language experiences. However, acknowledging the complexity of Asian multilingual contexts should not deter us from the crucial task of resituating the bi/multilingual repertoires of learners more centrally, even foundationally, in our teaching practices. In that, and much else as well, we still have much to learn in addressing multilingual learning from the perspective of motivation and identity.

We hope that this book has illustrated these key themes in an approachable and stimulating way and that it has helped develop an understanding of the many complex constructs involved in multilingual education. Above all, we hope that readers can appreciate that there is a possibility to learn an L3 while learning an L2 and develop new ideas that reflect the cultural norms while meeting the functional needs of multilingual education. Therefore, in multilingual education, learners' identity development and motivation change are key concerns. Multilingual education is related to its sociolinguistic, political, historical and economic context. We hope that this book, through addressing key issues in multilingual learning and presenting related research findings, could provide useful information for various contexts involving different forms of multilingual education. There are surely important ecological, historical, economic, cultural, motivational and emotional reasons to go on promoting multilingual education and offer learners opportunities to learn and use English along with other languages.

References

Abello-Contesse, C. (2013), 'Bilingual and Multilingual Education: An Overview of the Field', in C. Abello-Contesse, P. M. Chandler, M. D. Lopez-Jimenez and R. Chacon-Beltran (eds), *Bilingual and Multilingual Education in the 21st Century: Building on Experience*, 3–23, Bristol: Channel View Publications Ltd.

Adamson, B. and W. A. Y. Lai (1997), 'Language and the Curriculum in Hong Kong: Dilemmas of Triglossia', in M. Bray and W. O. Lee (eds), *Education and Political Transition: Implications of Hong Kong's Change of Sovereignty*, 87–100, Hong Kong: Comparative Education Research Centre, University of Hong Kong.

Ahn, H. (2013), 'English Policy in South Korea: A Role in Attaining Global Competitiveness or A Vehicle of Social Mobility?' *Journal of English as an International Language*, 8 (1): 1–20.

Alis, P. (2006), *Language and National Building: A Study of the Language Medium Policy in Malaysia*, Petaling Jaya: SIRD.

Allen, H. (2010), 'Interactive Contact as Linguistic Affordance during Short-term Study Abroad: Myth or Reality?', *Frontiers: The Interdisciplinary Journal of Study Abroad*, 19: 1–26.

Anderson, B. (2006), *Imagined Communities: Reflections on the Origin and Spread of Nationalism*, London: Verso Books.

Aronin, L. and M. Ó Laoire (2004), 'Exploring Multilingualism in Cultural Contexts: Towards a Notion of Multilinguality', in C. Hoffmann and J. Ytsma (eds), *Trilingualism in Family, School and Community*, 11–29, Clevedon: Multilingual Matters.

Aspinall, R. W. (2006), 'Using the Paradigm of 'Small Cultures' to Explain Policy Failure in the Case of Foreign Language Education in Japan', *Japan Forum*, 18 (1): 255–74.

Auer, P. and W. Li, eds (2007), *Handbook of Multilingualism and Multilingual Communication*, Berlin: De Gruyter.

Bacon-Shone, J. and K. Bolton (2008), 'Bilingualism and Multilingualism in the HKSAR: Language Surveys and Hong Kong's Changing Linguistic Profile', in K. Bolton and Y. Han (eds), *Language and Society in Hong Kong*, 25–51, Hong Kong: Open University of Hong Kong Press.

Baker, C. (2006), *Foundations of Bilingual Education and Bilingualism*, Clevedon: Multilingual Matters.

Baker, W. (2011), 'Culture and Identity through ELF in Asia: Fact or Fiction?', in A. Archibald, A. Cogo and J. Jenkins (eds), *Latest Trends in ELF Research*, 32–52, Newcastle upon Tyne: Cambridge Scholars.

Bandura, A. (1997), *Self-efficacy: The Exercise of Control*, New York: W.H. Freeman.

Bardel, C. and Y. Falk (2007), 'The Role of the Second Language in Third Language Acquisition: The Case of Germanic Syntax', *Second Language Research*, 23 (4): 459–84.

Barkhuizen, G. (2017), 'Investigating Multilingual Identity in Study Abroad Contexts: A Short Story Analysis Approach', *System*, 71: 102–12.

Barkhuizen, G., Benson, P. and Chik, A. (2014), *Narrative Inquiry in Language Teaching and Learning Research*. New York: Routledge.

Benson, P. (2005), '(Auto)biography and Learner Diversity', in P. Benson and D. Nunan (eds), *Learners' Stories: Difference and Diversity in Language Learning*, 4–21, Cambridge: Cambridge University Press.

Benson, P. and D. Nunan, eds (2005), *Learners' Stories: Difference and Diversity in Language Learning*, Cambridge: Cambridge University Press.

Berry, V. and A. McNeil (2005), 'Raising English Language Standards in Hong Kong', *Language Policy*, 4: 371–94.

Bhatia, T. and W. Ritchie (2013), *The Handbook of Bilingualism and Multilingualism*, 2nd edn, London: Blackwell.

Blackledge, A. (2004), *Negotiation of Identities in Multilingual Contexts*, Clevedon: Multilingual Matters.

Blackledge, A. and A. Pavlenko (2001), 'Negotiation of Identities in Multilingual Contexts', *International Journal of Bilingualism*, 5: 243–57.

Block, D. (2002), 'Destabilised Identities across Language and Cultural Borders: Japanese and Taiwanese Experiences', *Hong Kong Journal of Applied Linguistics* 7: 1–19.

Block, D. (2007), 'The Rise of Identity in SLA Research, post Firth and Wagner (1997)', *The Modern Language Journal*, 91: 863–876.

Blommaert, J. (2010), *The Sociolinguistics of Globalisation*, Cambridge: Cambridge University Press.

Bokhorst-Heng, W. D. and I. S. Caleon (2009), 'The Language Attitudes of Bilingual Youth in Multilingual Singapore', *Journal of Multilingual and Multicultural Development*, 30 (3): 235–51.

Bonfiglio, T. P. (2010), *Mother Tongues and Nations: The Invention of the Native Speaker*, New York: De Gruyter.

Boud, D., R. Keogh and D. Walker (1985), 'Promoting Reflection in Learning: A Model', in D. Boud, R. Keogh and D. Walker (eds), *Reflection: Turning Experience into Learning*, 18–40, London: Kogan.

Bourdieu, P. (1991), *Language and Symbolic Power*, Cambridge: Polity Press and Harvard University Press.

Bray, M. and R. Koo (2004), 'Language and Education', in M. Bray and R. Koo (eds), *Education and Society in Hong Kong and Macao: Comparative Perspectives on Continuity and Change*, 141–58, Hong Kong: Kluwer Academic Publishers.

Brigitta, B. (2011), 'Trends and Innovative Practices in Multilingual Education in Europe: An Overview', *International Review of Education*, 57 (5–6): 541–9.

Broughton, G., C. Brumfit, A. Pincas and R. D. Wilde (2002), *Teaching English as a Foreign Language*, New York: Routledge.

Brunei Ministry of Education (2009), 'The National Education System for the 21st Century', Available online: http://www.moe.gov.bn/Pages/spn21.aspx (accessed 9 December 2018).

Bui, G. and Teng, F. (2019), 'Exploring Complexity in L2 and L3 Motivational Systems: A Dynamic Systems Theory Perspective', *The Language Learning Journal*. DOI: 10.1080/09571736.2019.1610032.

Bui, G., F. Teng and L. Man (forthcoming), *Motivational Dynamics in L2 and L3 Learning*, Singapore: Springer.

Butler, Y. G. (2007), 'Foreign Language Education at Elementary Schools in Japan: Searing for Solutions amidst Growing Diversification', *Current Issues in Language Planning*, 8 (2): 129–47.

Camilleri, A. (1996), 'Language Values and Identities: Code-switching in Secondary Classrooms in Malta', *Linguistics and Education*, 8 (1): 85–103.

Cenoz, J. (2001), 'The Effect of Ldistance, L2 Status and Age on Cross-linguistic Influence in L3 Acquisition', in J. Cenoz, B. Hufeisen and U. Jessner (eds), *Cross-linguistic Influence in Third Language Acquisition*, 8–20, Clevedon: Multilingual Matters.

Cenoz, J. (2003), 'The Additive Effect of Bilingualism on Third Language Acquisition: A Review', *International Journal of Bilingualism*, 7: 71–88.

Cenoz, J. (2009), *Towards Multilingual Education: Basque Educational Research from an International Perspective*, Bristol: Multilingual Matters.

Cenoz, J., B. Hufeisen and U. Jessner, eds (2001), *Cross-linguistic Influence in Third Language Acquisition: Psycholinguistic Perspectives*, Clevedon: Multilingual Matters.

Census and Statistics Department (1996), *1996 Population By-census – Main Report*, Available online: https://www.statistics.gov.hk/pub/hist/1991_2000/B1120083199 6XXXXE0100.pdf (accessed 9 December 2018).

Census and Statistics Department (2011), *2011 Population Census – Summary Results*, Available online: http://www.census2011.gov.hk/pdf/summary-results.pdf (accessed 9 December 2018).

Census and Statistics Department (2017), *2016 Population By-census: Main Results*. HKSAR Government: Government Logistics Department.

Census and Statistics Department (2018), *Hong Kong 2018 Population By-census: Summary Results*, Available online: https://www.censtatd.gov.hk/hkstat/sub/so20.jsp (accessed 9 December 2018).

Chan, B. (2006), 'Virtual Communities and Chinese National Identity', *Journal of Chinese Overseas*, 2: 1–32.

Chan, E. (2002), 'Beyond Pedagogy: Language and Identity in Post-Colonial Hong Kong', *British Journal of Sociology of Education*, 23 (2): 271–85.

Cheng, Y. C. (2005a), *A New Paradigm for Re-engineering Education: Globalisation, Localisation and Individualisation*, Dordrecht: Springer.

Cheng, Y. C. (2005b), 'Globalisation and Educational Reforms in Hong Kong: Paradigm Shift', in J. Zaida, K. Freeman, M. Geo-JaJa, S. Majhanovich, V. Rustand R. Zajda (eds), *The International Handbook on Globalisation and Education Policy Research*, 165–87, Dordrecht: Springer.

Cheng, Y. C. (2009), 'Hong Kong Educational Reforms in the Last Decade: Reform Syndrome and New Developments', *International Journal of Education Management*, 23: 65–86.

Chik, A. and P. Benson (2008), 'Frequent Flyer: A Narrative of Overseas Study in English', in P. Kalaja, V. Menezes and A. M. Barcelos (eds), *Narratives of Learning and Teaching EFL*, 155–70, London: Palgrave.

Christensen, P. (2011), 'Ethnographic Encounter with Children', in D. Hartas (ed.), *Educational Research and Inquiry: Qualitative and Quantitative Approaches*, 185–200, London: Continuum.

Clem, W. (2008), 'Research Casts Doubts on Mother-tongue Education', *South China Morning Post*, 15 March, Available online: https://www.scmp.com/article/629969/research-casts-doubts-mother-tongue-education (accessed 9 December 2018).

Cogo, A. and M. Dewey (2012), *Analysing English as a Lingua Franca: A Corpus-Driven Investigation*, London: Continuum.

Coluzzi, P. (2012), 'Modernity and Globalisation: Is the Presence of English and of Cultural Products in English a Sign of Linguistic and Cultural Imperialism? Results of a Study Conducted in Brunei Darussalam and Malaysia', *Journal of Multilingual and Multicultural Development*, 33 (2): 117–31.

Constitution of Nepal (2015), Available online: https://en.wikipedia.org/wiki/Constitution_of_Nepal (accessed December 9, 2018).

Corbin, J. and A. Strauss (2014), *Basics of Qualitative Research: Techniques and Procedures for Developing Grounded Theory*, 4th edn, Oakwood, CA: SAGE.

Creswell, J. W. (2013), *Research Design: Qualitative, Quantitative, and Mixed Methods Approaches*, London: Sage.

Crookes, G. and R. W. Schmidt (1991), 'Motivation: Reopening the Research Agenda', *Language Learning*, 41: 469–512.

Crystal, D. (2003), *English as a Global Language*, Cambridge: Cambridge University Press.

Crystal, D. (2008), 'Two Thousand Million?', *English Today*, 24: 3–6.

Csizér, K. and Z. Dörnyei (2005), 'Language Learners' Motivational Profiles and Their Motivated Learning Behaviour', *Language Learning*, 55 (4): 613–59.

Cummins, J. (2001), *Negotiating Identities: Education for Empowerment in a Diverse Society*, 2nd edn, Los Angeles: California Association for Bilingual Education.

Dagenais, D. (2003), 'Assessing Imagined Communities through Multilingualism and Immersion Education', *Journal of Language, Identity, and Education*, 2 (4): 269–83.

Darvin, R. and B. Norton (2015), 'Identity and a Model of Investment in Applied Linguistics', *Annual Review of Applied Linguistics*, 35: 36–56.

Davison, C. and A. Y. Lai (2006), 'Competing Identities, Common Issues: Teaching (in) Putonghua', *Language Policy*, 6: 119–34.

Decca, E. L. and Ryan, R. M. (1987), 'The Support of Autonomy and the Control of Behavior', *Journal of Personality and Social Psychology*, 53: 1024–37.

de la Fuente, A. and H. Lacroix (2015), 'Multilingual Learners and Foreign Language Acquisition: Insights into the Effects of Prior Linguistic Knowledge', *Language Learning in Higher Education*, 5: 45–57.

Demick, B. (2002, March 31), *Some in S. Korea Opt for a Trim when English Trips the Tongue. Los Angeles Times*, Available online: http://articles.latimes.com/2002/mar/31/news/mn-35590 (accessed December 9, 2018).

Dewaele, J. (2001), 'Activation or Inhibition? The Interaction of LI, L2 and L3 on the Language Mode Continuum', in J. Cenoz, B. Hufeisen and U. Jessner (eds), *Cross Linguistic Influence in Third Language Acquisition: Psycholinguistic Perspectives*, 69–89, Clevedon: Multilingual Matters.

Dicker, S. J. (2003), *Languages in America: A Pluralistic View*, 2nd edn, Bristol: Multilingual Matters.

Dörnyei, Z. (1994), 'Motivation and Motivating in the Foreign Language Classroom', *Modern Language Journal*, 78: 273–84.

Dörnyei, Z. (1998), 'Motivation in Second and Foreign Language Learning', *Language Teaching*, 31: 117–35.

Dörnyei, Z. (2001), *Teaching and Researching Motivation*, Harlow: Longman.

Dörnyei, Z. (2005), *The Psychology of the Language Learner: Individual Differences in Second Language Acquisition*, Mahwah: Lawrence Erlbaum.

Dörnyei, Z. (2009), 'The L2 Motivational Self System', in Z. Dörnyei and E. Ushioda (eds), *Motivation, Language Identity and the L2 Self*, 9–42, Bristol: Multilingual Matters.

Dörnyei, Z. (2010), 'Researching Motivation: From Integrativeness to the Ideal L2 Self', in S. Hunston and D. Oakey (eds), *Introducing Applied Linguistics: Concepts and Skills*, 74–83, London: Routledge.

Dörnyei, Z. (2014), 'Motivation in Second Language Learning', in M. Celce-Murcia, D. M. Brinton and M. A. Snow (eds), *Teaching English as a Second or Foreign Language*, 4th edn, 518–31, Boston: National Geographic Learning/Cengage Learning.

Dörnyei, Z. and L. Chan (2013), 'Motivation and Vision: An Analysis of Future L2 Self Images, Sensory Styles, and Imagery Capacity Across two Target Languages', *Language Learning*, 63 (3): 437–662.

Dörnyei, Z., A. Henry and C. Muir (2016), *Motivational Currents in Language Learning: Frameworks for Focused Interventions*, New York: Routledge.

Dörnyei, Z., Z. Ibrahim and C. Muir (2015), '"Directed Motivational Currents": Regulating Complex Dynamic Systems through Motivational Surges', in Z. Dörnyei, P. D. MacIntyre and A. Henry (eds), *Motivational Dynamics in Language Learning*, 95–105, Bristol: Multilingual Matters.

Dörnyei, Z. and M. Kubanyiova (2014), *Motivating Learners, Motivating Teachers*, Cambridge: Cambridge University Press.

Dörnyei, Z., P. D. MacIntyre and A. Henry, eds (2015), *Motivational Dynamics in Language Learning*, Bristol: Multilingual Matters.

Dörnyei, Z. and E. Ushioda, eds (2009), *Motivation, Language Identity and the L2 Self*, Clevedon: Multilingual Matters.

Dörnyei, Z. and E. Ushioda (2011), *Teaching and Researching Motivation*, 2nd edn, Harlow: Longman.

Du, H. (2015), 'American College Students Studying Abroad in China: Language, Identity, and Self-presentation', *Foreign Language Annals*, 48 (2): 250–66.

Education Commission (1990), *Education Commission Report No. 4*, Hong Kong: Hong Kong Government Printer.

Education Commission (2005), *Report on Review of Medium of Instruction for Secondary Schools and Secondary School Places Allocation*, Hong Kong: Hong Kong Printing Department.

Education Department (1997), *Medium of Instruction Guidance for Secondary Schools*, Hong Kong: Hong Kong Government Printer.

Edwards, J. (2007), 'Societal Multilingualism: Reality, Recognition and Response', in P. Auer and L. Wei (eds), *Handbook of Multilingualism and Multilingual Communication*, 447–67, Berlin: Mouton de Gruyter.

Edwards, V. (2009), *Learning to be Literate: Multilingual Perspectives*, Clevedon: Multilingual Matters.

Ellis, R. and G. Barkhuizen (2005), *Analysing Learner Language*, Oxford: Oxford University Press.

Emerson, R. M., R. I. Fretz and L. L. Shaw (1995), *Writing Ethnographic Fieldnotes*, Chicago: University of Chicago Press.

Evans, S. (2002), 'The Medium of Instruction in Hong Kong: Policy and Practice in the English and Chinese Streams', *Research Papers in Education*, 17: 97–120.

Falk, Y. and C. Bardel (2011), 'Object Pronouns in German L3 Syntax: Evidence for the L2 Status Factor', *Second Language Research*, 27: 59–82.

Feng, A. W., ed. (2007), *Bilingual Education in China: Practices, Policies and Concepts*, Clevedon: Multilingual Matters.

Ferguson, G. (2003), 'Classroom Code-Switching in Post-colonial Contexts: Functions, Attitudes and Policies', *AILA Review*, 16 (1): 38–51.

'Fine-Tuning of MOI Will Defer for Six Years' (2015), *Ming Pao Daily*, July 4.

Firth, A. and J. Wagner (1997), 'On Discourse, Communication, and (Some) Fundamental Concepts in SLA Research', *Modern Language Journal*, 81: 286–300.

Fishman, J. A. (1971), *Advances in Sociology of Language*, The Hague: Mouton.

Fishman, J. A. (1976), *Bilingual Education: An International Sociological Perspective*, Rowley: Newbury House.

Flynn, S., C. Foley and I. Vinnitskaya (2004), 'The Cumulative-Enhancement Model for Language Acquisition: Comparing Adults' and Children's Patterns of Development in First, Second and Third Language Acquisition of Relative Clauses', *International Journal of Multilingualism*, 1: 3–16.

Fujimoto-Adamson, N. (2006), 'Globalization and History of English Education in Japan', *Asian EFL Journal*, 8 (3): 259–82.

Fuller, Janet M. (2007), 'Language Choice as A Means of Shaping Identity', *Journal of Linguistic Anthropology*, 17 (1): 105–29.

Gao, F. (2012), 'Imagined Identity of Ethnic Koreans and Its Implication for Bilingual Education in China', *International Journal of Bilingual Education and Bilingualism*, 15 (3): 343–53.

García-Mayo, M. (2012), 'Cognitive Approaches to L3 Acquisition', *International Journal of English Studies*, 12: 1–20.

Gardner, R. C. (1985), *Social Psychology and Second Language Learning*, London: Edward Arnold.

Gardner, R. C. (2001), 'Integrative Motivation and Second Language Acquisition', in Z. Dörnyei and R. Schmidt (eds), *Motivation and Second Language Acquisition*, 1–20, Honolulu: University of Hawai'i Press.

Gardner, R. C. (2010), *Motivation and Second Language Acquisition: The Socio-educational Model*, Bern: Peter Lang.

Gardner, R. C. and W. E. Lambert (1972), *Attitudes and Motivation in Second Language Learning*, Rowley: Newbury House.

Gardner, R. C. and P. D. MacIntyre (1995), 'An Instrumental Motivation in Language Study: Who Says It Isn't Effective?', in H. D. Brown and S. Gonzo (eds), *Readings on Second Language Acquisition*, 206–25, Englewood Cliffs: Prentice Hall Regents.

Gauci, H. and A. Camilleri Grima (2013), 'Code-Switching as a Tool in Teaching Italian in Malta', *International Journal of Bilingual Education and Bilingualism*, 16 (5): 615–31.

Giddens, A. (1990), *The Consequences of Modernity*, Stanford: Stanford University Press.

Gollnick, D. M. and P. C. Chinn (2006), *Multicultural Education in a Pluralistic Society* 7th edn, Upper Saddle River: Pearson Prentice Hall.

Gonzalez, A. (1998), 'The Language Planning Situation in the Philippines', *Journal of Multilingual and Multicultural Development*, 19 (5): 487–525.

Grosjean, F. (1985), 'The Bilingual as a Competent but Specific Speaker-Hearer', *Journal of Multilingual and Multicultural Development*, 6: 467–77.

Gu, M., B. Mak and X. Qu (2017), 'Ethnic Minority Students from South Asia in Hong Kong: Language Ideologies and Discursive Identity Construction', *Asia Pacific Journal of Education*. DOI: 10.1080/02188791.2017.1296814.

Gu, M. Y. (2009), *The Discursive Construction of Second Language Learners' Motivation: A Multi-level Perspective*, Bern: Peter Lang Publishing Group.

Gu, M. Y. (2010), 'Identities Constructed in Difference: English Language Learners in China', *Journal of Pragmatics*, 42: 139–52.

Hadfield, J. and Z. Dörnyei (2013), *Motivated Learning*, Harlow: Pearson.

Hall, S. (1990), *Cultural Identity and Diaspora: Identity: Community, Culture, Difference*, London: Lawrence & Wishart.

Hammarberg, B. (2001), 'Roles of L1 and L2 in L3 Production and Acquisition', in J. Cenoz, B. Hufeisen and U. Jessner (eds), *Cross-Linguistic Influence in Third Language Acquisition: Psycholinguistic Perspectives*, 21–41, Clevedon: Multilingual Matters.

Harris, M. (1968), 'Emics, Etics, and the New Ethnography', in M. Harris (ed.), *The Rise of Anthropological Theory: A History of Theories of Culture*, Lanham: AltaMira.

He, F. and F. Teng (2019), 'Language Tug-of-War: When English Literacy Instruction Encounters the NMET Policy in Mainland China', in B. L. Reynolds and F. Teng (eds), *English Literacy Instruction for Chinese Speakers*, 299–316, London: Palgrave Macmillan.

Henry, A. (2011), 'Examining the Impact of L2 English on L3 Selves: A Case Study', *International Journal of Multilingualism*, 8: 235–55.

Henry, A., Z. Dörnyei and S. Davydenko (2015), 'The Anatomy of Directed Motivational Currents: Exploring Intense and Enduring Periods of L2 Motivation', *The Modern Language Journal*, 99 (2): 229–345.

Herdina, P. and U. Jessner (2000), 'The Dynamics of the Third Language Acquisition', in J. Cenoz and U. Jessner (eds), *English in Europe: The Acquisition of a Third Language*, 84–98, Clevedon: Multilingual Matters.

Higgins, E. T. (1987), 'Self-Discrepancy: A Theory Relating Self and Affect', *Psychological Review*, 94: 319–40.

Higgins, E. T., R. Klein and T. Strauman (1985), 'Self-Concept Discrepancy Theory: A Psychological Model for Distinguishing Among Different Aspects of Depression and Anxiety', *Social Cognition*, 3: 51–76.

Holliday, A. (2010), 'Complexity in Cultural Identity', *Language and Intercultural Communication*, 10 (2): 165–77.

Hong Kong Education Bureau (2013a), 'Overview on Primary Education', Available online: http://www.edb.gov.hk/mobile/en/edu-system/primary-secondary/primary/overview/index.html (accessed December 9, 2018).

Hong Kong Education Bureau (2013b), 'Overview on Secondary Education', Available online: http://www.edb.gov.hk/en/edu-system/primary-secondary/secondary/overview/index.html (accessed December 9, 2018).

Hong Kong Tourism Board (2016), *A Statistical Review of Hong Kong Tourism 2016*, Hong Kong: Hong Kong Tourism Board.

Hsieh, P. P. and D. L. Schallert (2008), 'Implications from Self-efficacy and Attribution Theories for an Understanding of Undergraduates' Motivation in a Foreign Language Course', *Contemporary Educational Psychology*, 33 (4): 513–32.

Hu, G. W. (2007), 'The Juggernaut of Chinese-English Bilingual Education', in A. Feng (ed.), *Bilingual Education in China*, 94–126, Clevedon: Multilingual Matters.

Humphreys, G. and M. Spratt (2008), 'Many Languages, Many Motivations: A Study of Hong Kong Students' Motivation to Learn Different Target Languages', *System*, 36: 313–35.

Husin, W. (2011), 'Nation-building and Malaysia Concept: Ethnic Relations Challenges in the Education Field', *International Journal of Humanities and Social Science*, 1: 228–37.

Ige, B. (2010), 'Identity and Language Choice: "We Equals I"', *Journal of Pragmatics*, 42: 3047–52.

Ishikawa, T. (2016), 'World Englishes and English as a Lingua Franca: Conceptualising the Legitimacy of Asian people's English', *Asian Englishes*, 18 (2): 129–40.

Jackson, J. (2008), *Language, Identity and Study Abroad: Social Cultural Perspectives*, London: Equinox.

Jay, T. (2003), *The Psychology of Language*, Upper Saddle River: Prentice Hall.

Jenkins, J. (2003), *World Englishes: A Resource Book for Students*, London: Routledge.

Jenkins, J. (2007), *English as a Lingua Franca: Attitude and Identity*, Oxford: Oxford University Press.

Jenkins, J. (2015), 'Repositioning English and Multilingualism in English as a Lingua Franca', *Englishes in Practice*, 2: 49–85.

Joseph, J. (2004), *Language and Identity*, Basingstoke: Palgrave Macmillan.

Kan, V. and B. Adamson (2010), 'Language Policies for Hong Kong Schools since 1997', *London Review of Education*, 8 (2): 167–76.

Kan, V. and B. Adamson (2016), 'A Matrix Approach to Language Policy Analysis: The Case of Hong Kong', in C. M. Lam and J. Park (eds), *Sociological and Philosophical Perspectives on Education in the Asia-Pacific Region*, 111–30, Dordrecht: Springer.

Kan, V., Lai, K. C., A. Kirkpatrick, and A. Law (2011), *Fine-tuning Hong Kong's Medium of Instruction Policy*, Hong Kong: Strategic Planning Office & Research Centre into Language Education and Acquisition in Multilingual Societies, Hong Kong Institute of Education.

Kane, D. (2006), *The Chinese Language: Its History and Current Usage*, North Clarendon: Tuttle.

Kanno, Y. and B. Norton (2003), 'Imagined Communities and Educational Possibilities: Introduction', *Journal of Language, Identity, and Education*, 2 (4): 241–9.

Kaplan, R. B. and Baldauf, Jr. R. B. (2008), *Language Planning and Policy in Asia. Japan, Nepal, Taiwan and Chinese characters*, Bristol and Buffalo: Multilingual Matters.

Kawai, Y. (2007), 'Japanese Nationalism and the Global Spread of English: An Analysis of Japanese Governmental and Public Discourses on English', *Journal Language and Intercultural Communication*, 7 (1): 37–55.

Ke, I. C. (2016), 'Deficient Non-Native Speakers or Translanguagers? Identity Struggles in a Multilingual Multimodal ELF Online Intercultural Exchange', *Journal of Asian Pacific Communication*, 26 (2): 280–300.

Kinginger, C. (2015), 'Student Mobility and Identity-related Learning', *Intercultural Education*, 26: 6–15.

Kirkpatrick, A. (2010), *English as a Lingua Franca in ASEAN: A Multilingual Model*, Hong Kong: Hong Kong University Press.

Kirkpatrick, A. (2011), 'English as a Medium of Instruction in Asian Education (from Primary to Tertiary): Implications for Local Languages and Local Scholarship', *Applied Linguistics Review*, 2: 99–119.

Kirkpatrick, A. (2014), 'The Language(s) of HE: EMI and/or ELF and/or Multilingualism?', *Asian Journal of Applied Linguistics*, 1: 4–15.

Kirkpatrick, A. and M. Chau (2008), 'One Country, Two Systems, Three Languages: A Proposal for Teaching Cantonese, Putonghua and English in Hong Kong's Schools', *Asian Englishes*, 11 (2): 32–45.

Kirkpatrick, A. and Z. Xu (2001), 'The New Language Law of the People's Republic of China', *Australian Language Matters*, 9 (2): 14–8.

Klapwijka, N. and Van der Walt, C. (2016), 'English-plus Multilingualism as the New Linguistic Capital? Implications of University Students' Attitudes towards Languages of Instruction in a Multilingual Environment', *Journal of Language, Identity, and Education*, 15 (2): 67–82.

Kubota, R. (2002), 'The Impact of Globalisation on Language Teaching in Japan', in D. Block and D. Cameron (eds), *Globalisation and Language Teaching*, 13–28, London: Routledge.

Kuo, E. C. Y. and B. H. Jernudd (1994), 'Balancing Macro- and Micro-sociolinguistic Perspectives in Language Management: The Case of Singapore', in S. Gopinathan, A. Pakir, W. K. Ho and V. Saravanan (eds), *Language, Society and Education in Singapore: Issues and Trends*, 25–46, Singapore: Times Academic Press.

Kuppens, A. H. (2013), 'Cultural Globalisation and the Global Spread of English: From "Separate Fields, Similar Paradigms" to a Transdisciplinary Approach', *Globalisations*, 10 (2): 327–42.

Lai, M. L. (2001), 'Hong Kong Students' Attitudes towards Cantonese, Putonghua and English After the Change of Sovereignty', *Journal of Multilingual and Multicultural Development*, 22 (2): 112–32.

Lai, M. L. (2012), 'Tracking Language Attitudes in Postcolonial Hong Kong: An Interplay of Localisation, Mainlandisation, and Internationalisation', *Multilingua*, 31: 83–111.

Larrinaga, A. and M. Amurrio (2015), 'Internationalisation in Higher Education and its Impact in Multilingual Contexts: Redefining Identities of Basque-speaking Academics', *Language, Culture and Curriculum*, 28 (2): 158–69.

Larson-Freeman, D. and L. Cameron (2008), *Complex Systems and Applied Linguistics*, Oxford: Oxford University Press.

Lave, J. and E. Wenger (1991), *Situated Learning: Legitimate Peripheral Participation*, Cambridge: Cambridge University Press.

Leary, M. R. and J. P. Tangney (2003), *Handbook of Self and Identity*, New York: Guilford Press.

Lee, P. (2016), 'English Most Common Home Language in Singapore, Bilingualism Also Up: Government Survey', Available online: http://www.straitstimes.com/singapore/english-most-common-home-language-in-singapore-bilingualism-also-up-government-survey (accessed December 9, 2018).

Lee, S. K. (2003), 'Multiple Identities in a Multicultural World: A Malaysian Perspective', *Journal of Language, Identity and Education*, 2 (3): 137–58.

Lee, S. K., K. S. Lee, F. F. Wong and Y. Azizah (2010), 'The English Language and its Impact on Identities of Multilingual Malaysian Undergraduates', *GEMA Online Journal of Language Studies*, 10: 87–101.

Leung, C., C. Davison and B. Mohan (2014), *English as a Second Language in the Mainstream: Teaching, Learning and Identity*, New York: Routledge.

Leung, Y.-K. I. (2007), 'Second Language English and Third Language French Article Acquisition by Native Speakers of Cantonese', *International Journal of Multilingualism*, 4 (2): 117–49.

Li, D. C. S. (1998), 'The Plight of the Purist', in M. C. Pennington (ed.), *Language in Hong Kong at Century's End*, 161–90. Hong Kong: Hong Kong University Press .

Li, D. C. S. (2000), 'Cantonese-English Code-switching in Hong Kong a Y2K Review', *World Englishes*, 19 (3): 305–22.

Li, D. C. S. (2008), 'Understanding Mixed Code and Classroom Code-switching: Myth and Realities', *New Horizons in Education*, 56 (3): 75–87.

Li, D. C. S. (2017), *Multilingual Hong Kong: Communities, Languages, Identities*, Berlin: Springer.

Lim, H. Y. (2002), 'The Interaction of Motivation, Perception, and Environment: One EFL Learner's Experience', *Hong Kong Journal of Applied Linguistics*, 7 (2): 91–106.

Lim, L. (2009), 'Beyond Fear and Loathing in SG. The Real Mother Tongues and Language Policies in Multilingual Singapore', *AILA Review*, 22: 52–71.

Lim, L., A. Pakir and L. Wee, eds (2010), *English in Singapore: Modernity and Management*, Hong Kong: Hong Kong University Press.

Lin, A. M. Y. and E. Y. F. Man (2009), *Bilingual Education: Southeast Asian Perspectives*, Hong Kong: Hong Kong University Press.

Locke, E. A. and G. P. Latham (1990), *A Theory of Goal Setting and Task Performance*, Englewood Cliffs: Prentice Hall.

Man, L., G. Bui, and F. Teng (2018), 'From Second Language to Third Language Learning: Exploring a Dual-Motivation System among Multilinguals', *Australian Review of Applied Linguistics*, 41 (1): 63–91.

Markus, H. and P. Nurius (1986), 'Possible Selves', *American Psychologist*, 41: 954–69.

Martin, P. and K. Abdullah (2002), 'English Language Teaching in Brunei Darussalam: Continuity and Change', *Asia Pacific Journal of Education*, 22 (2): 23–34.

Meinhof, U. H. and D. Galasinski (2005), *The Language of Belonging*, Basingstoke: Palgrave Macmillan.

Miller, J. (2003), *Audible Difference: ESL and Social Identity in Schools*, Clevedon: Multilingual Matters.

Ministry of Education (2014a), 'Guidelines by the MOE on Improving Outstanding Traditional Culture', Available online: http://www.moe.edu.cn/srcsite/A13/s7061/ 201403/t20140328_166543.html (accessed December 9, 2018).

Ministry of Education (2014b), 'Guidelines by the State Council on Deepening the Examination and Enrollment System Reform', Available online: http://www.moe.edu.cn/publicfiles/business/htmlfiles/moe/s7229/201409/174543.html (accessed December 9, 2018).

Ministry of Education and Sports (2007), National Curriculum Framework for school education in Nepal, Available online: http://www.moe.gov.np/assets/uploads/files/National-Curriculum-Framework-2007-English.pdf (accessed December 9, 2018).

Morgan, D. L. (1997), *Focus Groups as Qualitative Research*, Thousand Oaks: Sage Publications.

Murphey, T., J. Chen and L. C. Chen (2005), 'Learners' Constructions of Identities and Imagined Communities', in P. Benson and D. Nunan (eds), *Learners' Stories: Difference and Diversity in Language Learning*, 83–100, Cambridge: Cambridge University Press.

Murray, G., X. S. Gao, and T. Lamb (2011), *Identity, Motivation and Autonomy in Language Learning*, Bristol: Multilingual Matters.

Nakamura, T. (2015,) 'Motivations for Learning Japanese and Additional Languages: A Study of L2 Self-image across Multiple Languages', *New Voices in Japanese Studies*, 7: 39–58.

Ng, C. L. (2014), 'Mother Tongue Education in Singapore: Concerns, Issues and Controversies', *Current Issues in Language Planning*, 15 (4): 361–75.

Niederhauser, J. S. (2012), 'Motivating Learners at South Korean Universities', *English Teaching Forum*, 50 (3): 28–31.

Noels, K. A. (2001), 'New Orientations in Language Learning Motivation: Towards a Model of Intrinsic, Extrinsic and Integrative Orientations and Motivation', in Z. Dörnyei and R. Schmidt (eds), *Motivation and Second Language Acquisition*, 43–68, Honolulu: University of Hawai'i Press.

Noels, K. A. (2003), 'Learning Spanish as a Second Language: Learners' Orientations and Perceptions of their Teachers' Communication Style', *Language Learning*, 53 (1): 97–136.

Noels, K. A., L. Pelletier, R. Clément and R. J. Vallerand (2000), 'Why Are You Learning a Second Language? Motivational Orientations and Self-determination Theory', *Language Learning*, 50: 57–85.

Norton, B. (2000), *Identity and Language Learning: Gender, Ethnicity and Educational Change*, Harlow: Pearson Education/Longman.

Norton, B. (2001), 'Non-Participation, Imagined Communities, and the Classroom', in M. Breen (ed.), *Learner Contributions to Language Learning: New Directions in Research*, 159–71, Harlow: Pearson.

Norton B. (2013), *Identity and Language Learning: Extending the Conversation*, 2nd edn, Bristol: Multilingual Matters.

Norton, B. (2015), 'Identity, Investment, and Faces of English Internationally', *Chinese Journal of Applied Linguistics*, 38 (4): 375–91.

Norton, B. and C. McKinney (2011), 'An Identity Approach to Second Language Acquisition', in D. Atkinson (ed.), *Alternative Approaches to Second Language Acquisition*, 73–94, New York: Routledge.

Norton, B. and K. Toohey (2011), 'Identity, Language Learning and Social Change', *Language Teaching*, 44 (4): 412–46.

Omoniyi, T. (2006), 'Hierarchy of Identities', in T. Omoniyi and G. White (eds), *The Sociolinguistics of Identity*, 11–33, London: Continuum.

Omoniyi, T. and G. White, eds (2006), *Hierarchy of Identities*, London: Continuum.

Otsu, Y., ed. (2004), *Is English Education Necessary at Elementary Schools?* Tokyo: Keio University Press.

Oxford, R. L. (1996), *Language Learning Motivation: Pathways to the New Century*, Honolulu: University of Hawaii, Second Language Teaching.

Oxford, R. L. and J. Shearin (1994), 'Language Learning Motivation: Expanding the Theoretical Framework', *The Modern Language Journal*, 78: 12–28.

Paia, M., J. Cummins, I. Nocus, M. Salaün and J. Vernaudon (2015), 'Intersections of Language Ideology, Power, and Identity', in W. E. Wright, S. Boun and O. García (eds), *The Handbook of Bilingual and Multilingual Education*, 145–63, Malden: John Wiley & Sons, Ltd.

Pakir, A. (2004), 'Medium-of-Instruction Policy in Singapore', in J. W. Tollefson and A. Tsui (eds), *Medium of Instruction Policies: Which Agenda? Whose Agenda?*, 117 33, Mahwah: Lawrence Erlbaum Associates.

Pan, S. W. (2000), 'Hong Kong's Bilingual Past and Present', *Intercultural Communication Studies*, 10: 57–65.

Paradis, M. (2004), *A Neurolinguistic Theory of Bilingualism*. Amsterdam: John Benjamins Publishing.

Park, J. (2009), 'English Fever' in South Korea: Its History and Symptoms', *English Today*, 25 (1): 50–57.

Park, J. S. Y. (2012), 'A Brief Overview of Issues in Language and Identity Relevant to the Study of Globalisation', in M. Juergensmeyer and H. Anheier (eds), *The Encyclopedia of Global Studies*, 1080–4, Thousand Oaks: Sage.

Park, N. S. (1989), *Language Purism in Korea Today: The Politics of Language Purism Berlin*, New York: Mouton de Gruyter.

Pavlenko, A. (2001), 'Bilingualism, Gender and Ideology', *International Journal of Bilingualism*, 5 (2): 117–51.

Pavlenko, A. (2002), 'Poststructuralist Approaches to the Study of Social Factors in Second Language Learning and Use', in V. Cook (ed.), *Portraits of the L2 User*, 277–302, Clevedon: Multilingual Matters.

Pavlenko, A. (2003), '"I Never Knew I was a Bilingual": Reimagining Teacher Identities in TESOL', *Journal of Language, Identity, and Education*, 2: 251–68.

Pavlenko, A. and A. Blackledge (2004), *Negotiation of Identities in Multilingual Contexts*, Clevedon: Multilingual Matters.

Pavlenko, A. and B. Norton (2007), 'Imagined Communities, Identity, and English Language Learning', in J. Cummins and C. Davison (eds), *International Handbook of English Language Teaching*, 669–80, New York: Springer US.

Pennington, M. C. (1995), 'Pattern and Variation in Use of Two Languages in the Hong Kong Secondary English Class', *RELC Journal*, 26 (2): 80–105.

Pennington, M. C. and F. Yue (1994), 'English and Chinese in Hong Kong: Pre-1997 Language Attitudes', *World Englishes*, 13: 1–20.

Pennington, M. C. (1998), 'Perspectives on Language in Hong Kong at Century's End', in M. C. Pennington (ed.), *Language in Hong Kong at Century's End*, 3–40, Hong Kong: Hong Kong University Press.

Pennycook, A. (2005), 'Teaching with the Flow: Fixity and Fluidity in Education', *Asia Pacific Journal of Education*, 25: 29–44.

Pherali, T. and D. Garratt (2014), 'Post-conflict Identity Crisis in Nepal: Implications for Educational Reforms', *International Journal of Educational Development*, 34 (1): 42–50.

Poon, A. Y. K. (1999), 'Chinese Medium Instruction Policy and Its Impact on English Learning in Post-1997 Hong Kong', *International Journal of Bilingual Education and Bilingualism*, 2 (2): 131–46.

Poon, A. Y. K. (2000), *Medium of Instruction in Hong Kong: Policy and Practice*, Lanham: University Press of America.

Poon, A. Y. K. (2009), 'Reforming Medium of Instruction in Hong Kong: Its Impact on Learning', in C. H. Ng and P. D. Renshaw (eds), *Reforming Learning: Issues, Concepts and Practice in the Asian-Pacific Region*, 199–232, Dordrecht: Springer.

Poon, A. Y. K. (2010), 'Language Use, and Language Policy and Planning in Hong Kong', *Current Issues in Language Planning*, 11: 1–66.

Poon, A. Y. K. (2013), 'Will the New Fine-tuning Medium-of-instruction Policy Alleviate the Threats of Dominance of English-medium Instruction in Hong Kong?', *Current Issues in Language Planning*, 14: 34–51.

Poon, A. Y. K. (2016), 'Unlocking the Dilemma of Language Policy in the Post-1997 Era', in T. K. C. Tse and M. Lee (eds), *Making Sense of Education in the Post-handover Hong Kong: Achievements and Challenges*, 52–72, Oxford: Routledge.

Preston, D. R. (2005), 'How Can You Learn a Language that Isn't There?', in K. Dziubalska-Kolaczuk and J. Przedlacka (eds), *English Pronunciation Models: A Changing Scene*, 37–58, Frankfurt am Main: Peter Lang.

'Publicity of Mother Tongue Teaching Can Hardly Change Parents' Mind' (1997), *Ming Pao Daily*, May 3.

Reeve, J. (2009), *Understanding Motivation and Emotion*, 5th edn, Hoboken: Wiley.

Ribeiro, F. R. (2010), 'Complexities of Languages and Multilingualism in Post-Colonial Predicaments', in Z. Desai, M. Qorro and B. Brock-Utne (eds), *Educational Challenges in Multilingual Societies*, 15–48, Cape Town: African Minds Publisher.

Ringbom, H. (1987), *The Role of the First Language in Foreign Language Learning*, Clevedon: Multilingual Matters.

Ringbom, H. (2007), *Cross-linguistic Similarity in Foreign Language Learning*, Clevedon: Multilingual Matters.

Roadmap, I. (2008, January 30), *Immersion Roadmap: Thorough Preparations Needed for English-only Classes*, *The Korea Times*, Available online: http://www.koreatimes.co.kr/www/news/opinon/2013/08/202_18207.html (accessed 9 December 2018).

Robertson, D. (2000), 'Variability in the Use of English Article System by Chinese Learners of English', *Second Language Research*, 16: 135–72.

Rothman, J. (2011), 'L3 Syntactic Transfer Selectivity and Typological Determinacy: The Typological Primacy Model', *Second Language Research*, 27: 107–27.

Rothman, J. and B. Halloran (2013), 'Formal Linguistic Approaches to L3/Ln Acquisition: A Focus on Morphosyntactic Transfer in Adult Multilingualism', *Annual Review of Applied Linguistics*, 33: 51–7.

Ryan, S. (2006), 'Language Learning Motivation within the Context of Globalisation: An L2 Self within an Imagined Global Community', *Critical Inquiry in Language Studies*, 3: 23–45.

Ryan, R. M. and E. L. Deci (2000), 'Self-Determination Theory and the Facilitation of Intrinsic Motivation, Social Development, and Well-Being', *American Psychologist*, 55: 68–78.

Samimy, K. K. and C. Kobayashi (2004), 'Toward the Development of Intercultural Communicative Competence: Theoretical and Pedagogical Implications for Japanese English Teachers', *JALT Journal*, 26 (2): 245–61.

Samovar, L. A. and R. E. Porter (2004), *Communication between Cultures*, 5th cdn, Belmont: Wadsworth.

Schensul, S. L., J. J. Schensul and M. D. LeCompte, eds (1999), *Essential Ethnographic Methods: Observations, Interviews, and Questionnaires*, Walnut Creek: AltaMira Press.

Schmidt, R. W. and Y. Watanabe (2001), 'Motivation, Strategy Use, and Pedagogical Preferences in Foreign Language Learning', in Z. Dornyei and R. Schmidt (eds), *Motivation and Second Language Acquisition*, 313–59, Honolulu: University of Hawaii Press.

SCOLAR (2003), *Action Plan to Raise Language Standards in Hong Kong*, Hong Kong: SCOLAR, Education and Manpower Bureau.

Seidlhofer, B. (2011), *Understanding English as a Lingua Franca*, Oxford: Oxford University Press.

Seth, M. J. (2002), *Education Fever: Society, Politics, and the Pursuit of Schooling in South Korea*, Honolulu: University of Hawaii Press.

Sharma, B. and P. Phyak (2017), 'Neoliberalism, Linguistic Commodification, and Ethnolinguistic Identity in Multilingual Nepal', *Language in Society*, 46 (2): 231–56.

Shoaib, A. and Z. Dörnyei (2005), 'Affect in Lifelong Learning: Exploring L2 Motivation as a Dynamic Process', in P. Benson and D. Nunan (eds), *Learners' Stories: Difference and Diversity in Language Learning*, 22–41, Cambridge: Cambridge University Press.

Sing Tao Daily (2008), *Michael Suen: No Streaming between CMI and EMI Schools*. Sing Tao Daily, 17 March.

Skutnabb-Kangas, T. (2000), *Linguistic Genocide in Education or Worldwide Diversity and Human Rights?*, Mahwah: Lawrence Erlbaum.

So, D. W. (1998), 'One Country, Two Cultures and Three Languages: Sociolinguistic Conditions and Language Education in Hong Kong', in B. Asker (ed.), *Teaching Language and Culture: Building Hong Kong on Education*, 152–75. Hong Kong: Addison Wesley Longman China Ltd.

Stiglitz, J. E. (2003), *Globalisation and Its Discontents*, New York: W. W. Norton & Company.

Strauss, A. and J. M. Corbin (1990), *Basics of Qualitative Research: Grounded Theory Procedures and Techniques*, Thousand Oaks: Sage.

Sugita McEown, M., K. A. Noels and K. E. Chaffee (2014), 'At the Interface between the Socio-Educational Model, Self-Determination Theory, and the L2 Motivational System Models', in K. Czisér and M. Magid (eds), *The Impact of Self-Concept on Second Language Acquisition*, 19–50, Bristol: Multilingual Matters.

Sugita McEown, M., Y. Sawaki and T. Harada (2017), 'Foreign Language Learning Motivation in the Japanese Context: Social and Political Influences on Self', *The Modern Language Journal*, 101 (3): 533–46.

Sullivan, N. and R. T. Schatz (2009), Effects of Japanese National Identification on Attitudes toward Learning English and Self-Assessed English Proficiency, *International Journal of Intercultural Relations*, 33 (6): 486–97.

Sung, C. M. (2014), 'Global, Local or Glocal? Identities of L2 Learners in English as a Lingua Franca Communication', *Language, Culture and Curriculum*, 27: 43–57.

Sung, C. M. (2016), 'Experiences and Identities in ELF Communication. Insights from Hong Kong Students' Written Narratives', *Journal of Asian Pacific Communication*, 26 (2): 301–20.

Support Plan for Multicultural Education (2007), Available online: http://english.moe.g o.kr/boardCnts/view.do?boardID=265&boardSeq=70384&lev=0&searchType=S&s tatusYN=C&page=1&s=english&m=0301&opType= (accessed 9 December 2018).

Swann, Jr. W. B., L. P. Milton and J. T. Polzer (2000), 'Should We Create a Niche or Fall in Line? Identity Negotiation and Small Group Effectiveness', *Journal of Personality and Social Psychology*, 79: 238–50.

Teng, F. (2017), 'Imagined Community, Identity, and Teaching Chinese as a Second Language to Foreign Students in China', *Frontiers of Education in China*, 12 (4): 490–514.

Teng, F. (2018), *Autonomy, Agency, and Identity in Teaching and Learning English as a Foreign Language*, Singapore: Springer.

Teng, F. (2019a), 'Learner Identity and Learners' Investment in EFL Learning: A Multiple Case Study', *Iranian Journal of Language Teaching Research*, 7 (1): 43–60.

Teng, F. (2019b), 'Understanding Teacher Autonomy, Teacher Agency, and Teacher Identity: Voices from Four EFL Student Teachers', *English Teaching & Learning*, 43 (2): 189–212.

Teng, F. and B. Bui (2018), 'Thai University Students Studying in China: Identity, Imagined Communities, and Communities of Practice', *Applied Linguistics Review*. DOI: https://doi.org/10.1515/applirev-2017-0109.

Teng, F. and W. Yip (2019), 'Exploring Identities of Novice Mainland Chinese Teachers in Hong Kong: Insights from Teaching Creative Writing at Primary Schools across Borders', *Applied Linguistics Review*. DOI: https://doi.org/10.1515/applirev-2018-0128.

The Philippines Department of Education (2009), 'Institutionalizing Mother Tongue-based Multilingual Education (Order no. 74)', Available online: http://www.depe d.gov.ph/orders/do-74-s-2009 (accessed 9 December 2018).

The Philippines Department of Education (2012), 'Guidelines on the Implementation of the Mother Tongue-based Multilingual Education (MTB-MLE) (Order no. 16)', Available online: http://www.deped.gov.ph/orders/do-16-s-2012 (accessed 9 December 2018).

Thomas, M. (1990), 'Acquisition of the Japanese Reflexive Zibun by Unilingual and Multilingual Learners', in H. Burmeister and P. L. Rounds (eds), *Variability in Second Language Acquisition: Proceedings of the Tenth Second Language Research Forum*, 701–18, Eugene: University of Oregon Press.

Ting-Toomey, S. (1999), *Communicating across Cultures*, New York: Guilford Press.

Ting-Toomey, S. (2005), 'Identity Negotiation Theory', in W. B. Gudykunst (ed.), *Theorizing about Intercultural Communication*, 211–34, Thousand Oaks: Sage.

Tollefson, J. W. (2007), 'Ideology, Language Varieties, and ELT', in J. Cummins and C. Davison (eds), *International Handbook of English Language Teaching. Volume 1*, 25–36, New York: Springer Science + Business Media LLC.

Trentman, E. (2013), 'Imagined Communities and Language Learning during Study Abroad: Arabic Learners in Egypt', *Foreign Language Annals*, 46 (4): 545–64.

Tsang, W. K. (2008), *The Effect of Medium-of-Instruction Policy on Education Advancement*, Hong Kong: The Chinese University of Hong Kong.

Tse, A. (1992), 'Some Observations on Code-switching between Cantonese and English in Hong Kong', *Working Papers in Languages and Linguistics*, 4, 101–8, Department of Chinese, Translation and Linguistics, City University of Hong Kong.

Tsui, A. B. M. (2007), 'Language Policy and the Construction of Identity: The Case of Hong Kong', in A. B. M. Tsui and J. W. Tollefson (eds), *Language Policy, Culture, and Identity in Asian Contexts*, 121–41, Mahwah: Erlbaum.

Tucker, G. R. (1998), 'Multidisciplinary Perspectives on Multilingual Education: A Global Perspective on Multilingualism and Multilingual Education', in J. Cenoz and F. Genesee (eds), *Beyond Bilingualism: Multilingualism and Multilingual Education*, 3–15, Clevedon: Multilingual Matters.

Tupas, R. (2015), 'Inequalities of Multilingualism: Challenges to Mother Tongue-Based Multilingual Education', *Language and Education*, 29 (2): 112–24.

Turnbull, B. (2017), 'Learner Perspectives on National Identity and EFL Education in Japan: Report of a Questionnaire Study', *The Journal of Asia TEFL*, 14 (2): 211–27.

Umino, T. and P. Benson (2016), 'Communities of Practice in Study Abroad: A Four-year Study of an Indonesian Student's Experience in Japan', *The Modern Language Journal*, 100 (4): 757–74.

Ushioda, E. (1996), 'Developing a Dynamic Concept of L2 Motivation', in T. Hickey and J. Williams (eds), *Language, Education and Society in a Changing World*, 239–45, Clevedon: Multilingual Matters.

Ushioda, E. (2009), 'A Person-in-Context Relational View of Emergent Motivation, Self and Identity', in Z. Dornyei and E. Ushioda (eds), *Motivation, Language Identity and the L2 Self*, 215–28, Clevedon: Multilingual Matters.

Ushioda, E. (2011), 'Motivating Learners to Speak as Themselves', in G. Murray, X. Gao and T. Lamb (eds), *Identity, Motivation and Autonomy in Language Learning*, 11–24, Bristol: Multilingual Matters.

Ushioda, E., ed. (2013), *International Perspectives on Motivation: Language Learning and Professional Challenges*, Basingstoke: Palgrave Macmillan.

Ushioda, E. (2016), 'Language Learning Motivation through a Small Lens: A Research Agenda', *Language Teaching*, 49 (4): 564–77.

Ushioda, E. (2017), 'The Impact of Global English on Motivation to Learn Other Languages: Towards an Ideal Multilingual Self', *The Modern Language Journal*, 101 (3): 469–82.

Ushioda, E. and Z. Dörnyei (2012), 'Motivation', in S. Gass and A. Mackey (eds), *The Routledge Handbook of Second Language Acquisition*, 396–409, New York: Routledge.

van Lier, L. (2007), 'Action-Based Teaching, Autonomy and Identity', *Innovation in Language Learning and Teaching*, 1 (1): 46–65.

Wang, L. and A. Kirkpatrick (2013), 'Trilingual Education in Hong Kong Primary Schools: A Case Study', *International Journal of Bilingual Education and Bilingualism*, 16 (1): 100–16.

Wang, L. and A. Kirkpatrick (2015), 'Trilingual Education in Hong Kong Primary Schools: An Overview', *Multilingual Education*, 5 (3): 1–26.

Wee, L. (2003), 'Linguistic Instrumentalism in Singapore', *Journal of Multilingual and Multicultural Development*, 24 (3): 211–24.

Wenger, E. (1998), *Communities of Practice: Learning, Meaning, and Identity*, Cambridge: Cambridge University Press.

Whitehead, T. L. (2005), 'Basic Classical Ethnographic Research Methods', *Cultural Ecology of Health and Change*, 1: 1–29.

Williams, M. and R. Burden (1997), *Psychology for Language Teachers*, Cambridge: Cambridge University Press.

Wolcott, H. F. (2005), *The Art of Fieldwork*, Walnut Creek, CA: Rowman AltaMira.

Woo, K. H. (2015), 'Recruitment Practice in the Malaysian Public Sector: Innovations or Political Responses?', *Journal of Public Affairs Education*, 21 (2): 229–46.

Wright, W. E., S. Boun and O. García, eds (2015), *The Handbook of Bilingual and Multilingual Education*, Hoboken: Wiley-Blackwell.

Yim, H. (2002), 'Cultural Identity and Cultural Policy in South Korea', *The International Journal of Cultural Policy*, 8 (1): 37–48.

Yim, S. Y. (2016), 'EFL Young Learners: Their Imagined Communities and Language Learning', *ELT Journal*, 70: 57–66.

Young, J. T., R. Natrajan-Tyagi and J. J. Platt (2015), 'Identity in Flux: Negotiating Identity while Studying Abroad', *Journal of Experiential Education*, 38 (2): 175–88.

Zhou, M. L. (2003), *Multilingualism in China: The Politics of Writing Reforms for Minority Languages*, 1949–2002, Berlin: de Gruyter.

Zhou, M. and X. M. Wang (2017), 'Introduction: Understanding Language Management and Multilingualism in Malaysia', *International Journal of the Sociology of Language*, 244: 1–16.

Index

actional stage   145
alignment   11, 12, 26, 128
attribution theory   144

bilingual education   1, 7, 42, 63, 66, 71
The "biliterate and trilingual" policy   74, 83, 87

co-existence   49, 111
communities of practice   4, 12, 124, 127, 128, 131, 133, 134, 137, 138, 139, 140
competition   111, 119, 123, 124, 155, 156, 160
cross-cultural awareness   62
cross-linguistic influence   30, 31, 45
Cumulative Enhancement Model   32

dual-motivation system   14, 49

ELF communication   38, 39
engagement   12, 14, 36, 120, 133, 142, 153
English as a Lingua Franca   3, 28, 30, 36, 41, 43, 56, 161
external force   85, 92, 95, 106

global community   11, 28, 30, 38, 40, 45, 62, 120, 121,
global identity   30, 36, 38, 120, 122

hierarchies of identities   122

ideal self   14, 15, 49, 78, 86, 92, 95, 107, 119, 154
identity construction   38, 44, 109, 111, 112, 124, 133, 139, 161
identity flux   109, 120, 122, 124, 159
ideology   16, 54, 56, 59, 66, 67, 76
imagination   9, 10, 11, 12, 128, 133, 137, 138, 155
imagined communities   1, 3, 5, 7, 10, 11, 15, 16, 18, 24, 25, 26, 126, 129, 131, 133, 137, 138, 141, 142

imagined identity   68, 120, 126, 156
instrumental motivation   14, 103, 105, 108, 111, 152, 156, 157
integrative motivation   14, 85, 92, 95, 99, 104, 111, 118, 123, 141, 152, 156
integrative orientation   48, 49, 85, 107
internal force   85, 93, 95
investment   3, 10, 11, 12, 15, 26, 69, 85, 127, 128, 135, 154, 156, 160

L2 learning experience   14, 49
L2 motivational self   48, 49, 152
L2 status factor   32
language contact   7, 18, 27
language development   76, 94, 128
language learning capacity   155, 156, 160
language policy and planning   2, 3, 66, 68, 82
language shift   25
linguistic diversity   5, 7, 8, 10, 24, 51, 68
linguistic interference   7

mainlandization   73, 80
medium of instruction   9, 17, 19, 39, 41, 51, 64, 65, 69, 75, 84, 87, 102, 112
membership   11, 12, 28, 35, 37, 125, 126, 137, 138
minority speakers   28
misalignment   26, 128
monolingualism   10, 25, 46, 54, 60, 68
motivational transformation episodes   151
motivation change   28, 109, 112, 118, 145, 158, 159, 162
motivation dynamics   142
multiculturalism   59, 60
multilingual identity   27, 28, 36, 37, 38, 41, 44
multilingualism   5, 7, 8, 9, 10, 12, 14, 15, 16, 17, 22, 25, 27, 29, 34, 42, 53, 65, 66, 68, 161
multilingual learning   2, 3, 4, 36, 50, 156, 159, 160, 161, 162

multiple ideal L2 selves   124, 155
multiple L2 selves   119, 123, 124, 156, 160

negotiation   4, 11, 12, 25, 35, 37, 75, 110,
    122, 123, 126, 127, 128, 129, 131, 137,
    138, 139, 140, 161

ought-to self   14, 78, 85, 86, 92, 95, 106,
    107, 119, 152

postactional stage   145
power relationship   12, 123
pragmatic multilingualism   16

preactional stage   145
psychological growth   8

self-determination theory   48, 49
self-discrepancy theory   153
self-efficacy   95, 144, 156
social identity   123, 154
social power   12
Symbolic power   11, 77

trilingual education   63, 65, 66, 74, 75,
    76, 77, 81, 82, 84, 88, 89, 92, 96, 103
Typological Primacy Model   32, 34